Modern Critical Views

Edward Albee
Maya Angelou
Asian-American Writers
Margaret Atwood
Jane Austen
James Baldwin
Samuel Beckett
Saul Bellow
The Bible
William Blake
Jorge Luis Borges
Ray Bradbury
The Brontës
Gwendolyn Brooks
Robert Browning
Italo Calvino
Albert Camus
Lewis Carroll
Willa Cather
Cervantes
Geoffrey Chaucer
Anton Chekhov
Kate Chopin
Agatha Christie
Samuel Taylor Coleridge
Joseph Conrad
Contemporary Poets
Stephen Crane
Dante
Daniel Defoe
Charles Dickens
Emily Dickinson
John Donne and the 17th-Century Poets
Fyodor Dostoevsky
W. E. B. DuBois
George Eliot
T. S. Eliot
Ralph Ellison
Ralph Waldo Emerson
William Faulkner
F. Scott Fitzgerald
Sigmund Freud
Robert Frost
George Gordon, Lord Byron
Graham Greene
Thomas Hardy
Nathaniel Hawthorne
Ernest Hemingway
Hispanic-American Writers
Homer
Langston Hughes
Zora Neale Hurston
Henrik Ibsen
John Irving
Henry James
James Joyce
Franz Kafka
John Keats
Jamaica Kincaid
Stephen King
Rudyard Kipling
D. H. Lawrence
Ursula K. Le Guin
Sinclair Lewis
Bernard Malamud
Christopher Marlowe
Gabriel García Márquez
Carson McCullers
Herman Melville
Arthur Miller
John Milton
Toni Morrison
Native-American Writers
Joyce Carol Oates
Flannery O'Connor
Eugene O'Neill
George Orwell
Sylvia Plath
Edgar Allan Poe
Katherine Anne Porter
J. D. Salinger
Jean-Paul Sartre
William Shakespeare: Histories and Poems
William Shakespeare's Romances
William Shakespeare: The Comedies
William Shakespeare: The Tragedies
George Bernard Shaw
Mary Wollstonecraft Shelley
Percy Bysshe Shelley
Alexander Solzhenitsyn
Sophocles
John Steinbeck
Tom Stoppard
Jonathan Swift
Amy Tan
Alfred, Lord Tennyson
Henry David Thoreau
J. R. R. Tolkien
Leo Tolstoy
Mark Twain
John Updike
Kurt Vonnegut
Alice Walker
Robert Penn Warren
Eudora Welty
Edith Wharton
Walt Whitman
Oscar Wilde
Tennessee Williams
Thomas Wolfe
Tom Wolfe
Virginia Woolf
William Wordsworth
Richard Wright
William Butler Yeats

Modern Critical Views

GRAHAM GREENE

Edited and with an introduction by

Harold Bloom
Sterling Professor of the Humanities
Yale University

CHELSEA HOUSE PUBLISHERS
Philadelphia

The Chelsea House World Wide Web address is http://www.chelseahouse.com

Printed and bound in the United States of America

10 9 8 7 6 5 4

∞ The paper used in this publication meets the minimum requirements of the American National Standard for Permanence of Paper for Printed Library Materials, Z39.48-1984.

Library of Congress Cataloging-in-Publication Data
Graham Greene.
(Modern critical views)
Bibliography: p.
Includes index.
Summary: A selection of criticism devoted to the fiction of Graham Greene.
1. Greene, Graham, 1904– —Criticism and interpretation. [1. Greene, Graham, 1904– —Criticism and interpretation. 2. English literature—History and criticism] I. Bloom, Harold. II. Series.
PR6013.R44Z63345 1987 823'.912 86-24495
ISBN 0-87754-701-7 (alk. paper)

Contents

Editor's Note

This book gathers together a representative selection of the best criticism devoted to the fiction of Graham Greene. The critical essays are reprinted here in the chronological order of their initial appearance. I am grateful to David Parker for his dedicated labor as a researcher upon this volume.

My introduction first centers upon what I take to be Greene's real tradition as a writer of adventure stories, rather than his more equivocal heritage from the fiction of Henry James and Joseph Conrad, after which I give an exegesis of what I judge to be Greene's best work, *Brighton Rock*. The chronological sequence of criticism begins with R. W. B. Lewis, who brings together crucial moral and narrative elements in *Brighton Rock*, *The Power and the Glory*, and *The Heart of the Matter*.

Frank Kermode, reviewing *A Burnt-Out Case*, contributes a valuable overview of the major works that have marked Greene's career. Also beginning with *A Burnt-Out Case*, Elizabeth Hardwick follows Kermode's insights but departs into her own views as to what is most valid in Greene's fictive world.

Frederick R. Karl, diagnosing Greene's heroes, comes to rest upon the nameless priest in *The Power and the Glory* and finds an aesthetic limit in the juxtaposition between the priest's personal agonies, and his difficulties in finding a language adequate to his ideals. A kind of parallel limit in *The Quiet American* is explored by Miriam Allott, while A. A. DeVitis examines what is most problematical, gloomy, and reluctant about Greene's heroes throughout his work, despite their religious dimension. It is curious that the Marxist critic Terry Eagleton, starting from very different premises, arrives at very much the same conclusions.

J. A. Ward, taking Greene rather at his own word, examines the influence relationship between Henry James and Greene. In an analysis of *The Honorary Consul* and *The Human Factor*, Roger Sharrock praises Greene for a technical accomplishment that allows a representation of the possibility of human freedom. Concluding this book, Grahame Smith returns us to *A Burnt-Out Case*, which he regards as an unqualified aesthetic success. Clearly, Greene still presents an unresolved problem for critics, as my introduction rather strenuously argues.

Introduction

I

Though he is much honored as an eminent contemporary novelist, it is not yet clear that Graham Greene will survive among the greater masters of fiction, rather than among the masterful writers of adventure stories. Henry James and Joseph Conrad seem less relevant to their disciple's achievement than do Rider Haggard, John Buchan, and even perhaps Edgar Wallace. The true comparison may be to Robert Louis Stevenson, since neither author is demeaned by such an association, though I myself prefer Stevenson. Greene, always generous and candid, paid tribute to what he called "Rider Haggard's Secret."

> How seldom in the literary life do we pause to pay a debt of gratitude except to the great or the fashionable, who are like those friends that we feel do us credit. Conrad, Dostoevsky, James, yes, but we are too ready to forget such figures as A. E. W. Mason, Stanley Weyman, and Rider Haggard, perhaps the greatest of all who enchanted us when we were young. Enchantment is just what this writer exercised; he fixed pictures in our minds that thirty years have been unable to wear away: the witch Gagool screaming as the rock-door closed and crushed her; Eric Brighteyes fighting his doomed battle; the death of the tyrant Chaka; Umslopagaas holding the queen's stairway in Milosis. It is odd how many violent images remain like a prophecy of the future; the love passages were quickly read and discarded from the mind, though now they seem oddly moving (as when Queen Nyleptha declares her love to Sir Henry Curtis in the midnight hall), a little awkward and stilted perhaps, but free from ambiguities and doubts, and with the worn rhetoric of honesty.

To be "free from ambiguities and doubts and, with the worn rhetoric of honesty," to express love—that is the hopeless nostalgia of Greene's protagonists, and of Greene himself. Greene tells us that he had a happy childhood, and a sad adolescence, and what he finds in Rider Haggard is a childhood vision, rather than an adolescent fantasy. Of Haggard's life, Greene observed that it "does not belong to the unhappy world of letters; there are no rivalries, jealousies, nerve storms, no toiling miserably against the grain, no ignoble ambivalent vision which finds a kind of copy even in personal grief." I would observe, rather sadly, that what Greene describes so negatively here is indeed an inescapable aspect of the creative lives of strong writers. Inescapable because they have chosen to overcome mortality through, in, and by their work, and such an overcoming requires rivalries—with figures of the past, the present, the future.

"Rider Haggard's Secret" turns out to be, according to Greene, what Greene least led us to expect: an obsessive fear of mortality, expressed in an anecdote concerning Haggard and the much stronger Kipling:

> There are some revealing passages in his friendship with Rudyard Kipling. Fishing together for trout at Bateman's, these two elderly men—in some ways the most successful writers of their time, linked together to their honour even by their enemies ("the prose that knows no reason, and the unmelodious verse," "When the Rudyards cease from Kipling, and the Haggards ride no more"), suddenly let out the secret. "I happened to remark," Haggard wrote, "that I thought this world was one of the hells. He replied he did not think—he was certain of it. He went on to show that it had every attribute of hell; doubt, fear, pain, struggle, bereavement, almost irresistible temptations springing from the nature with which we are clothed, physical and mental suffering, etc., ending in the worst fate man can devise for man, Execution."

Kipling's nihilism, akin to Walter Pater's, was partly assuaged by Kipling's surprisingly Paterian devotion to stories for stories' sake, poems for poems' sake. Greene's novels and entertainments have one pervasive fault: tendentiousness. We are never given a narrative for the narrative's sake, or the representation of a person for that person's sake. I have read no stranger criticism of Henry James than that ventured by Graham Greene, who has contrived to persuade himself that James was essentially a *religious novelist. The Portrait of a Lady* is scarcely *The Heart of the Matter*, or *The Wings of the Dove* a version of *The End of the Affair*, yet Greene seems not to know the difference. His Henry James is hardly the son of Henry James, Senior, disciple of Emerson and of Swedenborg, but rather someone "near in spirit

. . . to the Roman Catholic Church." This is too high-handed to be funny, and too inaccurate to be excusable. As a critic, Greene remains a minor ephebe of T. S. Eliot, the "Are you worthy to be damned?" man, author of such tractates as *After Strange Gods* and *The Idea of a Christian Society.* In his egregious essay, "Henry James: The Religious Aspect," Greene approvingly quotes Eliot on our glorious capacity for damnation, in order to suggest that James shared Eliot's enthusiasm for so sublime a human possibility:

> human nature is not despicable in Osmond or Densher, for they are both capable of damnation. "It is true to say," Mr. Eliot has written in an essay on Baudelaire, "that the glory of man is his capacity for salvation; it is also true to say that his glory is his capacity for damnation. The worst that can be said of most malefactors, from statesmen to thieves, is that they are not men enough to be damned." This worst cannot be said of James's characters: both Densher and the Prince have on their faces the flush of the flames.

That is rather severe, and leads me to an apprehension that in Greene's hell there are many mansions. It leads Greene to the exuberant conclusion that Henry James "is only just prevented from being as explicitly religious as Dostoevsky by the fact that neither a philosophy nor a creed ever emerged from his religious sense." James and Dostoyevski? Why not James and G. K. Chesterton? Or James and Evelyn Waugh? My questions are extravagant, but not so extravagant as Greene's, since he really means to ask the question: James and Graham Greene? There is a ready answer which is the critical truth about Greene, despite his journalistic idolators. *The Heart of the Matter*, *The Power and the Glory*, *The Quiet American*, and Greene's other ambitious novels cannot sustain a close rereading, and are destroyed by being compared to the major novels of Henry James and Joseph Conrad. Greene is most himself only in the company of Anthony Hope's *The Prisoner of Zenda*, Rider Haggard's *She* and *King Solomon's Mines*, John Buchan's *The Thirty-Nine Steps*, Edgar Wallace's *The Four Just Men*, and more lastingly, Stevenson's *Weir of Hermiston*, *Treasure Island*, *Kidnapped.* Of Greene's "entertainments," the most famous are *The Third Man* and *Our Man in Havana*, but the best seem to me the early group that includes *This Gun for Hire*, *The Confidential Agent*, and *The Ministry of Fear*. These are finer achievements than anything by John Le Carré, Greene's haunted disciple, and they have retained a curious freshness that might turn out to be as permanent as the quality of Stevenson's romances.

Greene's most vital "entertainments" have a Jacobean quality, reminding us of his intense admiration for the tragedies of John Webster, the thrillers of their age, together with the plays of Marston, Ford, and Tourneur. The motto for Greene's thrillers could be Webster's: "I limned this night-piece, and it was my best." This could also be the epigraph to what seems to me Greene's most enduring novel, *Brighton Rock* (1938), which is on the border between an entertainment like *This Gun for Hire* and his "Catholic novels," such as *The Power and the Glory* and its companions. Crudely worked out as the book is, *Brighton Rock* has a Websterian intensity that is displaced by piety and moralizing, however inverted, in Greene's most ambitious attempts to be the Catholic Henry James or Joseph Conrad of his own time.

II

Brighton Rock's protagonist, the seventeen-year-old thug Pinkie, is at once the most memorable and the most vicious representation of a person in Greene's fiction. He may be regarded, ironically, as a considerable advance in malevolence over his immediate forerunner, the killer Raven in *This Gun for Hire*. Contrast the deaths of Raven and Pinkie, and you see that the essential Graham Greene came into full existence during 1936–38:

> Raven watched him with bemused eyes, trying to take aim. It wasn't a difficult shot, but it was almost as if he had lost interest in killing. He was only aware of a pain and despair which was more like a complete weariness than anything else. He couldn't work up any sourness, any bitterness, at his betrayal. The dark Weevil under the storm of frozen rain flowed between him and any human enemy. "Ah, Christ that it were possible," but he had been marked from his birth for this end, to be betrayed in turn by everyone until every avenue into life was safely closed: by his mother bleeding in the basement, by the chaplain at the home, by the soft kids who had left it with him, by the shady doctor off Charlotte Street. How could he have expected to escape the commonest betrayal of all, to go soft on a skirt? Even Kite would have been alive now if it hadn't been for a skirt. They all went soft at some time or another: Penrith and Carter, Jossy and Ballard, Barker and the Great Dane. He took aim slowly, absent-mindedly, with a curious humility, with almost a sense of companionship in his loneliness: the trooper and Mayhew. They had all thought at one time or another that their skirt was better than other men's skirts, that there was something exalted in *their* relation. The only problem when you were once born was to get

out of life more neatly and expeditiously than you had entered it. For the first time the idea of his mother's suicide came to him without bitterness, as he fixed his aim at the long reluctant last and Saunders shot him in the back through the opening door. Death came to him in the form of unbearable pain. It was as if he had to deliver this pain as a woman delivers a child, and he sobbed and moaned in the effort. At last it came out of him, and he followed his only child into a vast desolation.

A voice called sharply "Pinkie" and she heard somebody splashing in the puddles. Footsteps ran . . . she couldn't tell where. It seemed to her that this must be news, that this must make a difference. She couldn't kill herself when this might mean good news. It was as if somewhere in the darkness the will which had governed her hand relaxed, and all the hideous forces of self-preservation came flooding back. It didn't seem real that she had really intended to sit there and press the trigger. "Pinkie," the voice called again, and the splashing steps came nearer. She pulled the car door open and flung the revolver far away from her towards the damp scrub.

In the light from the stained glass she saw Dallow and the woman—and a policeman who looked confused as if he didn't quite know what was happening. Somebody came softly round the car behind her and said, "Where's that gun? Why don't you shoot? Give it me."

She said, "I threw it away."

The others approached cautiously like a deputation. Pinkie called out suddenly in a breaking childish voice, "You bloody squealer, Dallow."

"Pinkie," Dallow said, "it's no use. They got Prewitt." The policeman looked ill-at-ease like a stranger at a party.

"Where's that gun?" Pinkie said again. He screamed with hate and fear, "My God, have I got to have a massacre?"

She said, "I threw it away."

She could see his face indistinctly as it leant in over the little dashboard light. It was like a child's, badgered, confused, betrayed: fake years slipped away—he was whisked back towards the unhappy playground. He said, "You little . . ." he didn't finish—the deputation approached, he left her, diving into his pocket for something. "Come on, Dallow," he said, "you bloody

> squealer," and put his hand up. Then she couldn't tell what happened: glass—somewhere—broke, he screamed and she saw his face—steam. He screamed and screamed, with his hands up to his eyes; he turned and ran; she saw a police baton at his feet and broken glass. He looked half his size, doubled up in appalling agony: it was as if the flames had literally got him and he shrank—shrank into a schoolboy flying in panic and pain, scrambling over a fence, running on.
>
> "Stop him," Dallow cried: it wasn't any good: he was at the edge, he was over: they couldn't even hear a splash. It was as if he'd been withdrawn suddenly by a hand out of any existence—past or present, whipped away into zero—nothing.

Both scenes are Jacobean, and very much in the mode of Webster, but the second, from *Brighton Rock*, has learned better the aesthetic lesson that the poet of *The White Devil* and *The Duchess of Malfi* teaches so superbly. Webster's hero-villains—Bosola, Flamineo, Ludovico—flare out sublimely as they die. They are indeed the best night-pieces that they have limned, *and they know it*, which is a peculiarly negative glory, to them and to us, but a glory nevertheless. Raven dies badly; the Jacobean groundlings would have shrugged him off as a weak wastrel. If your only issue is your death, if your only mark is "to get out of life more neatly and expeditiously than you had entered it," why then you have no greatness, no bad eminence that might be called the stuff of tragedy in which someone high, however hollow, falls downward and outward into the dark backward and abyss of time.

But Pinkie, unlike Raven, dies in the mode of Webster's sublime Bosola. Pinkie has the true Jacobean hero-villain's inverted Puritanism: disgust for human sexuality, hatred of mere life, "his virginity straightened in him like sex." Born a Catholic, Pinkie is somewhere between a repressed Jansenist and a crazed Manichaean, always ready for one death after another, a more than Eliotic believer in the glory of his own damnation. Quite literally, Pinkie dies a flaming death as he falls into nothingness, his face on fire as he goes off the cliff, memorably consumed by his own hatred of every existence, his own most of all.

The strength of *Brighton Rock*, which is likely to assure its permanence, is that it is all one thing, Greene's shot out of hell, as it were. Pinkie persuades us as I believe that the nameless whiskey priest in *The Power and the Glory* and Scobie the colonial policeman in *The Heart of the Matter* cannot. The problem is hardly what several critics have asserted it to be: the difficulty of representing vexed goodness or flawed sainthood as contrasted with the absolute moral depravity of the young devil Pinkie. Rather, it is the aesthetic question of just what Greene's creative exuberance is, and just how such gusto contrives to manifest itself in the representation of human qualities. Scobie and the whiskey priest move Greene, but they do not enchant him. His imagination is moved by Pinkie, because only Pinkie sustains the vision of evil that kindled Greene into narrative art in his most vital years as a story-teller.

However out of sympathy one is with the Eliotic mode of neo-Christianity, and I cannot imagine a critic who cares less for its aesthetic embodiment than my sad self, *Brighton Rock* has the strength of pathos that overcomes the critic's resentment of theological tendentiousness. I think always, in this regard, of the end of part six of *Brighton Rock*, where Pinkie has "such a vision of the street / as the street hardly understands," a vision deeply indebted to Eliot's superb "Preludes," with their "notion of some infinitely gentle / Infinitely suffering thing," and their phantasmagoria in which "the worlds revolve like ancient women / Gathering fuel in vacant lots." Pinkie sees what can be seen, and experiences the "horrified fascination" of the damned, as they contemplate the saved:

> He was taken by a craving for air, walked softly to the door. In the passage he could see nothing: it was full of the low sound of breathing—from the room he had left, from Dallow's room. He felt like a blind man watched by people he couldn't see. He felt his way to the stair-head and on down to the hall, step by step, creakingly. He put out his hand and touched the telephone, then with his arm outstretched made for the door. In the street the lamps were out, but the darkness no longer enclosed between four walls seemed to thin out across the vast expanse of a city. He could see basement railings, a cat moving, and, reflected on the dark sky, the phosphorescent glow of the sea. It was a strange world: he had never been alone in it before. He had a deceptive sense of freedom as he walked softly down towards the Channel.
>
> The lights were on in Montpellier Road. Nobody was about, and an empty milk bottle stood outside a gramophone shop; far down were the illuminated clock tower and the public lavatories. The air was fresh like country air. He could imagine he had escaped. He put his hands for warmth into his trouser-pockets and felt a scrap of paper which should not have been there. He drew it out—a scrap torn from a notebook—big, unformed, stranger's writing. He held it up into the grey light and read—

> with difficulty. "I love you, Pinkie. I don't care what you do. I love you for ever. You've been good to me. Wherever you go, I'll go too." She must have written it while he talked to Cubitt and slipped it into his pocket while he slept. He crumpled it in his fist: a dustbin stood outside a fishmonger's—then he held his hand. An obscure sense told him you never knew—it might prove useful one day.
>
> He heard a whisper, looked sharply round, and thrust the paper back. In an alley between two shops, an old woman sat upon the ground; he could just see the rotting and discoloured face: it was like the sight of damnation. Then he heard the whisper, "Blessed art thou among women," saw the grey fingers fumbling at the beads. This was not one of the damned: he watched with horrified fascination: this was one of the saved.

This was Greene's true sense of the heart of the matter, and his abiding vision of what could touch him, with full authenticity, as the power and the glory. His more celebrated novels fade already into the continuum of literary tradition. *Brighton Rock*, a terrible crystal of a book, may well be *The White Devil* of our era.

R. W. B. LEWIS

The "Trilogy"

In Greene's early fiction, along with a definite but notably uneven development of style and vigor, there was an apparent failure to distinguish between various fictional genres. Even *Brighton Rock* betrays an initial confusion between what Greene calls an "entertainment" and what he finally offered as a tragedy; but here the confusion is unexpectedly exploited (as shall be seen) in the composition of an immensely impressive novel. The distinction of genres, in a somewhat Gallic manner, would become important for Greene, and in a sense the making of him; but prior to *Brighton Rock*, we observe an uncertainty of artistic purpose that led to an unstable treatment of the basic elements of fiction: setting, character and action. Part of the success of *Brighton Rock*, *The Power and the Glory*, and *The Heart of the Matter* is due to the preliminary sketching of elements in each of them—a process that, as it turned out, managed to release the special energy and "vision" that would characterize Greene as a writer of stature.

The settings of *The Power and the Glory* and *The Heart of the Matter*, for example, had already been explored by Greene personally and in two excellent travel books: *The Lawless Roads*, from which the whole passages are transcribed in the former; and *Journey Without Maps*, which concludes on the Gold Coast of poor Major Scobie. In the travel books, Greene's journalistic and photographic abilities exhausted themselves; and in the novels, consequently, physical settings could be managed so as to exude a meaning that transformed them into spiritual situations, into elaborated images of fate.

From *The Picaresque Saint: Representative Figures in Contemporary Fiction*. © 1956, 1958 by R. W. B. Lewis. Lippincott, 1959.

Mexico, however discolored, is still Mexico in *The Lawless Roads;* in *The Power and the Glory,* the country has been reduced and reshaped to fit a particular action, of which indeed it contains the particular secret. Similarly, each one of these three novels has its correlative entertainment; a mystery story, in the popular sense, that functions ably as trial run for a mystery drama in a more ancient and theological sense. Here we touch the crucial distinction underlying the other distinctions, for the unsolvable mystery of the human condition, beyond or beneath any sociological or historical or psychological explanation thereof, has become Greene's obsessive subject. Raven, the killer in *A Gun for Sale* (1936, U.S. title: *This Gun for Hire*), with his dumb conviction of injustice and his bleak yearning for a soul he can trust, is a purely human cartoon for the metaphysical monster, Pinkie, the killer of *Brighton Rock* (1938). In *The Confidential Agent* (1939), the weary and frightened fidelity to his mission of the Spanish agent, D., is a sketchy and political version of the behavior of the nameless Mexican priest, the agent of God, on his exclusively religious mission in *The Power and the Glory,* a year later. And *The Ministry of Fear* (1943), the most skillful of the entertainments and a very good story indeed, dramatizes what Greene regards as the most dangerous of human emotions—pity—the fatal flaw which would destroy Major Scobie in *The Heart of the Matter* (1948), but which is significantly contrasted in that novel with its real opposite, the primary attribute of God: mercy.

It can be said about the earlier novels, then, that the confusion of purpose and the blurry handling of the elements are rooted in a failure to disentangle the *mystery* of the mystery, to separate it out from the contingencies of melodrama and the staged surprises of the brain-twister. The disentanglement followed, as it seems, upon the Liberian experience [examined elsewhere]; for after that, the plot and the action of Greene's novels are increasingly given their meaning by the religious motif—a motif which, since it cannot always be called Christian, can scarcely be always called Catholic; a sort of shocked intuition of supernature. It is when the religious motif takes charge that Greene's resources—including his nervous, highly pressured style, and his uncommon talent for narrative—become ordered and controlled, and his artistic power fulfills itself. *The Man Within* has an appealing youthfulness of viewpoint; but the religious element remains shadowy and generalized, and the whole story wobbles uneasily to (in context) a rather pointless climax. The real source of complexity in human events, as Greene would eventually see it, is not detected in *The Name of Action,* though that is what the novel is about; as a result, we are introduced here only to shapeless movements in a nightmare world. And in *England Made Me,* which is otherwise a genuine achievement, Greene so far misunderstood himself as to insert stream-of-consciousness meditations ill-advisedly but patently borrowed from James Joyce. Nothing could be further from Greene's intentions than those of Joyce—which achieve the careful rendering of the behavior of the mind, with the ultimate aim of celebrating the shaping power of art, the "stasis" that imposes value and meaning upon the chaos of mental experience. Greene has never reverted to the Joycean technique. What Greene has envisaged and what he has become especially concerned with are better implied in the title of still another early book, *It's a Battlefield:* the human scene now described as a battlefield between transcendent warring forces. And in *Brighton Rock*, the metaphor of the battlefield is dominant: "It lay there always, the ravaged and disputed territory between the two eternities."

The three novels published between 1938 and 1948 are sometimes taken together as a trilogy; but the word should be enclosed in quotation marks, for the trilogic pattern, if it existed in Greene's awareness, took hold only belatedly. But it is worth juxtaposing the three books, to observe several striking aspects of Greene. All three show his affection for the primitive; like Silone, Greene often turns away from the relatively civilized to inspect human life in its cruder and more exposed conditions: in a dark corner of Brighton, the jungles and prisons of Tabasco, the coast of West Africa—all places where, as Scobie tells himself in *The Heart of the Matter*, "human nature hasn't had time to disguise itself"; places where there openly flourished "the injustices, the cruelties, the meanness that elsewhere people so cleverly hushed up." In these primitive scenes, we encounter the dramatis personae of Greene's recurring drama and of his troubled universe: the murderer, the priest, and the policeman, who are the heroes respectively of the three books. All three figures, in different embodiments, appear in all three novels; and they tend more and more to resemble each other. The murderer, Pinkie, is knowingly a hideously inverted priest; the policeman, Scobie, becomes involved with crime and criminals; the officer in *The Power and the Glory* has "something of a priest in his intent observant walk," while the priest in turn has queer points of resemblance with the Yankee killer whose photograph faces his in the police station. The three figures represent, of course, the shifting and interwoven attributes of the Greenean man: a being capable of imitating both Christ and Judas; a person who is at once the pursuer and the man pursued; a creature with the splendid potentiality either of damnation or salvation. The actualities of their fate exhaust, apparently, the major possibilities. If one can be sure of anything in the real world or in Greene's world, Pinkie Brown is damned—it is his special mode of triumph; the Mexican priest is saved—sainthood gleams at last through his bloodshot eyes; and the final end of Major Scobie is what is precisely in doubt, as difficult to determine as his own ambiguous last words, "Dear God, I love. . . ." Pinkie is a proud citizen of hell; Scobie's suffering is that of a man in purgatory; and the laughter in *The Power and the Glory* celebrates, perhaps, the entrance of a soul into paradise. The three careers are presented to us in three very different kinds of fiction: *Brighton Rock* just manages to escape melodrama and becomes a work *sui generis; The Power and the Glory* is, in its way, a divine comedy; and *The Heart of the Matter* is a tragedy in the classical tradition. These novels are, respectively, Greene's most strenuous, his most satisfying, and, artistically, his most assured.

Brighton Rock in particular is the most harrowing of Greene's stories about children; and Pinkie, the seventeen-year-old gangster (he is usually referred to simply as "the Boy") is "the most driven and 'damned' " of all Greene's characters, to quote his own words about the evil forces in that other fearful tale about children, James's *The Turn of the Screw*. There is, to be sure, a superficial movement in the novel from death to life: the narrative begins with the revenge-murder by Brighton racetrack hoodlums of Hale, the man who is working a publicity stunt for a newspaper among the holiday crowds; and it closes with the pregnancy of Rose, the wan underage wife whom Hale's killer, Pinkie, has been forced for protection to marry. So far, there is a momentary likeness to Moravia's *Woman of Rome*, which similarly concludes with the heroine's pregnancy by a now dead murderer. Moravia's novel quite definitely suggests the painful victory of life over death. But Greene's artistic and intellectual purposes are almost always dialectically opposite to those of Moravia; and in *Brighton Rock*, not only is the death legally avenged, the birth itself will be altogether darkened by Rose's discovery of Pinkie's true feeling about her—via the "loving message" he has recorded by phonograph, and which, "the worst horror of all," she is on her way to hear as the story ends: "God damn you, you little bitch, why can't you go back home for ever and let me be?" The implied denouement in *Brighton Rock* is as disagreeable as anything in modern fiction. But *Brighton Rock* is deliberately pitiless, and partly because it aims, by moving beyond human pity, to evoke the far faint light of an incomprehensible divine mercy.

Part of the disaster that threatens in this pitiless book is artistic: a threat to the shape and character of the book itself. Greene evidently began it as an "entertainment," and the first American edition announced itself as such. He began it, that is, as a melodrama of murder and detection in which contingency and coincidence would be allowed free play, the chase be exciting for its own sake, and with a larger and more kindly emphasis than the novel eventually allowed on Ida Arnold, the London lady of easy virtue who had known Hale in his last frightened hours and who sets herself to discover the criminal, an aim she formidably succeeds in. But evil has always stimulated Greene a good deal more than the righting of wrongs; and in this case, the figure and story of Pinkie Brown (unlike those of Raven in *A Gun for Sale*, of which *Brighton Rock* would otherwise have been a repetition) expanded in Greene's imagination until a recognizable tragedy took its place in the book alongside the well-made entertainment. The entertainment is Ida's; it begins with the first sentence ("Hale knew, before he had been in Brighton three hours, that they meant to murder him"), and ends with the police closing in on the culprit. The tragedy is Pinkie's; *it* begins more subtly in the atmosphere of the place (implied by the adjectives used for the jostling crowds: "bewildered," "determined," "cramped," "closed," "weary"); and its action is defined in advance by the book's motto, from *The Witch of Edmonton*, with overtones of *Macbeth:* "This were a fine reign: / To do ill and not hear of it again." In the open world of the entertainment, happenstances accumulate; but in the tragedy there is no space for contingency, no time for the accidental. Evil is fertile and is always heard from again; every move Pinkie makes—from the killing of Hale, through the further necessitated murders and the detested courtship and marriage, to the climax in which, like Oedipus, he blinds himself (with vitriol)—has a convulsive inevitability, the more dreadful since it seems rooted neither in private temperament nor in social background. It derives from the inexplicable power of evil, one of the two things that Pinkie believes in: *"Credo in unum Satanum." Brighton Rock* confirms Greene's statement in the preface to a book about him by the French critic, Paul Rostenne, that he has no a priori edifying purpose in writing his novels, but is carried along rather by the unpredictable energies of his characters. As Pinkie's perils increase and his ambitions enlarge, the very design of the book shifts and re-forms.

Brighton Rock could have been a kind of disaster, two different books, between the same covers only by mistake. But it emerges as an original and striking work: for the relation between the detective story and the tragedy expresses exactly what *Brighton Rock* is finally all about. It is a relation between modes of narrative discourse that reflects a relation between two kinds or levels of reality: a relation between incommensurable and hostile forces; between incompatible worlds; between the moral world of right and wrong, to which Ida constantly and confidently appeals, and the theological world of good and evil inhabited by Pinkie and Rose. It is, in short, the relation Greene had formulated for himself in Liberia, between the "sinless empty graceless chromium world" of modern Western urban civilization and the supernaturally infested jungle with its purer terrors and its keener pleasures. The abrupt superiority of *Brighton Rock* to anything Greene had yet written comes from the fact that for the first time he had separated the mystery from the mystery and confronted the one with the other.

Here, of course, the confrontation takes the form of deadly warfare: "She [Ida] stared out over the red and green lights, the heavy traffic of her battlefield, laying her plans, marshalling her cannon fodder." That sense of the universal drama is both ancient and modern; for *Brighton Rock*, to put the case in perhaps exaggerated and misleading theological terms, belongs with the early and late medieval tradition, the tradition now again in fashion: the tradition of Tertullian and the dark, negative, and incorrigibly paradoxical theology wherein everything supernatural stands in implacable hostility over against everything natural and human; and for the most part, vice versa. This is the view Albert Camus has identified and attacked as *the* Christian tradition. But in another tradition, in so-called theocentric humanism, there are intermediate ends, intermediate goods, and intermediate explanations: because there is an intermediate figure, the God-man, Christ, who reconciles the realms and makes sense out of human history. But about Pinkie and his small explosive world, there is nothing intermediate—here everything is sudden and ultimate. Pinkie has no great involvement with the things of this world, with money or with sexual love or even with Brighton. His Brighton is not a town or a "background" but a Fury-driven situation; and he is involved immediately with evil and catastrophe.

He is deeply implicated, too, of course, with good—with the forlorn waitress Rose, who has just enough information about Hale's murder to make Pinkie decide savagely to marry her in order to keep her quiet; and who is as doomed to salvation (that is how Greene prefers to describe it) as Pinkie is to damnation. He sees her as his necessary counterpart. "What was most evil in him needed her; it couldn't get along without her goodness. . . . Again he got the sense that she completed him." Their world, too, is a battlefield, but with a difference:

> Good and evil lived together in the same country, spoke the same language, came together like old friends, feeling the same completion, touching hands beside the iron bedstead. . . . [Their] world lay there always, the ravaged and disputed territory between two eternities. They faced each other as it were from opposing territories, but like troops at Christmas time they fraternised.

In *Brighton Rock*, the theme of companionship, which takes so many forms in the fiction of the second generation, appears as the reluctant fellowship between good and evil and is symbolized in the illegal marriage of Pinkie and Rose and the uncertain sexual union of the two virgins on their wedding night. There, touching hands beside the iron bedstead, they peer out together at the "glare and open world," the utterly alien world of Ida Arnold. "She was as far from either of them as she was from Hell—or Heaven."

In Ida's world, the religious impulse is softened into a comfortable moralism; but in Pinkie's world, the human impulse shrivels and looks ugly. Pinkie sees only extreme alternatives—not even sacred and profane love, for example, but the supernatural and the obscene. Normal love is reduced to the pornographic, and is opposed only by fidelity to supernature; here, as in *England Made Me*, religion becomes a substitute for or even a heightened form of pornography. Pinkie quotes venomously from the cheap literature, "the kind you buy under the counter. Spicer used to get them. About girls being beaten." But in choosing the alternative, in submitting to the supernatural, Pinkie attaches himself primarily to supernatural evil. "*Credo in unum Satanum*" is the violent admission elicited on the same page by the outburst against pornography; and though he tells Rose scornfully, "Of course there's Hell," about heaven he can only say "Maybe."

As Pinkie pursues his dream of damnation, the tragic dimension of *Brighton Rock* turns into a sort of saint's life in reverse. The seven sections of the book dramatize one by one an inversion of all or most of the seven sacraments, dramatize what we might call the seven deadly sacraments: as Pinkie is confirmed in the habit of murder ("Hell lay about him in his infancy. He was ready for more deaths"), is ordained as a priest of his satanic church ("When I was a kid, I swore I'd be a priest. . . . What's wrong with being a priest? They know what's what"), performs the act of matrimony (which here is a mortal sin), and receives the vitriolic unction in the moment of his death. The entire reversal accomplished in *Brighton Rock*, haphazard though it is, manages to dignify the repellent protagonist on the principle indicated to Rose, at the very end, by the sniffling old priest: *Corruptio optimi est pessima*. The worst is the corruption of the best; only the potentially very good can become so very evil, and only the sacraments that save can so effectively become the sacraments that blast.

Despite its singularly uninviting character, accordingly, the narrow and oppressive world of Pinkie Brown is clearly to be honored—in the terms of the novel—over the spiritual bourgeoisie of Ida Arnold. Her world, for all its robust good humor, is increasingly represented as sterile, and she as a hollow, heartless menace. Ida, with her big breasts and her warm enveloping body, remains childless; it is the angular, nearly sexless Rose who conceives at once, after a single sexual venture. And the final worldly victory of Ida, her destruction of Pinkie, coincides with a hidden defeat of her own world: a repudiation of it, accomplished relentlessly by the rhetoric of the book. That rhetoric aims at separating out and then destroying the moral domain, in the name of the theological; the conventional values of right and wrong are lured into prominence and then annihilated. This is done by a series of seeming contradictions that sometimes appear strained and perverse, but often make arresting similes. A remark about Pinkie—"his virginity straightened in him like sex"—aptly suggests the colliding opposites that animate his experience. Oxymorons are employed in the account of Ida and her behavior, and with the intention of transforming or "transvaluating" our judgment of her. When allusion is made to Ida's "remorseless optimism" or her "merciless compassion," the aim is to negate the familiar human attributes—in this case, cheerfulness and pity—by stressing their remoteness from the religious virtues: in this case, penitent humility and mercy. The adjective, from its higher plane, denies all value to the nouns on their lower human level. And the whole process culminates in the epilogue when the priest, coughing and whistling through the grille in that unattractive and seedy way Greene's priests almost always have, says to Rose about Pinkie—destroyed now by the ferocious pity of Ida Arnold—that no human being can conceive "the appalling strangeness of the mercy of God."

About this verbal technique, which may best be defined as a technique of befuddlement and concerning which one has the uneasy suspicion of mere cleverness, there will be more to say. Meanwhile, it is to be noted that as the detective story and the tragedy intertwine in *Brighton Rock*, we find ourselves in a universe wherein seeming opposites—good and evil—become closely allied, and seeming likenesses—the good and the right—are totally opposed. These paradoxes, too, are incarnate in the central figure. Pinkie, Greene's first memorable image of the character he had so cherished as a boy in *The Viper of Milan*—"perfect evil walking the world where perfect good can never walk again"—is a replica of Judas who nonetheless has faint confusing echoes about him of the perfectly good, of Christ. He is the worst *only* by virtue of being the corruption of the best. And so, when his unstable associate Cubitt is talking about him to Ida and when Cubitt denies being a friend of his—" 'You a friend of Pinkie's?' Ida Arnold asked. 'Christ, no,' Cubitt said and took some more whiskey"—there is the fleeting whisper of a memory: "A court-yard, a sewing wench beside the fire, the cock crowing." And Cubitt goes on to deny him thrice.

On numerous occasions Greene has quoted the lines from AE's poem, "Germinal":

In ancient shadows and twilights
Where childhood had strayed,
The world's great sorrows were born
And its heroes were made.
In the lost boyhood of Judas
Christ was betrayed.

It is not only the realm of supernatural good and its unlikely representative Rose which are betrayed by the lost boyhood of this demonic Judas; it is also the flickers of the Christ in himself. It is within such a context and by such insinuations that Greene earns Pinkie the right to be regarded, as though reflected in a crazy-mirror on Brighton pier, as an image of the tragic hero. There can be no doubt, finally, about the damnation of Pinkie Brown: except the enormous doubt that, according to Greene, must attend our every human judgment and prediction.

The motto of *The Power and the Glory* is from Dryden: "Th' inclosure narrow'd; the sagacious power / Of hounds and death drew nearer every hour." The lines could apply to *Brighton Rock* and with a little stretching to *The Man Within*, as well as to most of Greene's entertainments; they summarize Greene's settled view of human experience. But they are peculiarly appropriate to *The Power and the Glory*, which is, one could say, Greene's settled view of human experience. But they are peculiarly appropriate to *The Power and the Glory*, which is, one could say, Greene's most peculiarly appropriate novel and which comprises the adventures of a hunted man—the last Catholic priest in a totalitarian Mexican state—whom the hounds of power catch up with and to whom death does come by a firing squad. There is no complication of genres here: the novel has a single hero and a single action—and both are strikingly representative of the special kind of hero and heroic adventure that characterize the fiction of the second generation.

According to the laws of the godless Mexican state, the priest is an outlaw simply because he carries on his priestly duties; but he has also broken the laws of his Church. He is a rogue, a *pícaro*, in several kinds of ways; his contradictory character includes much of the comical unpredictability of the traditional *pícaro;* and the narrative Greene has written about him is perhaps the most patently picaresque of any we are considering—the lively story of the rogue on his travels, or better, on his undignified flights from and toward the forces of destruction. In no other novel of our time, moreover, are the paradoxes of sainthood more expertly handled. The priest—who is a slovenly drunkard and the father of a devilish little child who giggles a good deal and is often helplessly weak at the knees—is also a potential, perhaps finally an actual saint. He feels at the end that he has failed: "It seemed to him, at that moment, that it would have been quite easy to have been a saint. . . . He felt like someone who has missed happiness at an appointed place." But other evidence throughout the book suggests that all unwittingly he had kept his appointment with beatitude. *The Power and the Glory* stands beside Silone's *Bread and Wine.* And the so-called "whiskey-priest," disguised as a layman and fumbling his way toward disaster, is, if not the twin, at least a brother of Pietro Spina, a layman (a revolutionist) disguised as a priest, and similarly the last lonely witness to truth in his own neighborhood, who is equally pursued by the forces of oppression and who is likewise the attractive, incompetent, and saintly source of damage and of death to almost everyone involved with him. These two novels give the most revealing account in second generation fiction of the hero as outlaw, fleeing and transcending the various forms that power currently assumes.

In terms of Greene's artistic and intellectual development, however, another motto, in place of Dryden's, might be drawn from the book itself: when the priest, heading bumpily into the hills of Tabasco on mule-back, daydreams in the imagery of a "simplified mythology"—"Michael dressed in armour slew the dragon, and the angels fell through space like comets with beautiful streaming hair because they were jealous, so one of the Fathers had said, of what God intended for men—the enormous privilege of life—this life." *This life.* In this novel, by a refreshing contrast with *England Made Me* and *Brighton Rock,* the religious impulse no longer denigrates and undermines the human but serves rather to find in it or to introduce into it a kind of beauty and a kind of goodness. "I tell you that heaven is here," the priest cries out to the vacant-faced peasants gathered dumbly in a hut on the mountainside at dawn. It is, of course, characteristic of Greene that, in *The Power and the Glory,* where the divine image for once irradiates and redeems the human, it is seen doing so only to the most squalid, repellent and pain-racked of human conditions—just as omens of sanctity are seen only in an unshaven brandy-bibber. Natural beauty is not enhanced, but natural ugliness is touched by grace.

> At the center of his own faith there always stood the convincing mystery—that we were made in God's image—God was the parent, but He was also the policeman, the criminal, the priest, the maniac and the judge. Something resembling God dangled from the gibbet or went into odd attitudes before the bullets in a prison yard or contorted itself like a camel in the attitude of sex. He would sit in the confessional and hear the complicated

> dirty ingenuities which God's image had thought out: and God's image shook now, up and down on the mule's back, with the yellow teeth sticking out over the lower lip, and God's image did its despairing act of rebellion with Maria in the hut among the rats.

Characteristically, too, it is less the splendor than the almost ridiculous *mystery* of the thing that Greene wants to dramatize. But let him do so in his own manner: in *The Power and the Glory* a compassionate and ultimately a very charitable manner. For it is by seeking God and by finding Him in the darkness and stench of prisons, among the sinners and the rats and the rascals, that the whiskey-priest arrives at the richest emotion second generation fiction has to offer: the feeling of companionship, and especially the companionship of the commonly guilty and wretched. Arrested for carrying brandy, crowded into a pitch-black cell, crushed between unseen odorous bodies, with a woman on one side hysterically demanding to make her trivial confession and an unseen couple copulating somewhere on the floor, announcing their orgasms with whimpering cries of pleasure, the priest is touched suddenly "by an extraordinary affection. He was just one criminal among a herd of criminals. . . . He had a sense of companionship which he had never experienced in the old days when pious people came kissing his black cotton glove."

To appreciate this scene—it is the whole of chapter three of part two, and in my opinion the most effective scene Greene has yet written—we should locate it in the structure of the novel. It begins a few pages beyond the mathematical center of the book; but it constitutes the center as well of an action that has its clear beginning and its firmly established end. The basic unit in the structure of *The Power and the Glory* is the encounter: as it is in so many other novels of the second generation with their picaresque tendency and their vision of man as an outlaw wandering or hastening through an anarchic and hostile world. In *The Power and the Glory*, as in *Bread and Wine*, the plot is episodic and consists of a succession of encounters between the harried protagonist and a number of unrelated persons—while within that succession, we observe a pattern of three dominant and crucially meaningful encounters.

We first see the priest when, in disguise, he sips brandy in the office of Mr. Tench, the morose expatriate dentist. We follow him, episode by episode, as he is hidden and given food by Coral, the precocious daughter of an agent for a banana company, Captain Fellowes, and his miserable death-haunted wife; as he arrives in the village which is the home of the woman, Maria, by whom he has had the child Brigitta; as he travels onward in the company of a mestizo, the yellow-toothed ignoble Judas who will betray him to the police; as he is arrested and released and fights his way over the mountains to freedom in a neighboring state and the comfortable home of Mr. Lehr and his sister, German-Americans from Pittsburgh, in charge of a mining operation; as he is enticed back across the border of Tabasco to attend the death of James Calver, an American murderer who has been fatally wounded by the police; is arrested again by the police lieutenant, taken back to the capital city, and executed. Tench, Coral, Maria, the Lehrs, Calver: these are all strangers to each other. The episodes with each of them thicken and expand the novelistic design (Coral, for instance, is the priest's good spiritual daughter, while Brigitta is his evil actual daughter). But the design itself is created by the three encounters between the priest and the lieutenant.

These occur at carefully spaced intervals, about one third and two thirds through the book, and then at length in the climax. The first time, the lieutenant—whose whole energy and authority are directed exclusively to capturing this last remaining agent of the Church—sees the priest and interrogates him; but he neither recognizes nor arrests him. The second time, the priest is arrested, but he is not recognized: the charge is carrying liquor. The third time, recognition is complete and the arrest final. But these encounters are mere indicators of a carefully constructed plot; the action is something different and more telling, and we are made conscious of it from the outset when—in separate, successive views of them—paradoxical resemblances are registered about the two men. The priest disappears wearily into the interior, giving up a chance to escape in order to minister to a sick peasant woman and feeling "like the King of a West African tribe, the slave of his people, who may not even lie down in case the winds should fail." On the next page, the lieutenant marches by with a ragged squad of police, looking as though "he might have been chained to them unwillingly: perhaps the scar on his jaw was the relic of an escape." Later, as he walks home alone, dreaming of a new world of justice and well-being for the children of Tabasco, "there was something of a priest in his intent observant walk—a theologian going back over the errors of the past to destroy them again." The exhausted and sometimes drunken soldier of God, the chaste and fiercely dedicated priest of the godless society: each one enslaved to his mission, doomed to his role and its outcome: these are the beings, the systole and diastole, between whom the force of the novel is generated.

Readers of Dostoyevski or of the Book of Revelation will easily identify them. They are the "hot" and the "cold" bespoken by the angel in lines quoted twice in *The Possessed:* "These things saith the Amen . . . I know thy works, that thou art neither cold nor hot: I would thou wert cold or hot. So then, because thou art lukewarm, and neither cold nor hot, I will spue thee out of my mouth" (Rev. 3: 14–16). The lieutenant has had the chilling vision of absurdity: "He was a mystic, too, and what he had experienced was a vacancy—a complete certainty in the existence of a dying, cooling world, of human beings who had evolved from animals for no purpose at all. . . . He believed against the evidence of his senses in the cold empty ether spaces." With a devotion only to the reality of the here and now, he is a rebel against all the misery and injustice and unhappiness he associates with the rule of a greedy Church and its insistence on the unimportance of the human lot in this world. He watches the children in the street, his love for them hidden beneath his hatred of the Church and its priests: "He would eliminate from their childhood everything which had made him miserable, all that was poor, superstitious and corrupt."

The lieutenant, in a word, in *l'homme révolté* of Albert Camus, seen—with respect—in the unorthodox religious perspective of Graham Greene. François Mauriac was right, in his preface to the French edition of *The Power and the Glory*, to call the novel an answer in narrative terms to the widespread European sense of absurdity—to that sense as somehow the one necessary prerequisite to the struggle for social justice. *The Power and the Glory* is not perhaps *the* answer; but it does contain, among other things, a potent allegory of one of the major intellectual debates of our time. Greene, too, it should be said, gives fairer and more substantial play to what he regards as the opposition—embodied in the lieutenant—than Camus gives to *his* opponent, the crudely drawn cleric Paneloux in *The Plague.* Camus contrasts Paneloux, and his helpless appeal to divine irrationality, with the rational and dignified Rieux and Tarrou; while Greene joins the upright police officer in a contest with the wavering and incompetent whiskey-priest. Yet the nameless priest, consecrating moistly amidst the unspeakable heat and the detonating beetles of Tabasco, sweating his way toward a sort of befuddled glory, is of course the representative of the "hot," and the lieutenant's proper adversary.

These two are the persons of stature in the universe of the novel, and eventually they acknowledge each other. "You're a good man," the priest says in astonishment when, at the moment of his release from prison, the lieutenant gives him five pesos. And: "You aren't a bad fellow," the lieutenant concedes grudgingly, during the long conversations after the final arrest. Most of the other characters, those whom Greene calls "the bystanders," are the lukewarm, and their artistic purpose is, by a variety of contrasts, to illuminate the nature of the hunt. A good many of the more "regular" members of the Church, in fact, both in the past and now in the pleasant safety of another state, appear as lukewarm; *The Power and the Glory* may be a religious novel, but it is decidedly not an ecclesiastical one. The priest himself had been lukewarm in the old days, going smugly on his parochial rounds and attending the meetings of the guilds. It is only in his moment of degradation, arrested not even for being the last priest with the courage to remain in Tabasco but only as a common citizen carrying contraband, that the priest reveals the "hot," the heroic side. He does so unconsciously, out of humility and a conviction of his own unworthiness and an irrepressible sense of humor. We return to the prison scene mentioned above: it occurs just before the second of the three major encounters.

The whole of it should be studied, from the entrance into the cell to the departure next morning and the sudden sense of companionship even with the lieutenant. But perhaps the following fragments can suggest the remarkable interplay—not, in this case, the remote opposition—of sacred and obscene love, of beauty and extreme ugliness, of comedy and deadly peril: all of which gives the scene a rich multiplicity of action beyond anything Greene had previously achieved. Just as the key moment in *Bread and Wine* occurs in the darkness of a squalid hut, so here the "epiphany" takes place in the blackness and stench of a prison.

> Among the furtive movements came again the muffled painless cries. He realised with horror that pleasure was going on even in this crowded darkness. Again he put out his foot and began to edge his way inch by inch from the grill.
>
> "They'll shoot you, father," the woman's voice said.
> "Yes."
> "Are you afraid?"
> "Yes. Of course."
> A new voice spoke, in the corner from which the sounds of pleasure had come. It said roughly and obstinately, "A man isn't afraid of a thing like that."
> "No?" the priest asked.
> "A bit of pain. What do you expect? It has to come."
> "All the same," the priest said, "I *am* afraid."
> "Toothache is worse."
> "We can't all be brave men."
> The voice said with contempt, "You believers are all the same. Christianity makes you cowards."
> "Yes. Perhaps you are right. You see I am a bad priest and a

bad man. To die in a state of mortal sin"—he gave an uneasy chuckle—"it makes you think."

A long train of thought began, which led him to announce after a while, "They are offering a reward for me. Five hundred, six hundred pesos, I'm not sure." Then he was silent again. He couldn't urge any man to inform against him—that would be tempting him to sin—but at the same time, if there was an informer here, there was no reason why the wretched creature should be bilked of his reward. To commit so ugly a sin—it must count as murder—and to have no compensation in this world. . . . He thought: it wouldn't be fair.

"Nobody here," a voice said, "wants their blood money."

Again he was touched by an extraordinary affection. He was just one criminal among a herd of criminals. . . . He had a sense of companionship which he had never experienced in the old days, when pious people came kissing his black cotton glove.

The pious woman's voice leapt hysterically out at him. "It's so stupid to tell them that. You don't know the sort of wretches who are here, father. Thieves, murderers. . . ."

"Well," an angry voice said, "why are you here?"

"I had good books in my house," she announced, with unbearable pride. He had done nothing to shake her complacency. He said, "They are everywhere. It's no different here."

"Good books?"

He giggled. "No, no. Thieves, murderers. . . . Oh, well, my child, if you had more experience, you would know there are worse things to be."

Somewhere against the far wall pleasure began again: it was unmistakeable: the movements, the breathlessness, and then the cry. The pious woman said aloud with fury, "Why won't they stop it? The brutes, the animals!"

"What's the good of your saying an Act of Contrition now in this state of mind?"

"But the ugliness. . . ."

"Don't believe that. It's dangerous. Because suddenly we discover that our sins have so much beauty."

"Beauty," she said with disgust. "Here. In this cell. With strangers all around."

"Such a lot of beauty. Saints talk about the beauty of suffering.

Well, we are not saints, you and I. Suffering to us is just ugly. Stench and crowding and pain. *That* is beautiful in that corner—to them. It needs a lot of learning to see things with a saint's eye: a saint gets a subtle taste for beauty and can look down on poor ignorant palates like theirs. But we can't afford to."

"It's a mortal sin."

"We don't know. It may be. But I'm a bad priest, you see. I know—from experience—how much beauty Satan carried down with him when he fell. Nobody ever said the fallen angels were the ugly ones. Oh no, they were just as quick and light and . . ."

Again the cry came, an expression of intolerable pleasure. The woman said, "Stop them. It's a scandal." He felt fingers on his knees, grasping, digging. He said. "We're all fellow prisoners. I want drink at this moment more than anything, more than God. That's a sin too."

"Now," the woman said, "I can see you're a bad priest. I wouldn't believe it before. I do now. You sympathise with these animals. If your Bishop heard you . . ."

"Ah, he's a very long way off." He thought of the old man now—in the capital: living in one of those ugly comfortable pious houses, full of images and holy pictures, saying Mass on Sundays at one of the Cathedral altars.

"When I get out of here, I shall write . . ."

He couldn't help laughing: she had no sense of change at all. He said, "If he gets the letter he'll be interested—to hear I'm alive."

Pinkie Brown and Major Scobie, the protagonists of *Brighton Rock* and *The Heart of the Matter*, are never seen to smile, much less to laugh; the former is in a constant state of fury, the latter of apprehension. It is the laughter, almost more than anything else, that distinguishes *The Power and the Glory:* laughter based on the recognition of God's image in man, evoked by the preposterous incongruity of it and yet leading naturally to a warmth of fellow-feeling. Here again, a similarity may be noted with the comedy and the companionship of *Bread and Wine;* and perhaps Silone was not wrong, after all, to turn the ridiculous Sciatàp of that novel into the treacherous figure of *The Seed beneath the Snow*. In this particular comic vision, even the traitors—even the Judases—have a clownish aspect. Contemplating the mestizo (in another passage) and recognizing him as a Judas, Greene's priest remembers a Holy Week carnival where a stuffed Judas was hanged from the belfry and pelted with bits of tin: "it seemed to him a good thing that the world's traitor should be made a figure of fun. It was too easy otherwise to idealise him as a man who fought with God—a Prometheus, a noble victim in a hopeless war" (the very archetype, in short, of Camus's rebel). But the force of the comic consciousness in *The Power and the Glory* is indicated, properly enough, at the end, when the lieutenant, having completed his mission and arranged for the priest's execution, sits down at his desk and falls asleep. "He couldn't remember afterwards anything of his dream except laughter, laughter all the time, and a long passage in which he could find no door." It is the lieutenant, Greene suggests, who is the trapped man, the prisoner; and the laughter he hears is like that laughter recorded by Dante on the upper slopes of purgatory, the chorus celebrating the release of a captive human soul from punishment and its entrance into paradise.

The priest himself hears none of that laughter and goes to his death persuaded of practical and spiritual failure: "I don't know a thing about the mercy of God," he tells the lieutenant, in the phrase that also rounds out *Brighton Rock* and *The Heart of the Matter*; ". . . But I do know this—that if there's ever been a single man in this state damned, then I'll be damned too. . . . I wouldn't want it any different." It never occurs to the priest that if he should so far honor the mestizo as to call him a Judas, he might himself appear as a version of the man Judas betrayed. The book has been hinting as much all along, in the pattern and style of the priest's adventures. The relationship is far more pressing and elaborate here than in *Brighton Rock* or *The Heart of the Matter*, where the vigor of supernature is hardly sweetened by the figure of intermediary and reconciler. The priest, accordingly, preaches to the poor and the meek and downtrodden across the hilly countryside; is tempted in the wilderness; is betrayed, tried, and executed. Toward the end, he, too, is juxtaposed with a common criminal—the Yankee killer, whose name, James Calver, echoes two syllables of the mount on which Christ was crucified, and opposite whose picture in the prison office there is a picture of the priest, grinning within the halo someone had inked around the face for identification. There is even a kind of resurrection in the little epilogue—about which one has mixed feelings—when a new, frightened priest arrives in town and is greeted with reverence by the boy Juan, who, prior to the martyrdom, had been a disciple of the lieutenant. That epilogue, offering presumably the first of the priest's miracles after death, insists perhaps too much. But if the priest is associated not only with Christ but with non-Christian divinities—the god-king of an African tribe, and the surrogate for the god, the bull that was slaughtered in the early Greek ritual of sacrifice and rebirth ("Then there was a single shot . . . the bull was dead")—the entire pattern is nevertheless artistically redeemed by a full awareness of the grotesque disproportion between the model and its re-enactment. "The priest giggled: he couldn't stop himself. He said, 'I don't think martyrs are like this.' " It is the giggle that saves both the priest and the novel Greene has written about him. For it is when he laughs that we know this slovenly rogue, this unshaven *pícaro,* to be also a saint; and we know that here for once—as in only one or two other novels—the paradoxes have held firm and the immense delicate balance has been maintained.

The Heart of the Matter is the most traditional of Greene's novels, in both content and construction. As such, it is obviously less representative than *The Power and the Glory;* and as such, it has a special appeal for those who mean by the word *novel* the kind of work that was typical in the nineteenth century. We note a major paradox about second generation writers: they are developing a rather new sort of fiction—the novel as an act of inquiry or of rebellion or of expiation, rather than as a direct and unprejudiced impression of life; but at the same time, most of them turn for support not to the experimental achievements of the first generation but to the literary forms of the nineteenth century.

The paradox is further strained in the case of *The Heart of the Matter.* Here, for example, is the careful delineation, not altogether unworthy of Trollope, of various discordant elements in a multicolored society, the society of the coastal city in West Africa that Greene had known on his journey in 1935 and again as a government official during the war in 1942–43, the date of the novel's action. In *The Heart of the Matter,* there is no savage eruption out of animal holes into the glare and open world that characterized *Brighton Rock,* and none of the rhythmic peregrinations through anarchy of *The Power and the Glory.* The incidents take place very much *within* the society of the book and involve—not proscribed outlaws but—persons of significance and authority whose intimate knowledge of each other provides much of the hero's tragic dilemma. Here, too, there is a narrative pace, leisurely but never slack, reminiscent of Greene's distant relation, Robert Louis Stevenson. Greene may not be a master of all the elements of fiction, but that he is a master of narrative can be doubted only by those too little interested in storytelling to be capable of discrimination; *The Heart of the Matter* is very handsomely told. And here, too, is an array of characters in the old tradition—and including one especially, the merchant Yusef, whose fat and candid dishonesty would have pleased Dickens and even more, Wilkie Collins. Here, in short, is a traditional, almost a conventional *novel* that is yet a novel by

Graham Greene, and something the nineteenth century could scarcely have imagined. For what the action serves to expose is not the habits of a society or the nature of the human heart (no one, says Father Rank in the epilogue, knows "what goes on in a single human heart"); but, going beyond all that, the absolute mystery of the individual destiny.

"Why, why did he have to make such a mess of things?" This is the hopeless and embittered question raised on the last page by Major Scobie's wife, Louise: not "Why did he?" but "Why did he *have to?*" That Scobie, the late Assistant Commissioner of Police, had made an appalling mess of things cannot be denied. *The Heart of the Matter* is the progressive account of it, from the first moment when he is passed over for promotion, through the disappointment of his restless, vaguely artistic wife—a disappointment so great that Scobie makes a dubious if not illegal transaction with the diamond-smuggler, Yusef, to get enough money to send her on a trip to South Africa; through the adulterous affair with the schoolgirlish widow, Helen Rolt, on which he embarks during his wife's absence; through the now rapid deterioration of his public and private life; through the agony—for a Catholic of his temperament—of receiving the sacrament in a condition of mortal sin; to the still graver sin of despair and suicide by which Scobie ends his career. The mess is so great and Scobie's talent, at every turn, for making bad matters worse is so remarkable that the novel has occasionally been dismissed as implausible. George Orwell once wrote to the effect that no one who could get into such deep trouble so quickly could ever have had the honorable career Scobie is alleged to have had in the first place. In the sane and skeptical humanism of Orwell, the contention is reasonable; but it is a point made outside the world of the book; within that world, the issue of plausibility does not arise.

As a matter of fact, the novel offers a definite though still typically mysterious answer to Louise Scobie's question. It would not have satisfied Orwell, for it is not drawn, finally, from psychology: that, Greene thinks, is not where the real mystery lies. But, before approaching the real mystery, it should be said that *The Heart of the Matter* does also offer clues for a purely psychological explanation of Scobie and his conduct. He has the ingredients of a genuine tragic hero. He is presented as a good man, rather better than most, with an inviolable sense of justice irritating to some of his colleagues. "You're a terrible fellow, Scobie," the commissioner tells him affectionately. "Scobie the Just." He is an able man and within limits a forceful one; and he is a strong Catholic with that special religious intensity that only Greene's Catholics (not, that is, the Catholics one thought one knew) betray. And he has a fatal flaw: but it is not arrogance or any normal form of pride; Scobie calls down ruin on himself, plainly and articulately, but not through *hubris*. His flaw is an excess of the quality Greene calls pity—an inability to watch disappointment or suffering in others—with this portion perhaps of pride (in Greene's view), that he feels it peculiarly incumbent upon himself to relieve the pain. In *The Ministry of Fear*, the entertaining trail run for *The Heart of the Matter*, Arthur Row's troubles begin when he commits a mercy killing—or, to stick to Greene's verbal distinctions, a "pity-killing"—to end the intolerable physical suffering of his wife. Scobie kills no one, though he feels himself implicated in several deaths; like some other heroes of second generation fiction, it is his misfortune to harm most of those he longs to help or even to save.

Scobie's troubles begin with his attempt to alleviate the painful disappointment of his wife. His feeling of guilt about her is due partly to his failure to be promoted; but it is rooted more deeply in another failure, an inability any longer to love his wife; and it goes back, too, to the moment when Scobie was unable to be present at the death of his child. He is a man clearly given to self-accusation, and the pattern of it thickens as the story moves forward. It might well be that the suicide, a third of the way through, of Dick Pemberton—an assistant district commissioner at Bamba who hangs himself and whose mode of death affects Scobie enormously—may have released in Scobie a congenital self-destructive impulse. Pemberton's name, Dicky, with which he signed the suicide note, and the nickname Louise has coyly pinned on her husband—Ticki (his real name is Henry)—blur in Scobie's mind while he lies ill with fever after the Pemberton affair; and from then on, the pace of his decline grows more rapid. Scobie, in summary, is an affecting human being, whose sorry career is all too understandable. He is burdened by his own habit of pity for others. But we can ally ourselves with him in that other kind of pity that Aristotle called one of the two emotions properly evoked by tragedy. Still, it is the second of the emotions named by Aristotle—the emotion of tragic terror—that is the more deeply aroused in us by this novel, according to Greene's intention. Tragic pity (to borrow Joyce's definitions of these ancient terms) associates us with the human sufferer, during his grave and terrible experience. Tragic terror springs rather from our stimulated awareness of the secret cause of the suffering; and in *The Heart of the Matter*, as traditionally, that secret cause is the action of God.

The "heart of the matter," as a phrase, occurs after the opening of the novel's second part, when Scobie, momentarily alone and looking up at the stars, wonders whether "If one knew . . . would one have to feel pity even for the planets? if one reached what they called the heart of the matter?"

Less than ten minutes later, unknowingly—though he does suddenly feel cold and strange—Scobie reaches the heart of the matter and gives up the peace of his own soul. Coming in from his reverie, into the resthouse where they have brought the stretcher-cases from a torpedoed ship, Scobie is asked to stand watch over two victims who lie unconscious on two beds divided by a screen. One is a six-year-old girl. Looking at her, Scobie thinks again of his own dead daughter; and he begins to pray. "Father . . . give her peace. Take away my peace for ever, but give her peace." We are to understand, I believe, that God does exactly that. He gives the child the peace of death and a release from suffering, and Scobie's peace is taken away for the remainder of his earthly career. This is the book's major turning point, when pity deepens into terror. And the human agent through whom God acts is the patient on the other side of the screen, "the young woman lying unconscious on her back, still grasping the stamp-album." It is Helen Rolt, whom pity and loneliness will drive Scobie to make love to, in an affair that so torments Scobie's Catholic conscience that only an overdose of tablets can rescue him.

Here, as in *The End of the Affair* and *The Potting Shed,* God moves in a singularly Mephistophelean manner, His wonders to perform—a deity with whom one bargains away one's peace or love or beliefs, for the life of someone else. In a letter to the French Christian existentialist Marcel Moré, Greene put Scobie's case plainly enough: "Obviously one did have in mind that when he offered up his peace for the child it was genuine prayer and had the results that followed. I always believe that such prayers, though obviously a God would not fulfill them to the limit of robbing him of a peace for ever, are answered up to the point as a kind of test of a man's sincerity and to see whether in fact the offer was merely based on emotion." Literary criticism does not invite us to scruple over Greene's religious orthodoxy or lack of it; our concern is simply the dramatic effectiveness of any religious opinion he happens to show. On this ground, *The Heart of the Matter* should be reckoned as successful precisely by implying a terrible tension between the divine and the human—a somber and disturbing modern version of the Greek tragic tension between fate and freedom. As in almost everything Greene has written except *The Power and the Glory*, the supernatural power and the human religious impulse work against the purely human inclination: even when the result is an awe-inspiring fulfillment, the granting of a wish. We may be dismayed that things are seen to be happening so, but that they are seen dramatically cannot be doubted.

Greek classical tragedy customarily ended by a choral acknowledgment of the unsolvable mystery and the purgatorial terror. Father Rank performs a similar function in *The Heart of the Matter,* in the epilogue Greene has characteristically added to ensure our befuddlement over the exact meaning of the events. "For goodness' sake, Mrs. Scobie, don't imagine you—or I—know a thing about God's mercy. . . . The Church knows all the rules. But it doesn't know what goes on in a single human heart." Again, the institutionalized Church is opposed in the name of the religious mystery; and again, the sheer incomprehensibility of God's mercy and grace is the aspect insisted upon. Again, too, the hero, moving doggedly toward disaster, is oddly associated with the figure of Christ: in the manner of *Brighton Rock* rather than *The Power and the Glory,* for we are once more in a universe without intermediaries. The role of Judas is played out by the English government spy, Wilson, who covets Scobie's wife as well as his reputation for integrity; and Scobie tries desperately to condone his act of despair by seeing in it an imitation of Christ: "Christ had not been murdered: Christ had killed himself: he had hung himself on the Cross as surely as Pemberton from the picture rail"—a notion that turns up again after the suicide in *The Living Room.* All these items provide the reader, as planned, with a full measure of uncertainty about Scobie's conduct in this world and his chances in the next. It is suggested in the last lines that Scobie may really have loved God; and it is suggested that God may be the only being he did love. The night before he encounters the dying child and Helen Rolt, we hear Scobie murmuring the incomplete phrase as he falls asleep, "O God, bless—," and later, another incomplete phrase as he falls senseless and dying: "Dear God, I love . . ." Not even the reader, who knows more about Scobie than anyone else, can be sure of the objects of those verbs.

Psychology thus yields to a dark theology, the pity to the terror, the human sufferer to the secret cause. All we are meant to know is that we know nothing; that is the answer to Louise's question. Pinkie Brown *almost* certainly is damned, and he was without any doubt a vicious and wicked young man. The Mexican priest is almost certainly saved, and he was one of the most curiously sympathetic figures in modern fiction. We conclude, about Henry Scobie, in a purging sense of the unguessable nature of human conduct and divine intervention. Insofar as they do constitute a trilogy, Greene's three novels reverse the direction of the greatest religious trilogy, *The Divine Comedy.* Dante's poem moves from ignorance to knowledge, from discord to harmony, from unspeakable darkness to overwhelming light. Greene's "trilogy" moves stealthily deeper into the darkness, moves through the annihilation of our confidence in human knowledge to an awareness of impenetrable mystery, moves from the deceptive light to the queerly nourishing obscurity. All the truth of things, for Greene, lies hidden in the darkness: whether of slum-ridden Brighton, of a squalid prison cell, or of a West African night of wonder and despair. Scarcely less mysterious is Greene's achievement of making visible in that darkness, and exactly by means of it, the unforgettable dramas of extraordinarily living human beings.

FRANK KERMODE

Mr. Greene's Eggs and Crosses

Oh, is God prodigall? hath he spent his store
of plagues on us, and only now, when more
Would ease us much, doth he grudge misery,
And will not let's enjoy our curse, to dy?

Mr. Graham Greene's new novel is so far below one's expectation that the questions arise, was the expectation reasonable, and has there been any previous indication that a failure of this kind was a possibility? So I have been reading the novels since *The Power and the Glory* (1940) and taking some note of what Mr. Greene's by now numerous commentators have said about them. Here one jostles uncomfortably with Waterbury, the critic in *The End of the Affair,* who loses his girl to Bendrix the novelist, which is an allegory and explains what critics (men of limited potency) may expect if they are unpleasant to their betters. Hence their refined envy; it is very noticeable that the best criticism of Mr. Greene is hostile. He himself seems to find it all distasteful, whether it is the adulatory sort that discovers "buried significance . . . of which I was unaware" or the nasty sort that finds "faults I was tired of facing." But critics write for people, not for novelists; a poet commenting on another's work is far more likely to say a line won't do than that it suggests a corruption of consciousness which ought to be purged; the novelist does not need to be told that his technical shortcomings have large moral implications. If Mr. Greene, as I think, was always, on the evidence of his earlier work, likely to write a big serious novel that would die at birth, he knew better than anybody that it was so; this, however, does not excuse Waterbury from doing his bit.

A Burnt-Out Case seems to be this novel. Querry, a famous Catholic

---

From *Encounter* 16, no. 4 (April 1961).

architect, takes flight from his old life and stops only when he can go no farther, having reached the heart of darkness, a *leproserie* deep in the Congo. His spiritual condition, as he and the devoted but rationalist doctor Colin see it, is parallel to the physical state of a leper in whom the disease, treated too late, has had to run its course; though technically cured he is mutilated, a burnt-out case. Querry is given such a patient as his servant; and when this man runs off into the bush, in search of some lost paradise, Querry follows him and saves his life, watching with him all night. This act, and some modest building operations undertaken for the priests who run the settlement, seem to be working for the restoration of Querry's humanity. But the diagnosis of Querry and Colin is not accepted by some other characters, notably Fr. Thomas, an unstable priest, Rycker, a detestably pious margarine manufacturer, once a seminarist, and Parkinson, a corrupt English journalist. In pressing home his complaint against Rycker, whose high-minded gossip has proved a serious nuisance, Querry is involved with Rycker's unhappy young wife; instead of seducing her he spends the night telling her the story of his life, got up rather archly as a sort of fairy tale. Hating her husband, she announces that Querry is the father of the child she is carrying, and the consequence of this affair, totally anomalous because Querry has been a selfish and successful lover of women, is that Rycker shoots his rival. Querry dies amused at the irony of this; his power over women was always an index of his worldly success, and when he renounced success he renounced women too; but he dies their victim.

This fable is constructed with economy and skill. It is a characteristic Greene plot (though less complex than some), for it turns upon a point of comedy, or farce—the husband-wife-lover situation which occurs in a considerable variety of manifestations in the later Greene, and with special ingenuity in *The End of the Affair* and *The Complaisant Lover*. (This time the lover is pitying, impotent, and bores the wife all night.) The timing of the story is very exact; the burnt-out leper is not too obtrusive, the talk with the girl is dramatically well-placed, and the catastrophe is arranged like an expert final act: an innocent champagne party with the priests celebrating the erection of a roof-tree on Querry's building, the approaching storm, the arrival of the Ryckers, which ends the story by destroying not only Querry's life but his growing reputation for sanctity. The clinical details of leprosy are tactfully disposed though shocking in the right degree ("the sweet smell of sloughed skin") and the descriptions of tropical river and bush have the moody accuracy one has learned to expect. The idiom is often satisfyingly Greeneian—there is an ample provision of those new proverbs of hell: "it was God's taste to be worshipped and their taste to worship, but only at stated hours like a suburban embrace on a Saturday night"; "suffering is something which will always be provided when required"; and there are some of those sad recondite conceits: "The pouches under his eyes were like purses that contained the smuggled memories of a disappointing life." Everywhere there is evidence of competent arrangements. It is arranged, for instance, that we should not like the priests, yet be forced to meditate on their view of the meaning of the events described. If the texture of these events is thinner than in, say, *The Heart of the Matter*, that merely makes clearer the theme of the book; the problem is not to find a way of saying what this is, but rather to account for the discrepancy between it and the story, the failure to give it a body.

The theme, to name it accurately but perhaps misleadingly, is Heroic Virtue. This term is used during a conversation between Colin and the dreadful, stubborn Fr. Thomas in the lull before the stormy climax of the book. Fr. Thomas is saying what a good thing it was for them that Querry had dropped in and put up this new building. Colin observes that it was an even better thing for Querry himself, who is now almost cured. Fr. Thomas at once reduces Querry's history to a familiar theological term: "the better the man the worse the aridity." He has been determined, ever since he found out who Querry was, to understand him in this language and no other. The doctor protests that they have no application to Querry's case; but the priest answers that whereas the doctor is trained to spot the early symptoms of leprosy, the priest is expert in detecting incipient Heroic Virtue. This is one of the best scenes in the book, full of ironies, little time-bombs planted with short fuses among the illusory satisfactions of the evening; and not the least striking of them is the implicit analogy between leprosy and Heroic Virtue. Fr. Thomas does not use the expression loosely; he has in mind the teaching of the Church on this subject, which, if I understand it, is pretty definite. Between the "political" or "social" virtues and the "divine" or "exemplary" virtues—between the human and the divine—there are intermediate virtues of two degrees of perfection, the first of which are called purifying (*purgatoriae*) and the second "the virtues of the purified soul" (*virtutes iam purgati animi*). Fr. Thomas presumably supposes Querry's bad time to have corresponded to the first of these states, and his present conduct to the second. The condition of Heroic Virtue is distinguished from that of sanctity, though officially described as "rare in this life." Fr. Thomas, in short, is putting Querry pretty high, and in terms of a doctrine which means nothing to Colin or to Querry himself. The situation is characteristic of the author, who is constantly pointing out that human behaviour acquires an entirely different and often disturbing valuation when you consider it in the light of religious doctrine; and the question here is whether you ought to do so, especially when that doctrine is applied mechanically by vulgar and imperceptive people, including priests.

For this religious interpretation of Querry's life is applied by others, and indeed it is the cause of the crisis of the plot. The practice was started by Rycker with his vulgar lust for holiness; then Fr. Thomas odiously takes it up, with his theory of aridity: "Perhaps even now you are walking in the footsteps of St. John of the Cross, the *noche oscura.*" He can't get it into their heads that he is merely burnt out. The journalist Parkinson, vulgarised beyond any hope that he might recognise distinctions between truth and falsehood, wants to make of Querry a Sunday-paper Schweitzer, even a saint if that will please Them (his readers). "I wouldn't be surprised if there were pilgrims at your shrine in twenty years, and that's how history's written. *Exegi monumentum.* Quote. Virgil." But divine intervention in human affairs is, as we could have learnt from Mr. Greene, apparently capricious, often tasteless, and quite capable of working through Rycker or Parkinson. Even Colin has his doubts about Querry: "You're too troubled by your lack of faith. . . . You keep on fingering it like a sore." And Querry himself remembers, "in moments of superstition," that there are religious explanations for his condition; for instance, he thinks that in choosing art he deliberately forfeited grace, a point Fr. Thomas would confute simply by indicating his good works.

On the whole, however, Querry offers naturalist explanations only, and these, of course, conflict with the others. This is the choice the book offers. Either Querry is right, or God is a plot-maker, working through his inferior priests, through the theological pervert Rycker, through innocence and pity (great enemies of human happiness in Greene); ready to use any degree of absurdity—an incompetent private detective, a preposterous Palais Royal bedroom scene, to get His way. And this is only the crisis; before it God has, on this view, been fostering Querry's self-disgust, making him more and more successful, more and more powerful with women, so as to get him ready for the last strategem.

This is perfectly all right; what goes wrong is the presentation of Querry's alternative explanation. He has recovered from the sickness of faith, and may be getting over the sickness of success. But his way of life has hardened all within and petrified the feeling. He has a dream (Mr. John Atkins in his book reminds us of the extraordinary number of explanatory dreams Mr. Greene's characters have) in which he makes this point: "I can't feel at all, I'm a leper." The one thing he is sure of is that his state has nothing to do with vitality, nobility, or spiritual depth, yet there is this conspiracy to enforce the theory that it has. His identity is discovered in the first place through a cover-drawing in *Time* magazine, which romanticised his features and gave him a soulful, mysterious quality; this is an experience Mr. Greene has had himself. And this is the really important point. Querry, the famous Catholic architect, is a famous Catholic writer thinly disguised; and if it was ever true—as Mr. Greene's hostile critics insist—that the earlier novels are sometimes flawed by the author's inability to stand clear of his hero or victim, it is certainly true of this book.

In one of his long conversations with Colin, Querry explains that he never built except for his own pleasure, and perhaps never loved a woman except for the same reason. "A writer doesn't write for his readers, does he? . . . The subject of a novel is not the plot." He makes buildings (books) in which people can be comfortable, but he is not interested in their use, and hardly minds when they are clogged with cheap ornaments (the irrelevant personal rubbish a reader might bring to a book to make it seem lived-in). The real object of writing (building) is selfish: "Self-expression is a hard and selfish thing. It eats everything, even the self. At the end you find you haven't even got a self to express. I have no interest in anything. . . . I don't want to sleep with a woman or design a building." The difficulty is that Querry's self-explanation is a mere diagram; he has chosen a self-consuming artist's life, perfection of the work. Even when he is drawn into the service of suffering he protests that "Human beings are not my country." For the doctrine of the priests he substitutes not nature but a myth of decadence; there is even a secular version of Fr. Thomas's smug theory of aridity in his talk of the artist's regress. One is driven towards the position taken up by Miss Elizabeth Sewell in a remarkable essay on Mr. Greene published a few years ago in the *Dublin Review:* he is a novelist of the Decadence, writing not as a Catholic but as a neo-Romantic. His heroes, all *maudits*, know nothing of the happiness and hope that are, after all, part of religion; his world is one in which only Faust can be saved, and the victimised postures of his heroes are ultimately Faustian. I should want to modify Miss Sewell's account of the basic myth, but there seems no doubt that Querry, more than any other of the heroes, is a poseur, and ought not to be if the conflict between religious and secular interpretations of his life is to have a valid basis.

This issue becomes very acute in the fairy-tale version of his life which Querry tells Mme. Rycker to put her to sleep. Reviewers have called this embarrassing; yet it is the marrow of the book. It exposes the falsity of Querry's position, not because the stupid priests are necessarily right, but because their view of the matter can be fully and ironically presented but this decadent mythology cannot. He speaks of a man who has not been able to detect the hand of God in human life; who sees virtue rewarded by the death of a child (the crucial test of God in *The Heart of the Matter*) and viciousness punished only invisibly. Instead of being a great artist he became a sort of Fabergé, making ingenious jewels and enjoying many women. God refused to allow him to suffer. But although people thought he must be very good to have such rewards from God—as others who got their legs cut off in accidents must be very bad—he found that, unable to suffer, he was unable to love. His jewels were fashionable, and people said he was not only a master-technician but dealt with serious subject-matter, because he made eggs with gold crosses on top, "set with precious stones in honour of the King." About this time a mistress committed suicide, without his being much disturbed. Then, as popular favour waned, the connoisseurs took him up. "They began to write books about his art; especially those who claimed to know and love the King" calling him, for instance, "the Jeweller of Original Sin." For "jeweller" one reads "architect = Querry = novelist = ?" (Mr. Greene has said before that a novel is always a kind of confession.) At this point the jeweller sees that his work has nothing to do with love, the love of the King for his people; and he wonders, as the whole plot of Mr. Greene's novel does, whether his unbelief and the ugliness of his success are not finally proof of the King's existence. While he has been talking the night away the King has in fact been at work, in the shape of the prying Parkinson, ensuring that this "success" will amount in the end to the same thing as failure, that so much more desirable fate. Only failures can be good, and God is a specialist in failure. Querry is to have his suffering; "with suffering we become part of the Christian myth." He dies not for his own crimes but for those of the Ryckers; as in *The Heart of the Matter* this is a case of *victimage*, like Huysmans refusing morphia for cancer of the throat.

The artist's lust for suffering can be called a leading theme of Mr. Greene's. There is a hint of it in the famous autobiographical piece, "The Revolver in the Corner Cupboard." Since the acceptance of God entails pain, it is a theme to be found in *The End of the Affair*. It is strongly present in this book, a dominant, but not fully embodied theme; and behind it is something less easy to extract, the persistent notion of God as the enemy, whose disastrous invasion of human life is called by theologians love. Let us look, without making too much of it, at the little emblem of the egg-jewel with the cross on top. On the world of natural generation is stuck, incongruous, the heraldic device of God. Mr. Greene's books are like that. We could get along, better perhaps since He is so interested in pain, without God. Scobie's situation would have been tolerable if the egg had no cross; his wife uses the pledge of God's love to torment him, and out of love he comes to death; even death is worse with God, since one cannot take it out of His hands without wounding Him. (To the non-believer like Fowler in *The Quiet American* death is something one may reasonably desire, like sex, though, virgins all, we may be scared of it as well as attracted.) The harshness of Mr. Greene's Christianity is that the unforgivable sins are the most tempting, and that however unreasonable God may be He is also strong, and has somehow convinced us that He is easily hurt. How much easier to be a Stoic! Sometimes it seems that the disaster—that aboriginal calamity—that fell upon us was not the Fall but God (who foresaw without willing it). Ever since His arrival on the scene the good human emotions, and chiefly pity, are dangerous, innocence an evil trap. Querry is only the last of Greene heroes to be caught in it. They belong only to the nursery paradise, not to the wild woods forlorn of the fallen. Scobie has to pray *not* to be a decent fellow, but to do the will of a master who allows children to die after surviving forty days in a ship's boat, so that he may save his soul; but pity frustrates him. The priest in *The Power and the Glory* is obsessed with the need to protect God from himself. Sin is the shadow thrown by the strong light of God; Mr. Greene is of the devil's party and comes near to knowing it. God's priests are rarely up to much; the natural man has little time for the voluntary eunuch. This only strengthens the case against Him; He has made us as we are and expects us, on terrible penalties, to behave otherwise; He would not leave us in the state of the amoeba, yet He denies us adult brains. "Why did He give us genitals if he wanted us to think clearly?" ("Vainly begot, and yet forbidden vanity, Created sick, commanded to be sound.") Once the intellect accepts God (Mr. Greene has emphasised that his reception into the Church was a result of intellectual rather than emotional conviction) a terrible incongruity invades human affairs; confronted with that image human sex becomes fury and mire. The natural man can scarcely act without alienating Him; there is even a feeling that the ugly shapes of the world are caused by this constraint. Yet if He wants heroes He has to find them among the dying generations; He must work in the fury and the mire. *A Burnt-Out Case* may be read as an account of His doing so, confronted with a naturalist account of the same events.

The resultant tension might make a great book; it does not have that effect here, or anywhere else except in *The End of the Affair*. The *Power and the Glory* sometimes comes near to a full realisation, with its well-placed sermon on pain and fear as "part of heaven," the paradoxical emphasis on the beauty of sin, especially sexual sin (as in the passage with the pious old maid and the shameless copulators in prison) and the perversely high valuation put upon suffering. The priest's surprised admission that his enemy, the lieutenant, is "a good man," and the determined irrationalism of his conduct, especially at the crisis, silently stress the obsessive theme, the use God makes of wantonly unsuitable material for humanly detestable ends. And, as nearly always in Mr. Greene, the concept of mortal sin, so incredible on the human view of decency, is continually eroded by reservations of all sorts. But it is true that this endless complaint about God seems less to be shaping the book than tearing it apart, and I think it is on this score that *The Power and the Glory* has had some damaging criticism, notably from F. N. Lees, who thinks it never becomes "the study of will and conduct," it seems to aim at being, but sinks into "self-condemnatory reverie"; instead of an "evaluating vision of a situation" we get a ventriloquial performance with an interesting dummy. Mr. Lees argues from evidences of strain in the language of the book; Mr. Hoggart, with a very nice understanding of its qualities, comes nevertheless, though from a different direction, to the same conclusion: "we are in the presence of an unusually controlled allegory. . . . The characters have a kind of life, but that life is always breathed into them by Greene's breath. In Greene's novels we do not 'explore experience'; we meet Graham Greene." Though I think both these criticisms are too severe, one sees what brought them into being; Mr. Greene's war against the intolerable God his intellect accepts is an extremely personal matter, and its obsessive presence is felt everywhere, colouring, distorting, taking the place of, more generalised "experience," suggesting that "will and conduct" are only defensive tactics in the struggle with omnipotence.

It would seem that the way out of this is to objectify the obsession, to embody the God-hatred in the fiction. *The Heart of the Matter* in a way does this; much of the torment comes from the position that natural knowledge, knowledge of sex, is real, and knowledge of God by comparison notional; if you abuse a woman she will be hurt or angry, but you can insult and debase God without His giving any sign. So a man damns himself out of pity for those who cry out; that, at any rate, is what the rules say, and if there is an escape clause ("the appalling strangeness of the mercy of God") we cannot be sure of its application. Scobie is Greene's greatest expert in proverbs of hell, in "the loyalty we all feel to unhappiness—the sense that that is where we really belong." He is cursed by an awareness of "the weakness of God" and by integrity-destroying pity; sufficiently of God's party to know that failure alone is lovable, but critical of the divine arrangements ("Couldn't we have committed our first major sin at seven, have ruined ourselves for love or hate at ten, have clutched at redemption on a fifteen-year-old death-bed?") Consequently, "as for God, he could speak to him only as one speaks to an enemy." In the end he propagates suffering instead of preventing it by total self-sacrifice, because God will not allow one to arrange the happiness of others as one wishes. As to the "eternal sentence" which our intellectual knowledge of God insists to have been Scobie's due, it is pronounced for an act of which the human significance is trivial, the theft of a little bread. But of course there is Fr. Rank to say we do not understand God, that Scobie's conduct may be divinely construed as love of God. Mr. Lees observes with severity that this remark is misplaced, since we know, as God does, what has gone on in Scobie's mind, and "if at his death we don't know that he *won't* go to Heaven, we most certainly don't know that he *will*." This is part of a charge that the novelist gives uncritical assent to Scobie's "shouldering of the world's whole weight," and indeed he is a classic case of *victimage*, with the priest brought in to say that nobody can affirm this "decadent" position to be erroneous. But I do not see that there is total identification of author and character here; the point of the revelation that Mrs. Scobie knew very well what she was doing when she coaxed her erring husband to Mass is that he was wanting in self-knowledge in a matter where you would expect a policeman not to be; he bungles an ordinary appraisal of human suspicion; and to this extent Mr. Greene is saying that Scobie had a *wrong* idea of himself. But the main issue of the book is not fully discussed: it is that Scobie's intolerable position is plotted by God; He demands more love and pity than anybody else and ought not to get them. Even specialists in Him know far more about his demands than about his benefactions; it is his mercy, not his justice, that is unfamiliar, "appallingly strange." A good man should not be treated as Scobie is. But all this lurks immediately under the surface of the book's argument; the egg is not allowed to speak out against the Cross.

This speaking out was delayed until *The End of the Affair*, and this seems almost beyond question Mr. Greene's masterpiece, his fullest and most completely realised book. Mr. Lees says the opening paragraph is uneasily slack; but in a deliberately tentative way it disposes of a remarkable amount of information. A novelist, a good technician launching what purports to be a straightforward narrative but at the same time foreseeing Conradian complexities, hesitates deliberately over the arbitrary but necessary starting-point; and he wants the essential fact of his being a writer, and the other essential fact of his new, odious, belief in God, to get said at once. Bendrix is not a Scobie but the hero Mr. Greene has needed: a natural man who sees this God as a natural man would, as unscrupulous rival, corrupter of human happiness, spoiler of the egg; and a novelist who hates Him as a superior technician. Bendrix's book is plotted by God, a testimony to His structural powers. And we get for the first and only time the real Satanic thing, the courage never to submit or yield. All this is germinal in the first page, which contains sentences crucial to the entire *oeuvre:* "If hate is not too large a term to use in relation to any human being, I hated Henry. . . . He surely must have hated his wife and that other, in whom in those days *we were lucky enough not to believe.*" Bendrix's fury in the end is that of the trapped: everything from onions to the absurd private detective, the rationalist lectures, Arbuckle Avenue, flying bombs, miracles that can be explained away, is economically employed by the Plotter. And just as Bendrix is a potent enough novelist to take away the critic's girl, God is a good enough one to take away his, even though she doesn't want to go; He plants in her not only love of him but His favourite Augustinian reluctance ("but not yet") to increase the pain. "Dear God, you know I want Your pain, but I don't want it now."

The unwilling sanctification of Sarah is a difficult theme, and leads the novelist into some expressions that may seem excessive, though hardly ever in the rapt context; and God's perversity and skill are remembered even by Sarah, who takes the deforming strawberry mark as His image, and remembers how unfairly He used Bendrix to His own ends. It is a mark of the difference of this book that the last words are shared between the frigid priest and Bendrix, and Bendrix is very explicit: "I know Your cunning. It's You who take us up to a high place and offer us the whole universe. You're a devil, God, tempting us to leap." He can no longer refuse to believe in the disastrous existence of God; but he can still separate the idea from love. But God may not have finished with him. This is another love-triangle, but even the hate necessarily generated may be converted by Him into an inhuman love. The book ends with Bendrix praying for the peace of the natural man, burnt out. It is the only novel to offer a full statement of the case for the fornicating human victim, for the energy as well as the sadness of hell, and the case against the God who inflicts, as with love, that pain from which the pleasure-loving flesh continually shrinks. Mr. Lees calls Bendrix an evil man, and the book gives him some right to do so; but this reminds one again of the genuine proverb of hell, that hell is energy; and the difference between the vicious energy of Bendrix and the rigidly self-conscious despair of Querry is a fair measure of the difference in quality between the two books. Querry is too clearly a surrogate; the argument about Heroic Virtue is also a substitute, too partial, too technical perhaps, to bear the weight of the real theme: natural happiness, defeated not by success or surfeit, but by God and His love.

ELIZABETH HARDWICK

Loveless Love

"The passenger wondered when it was that he had first begun to detest laughter like a bad smell."

". . . I suffer from nothing. I no longer know what suffering is. I have come to the end of all that, too."

"The boat goes no further."

". . . I am sorry, I am too far gone, I can't feel at all, I am a leper."

The passenger, a distinguished church architect named Querry, is the hero of Graham Greene's last novel, *A Burnt-Out Case.* Querry has been loved by many women; he is successful and famous—above all, *famous.* And from it he has ended up tired, morally despairing, filled with self-loathing, insisting upon his loss of feeling, his deadness. Loss of feeling? What does it mean? Fitzgerald's "Crack-up"—what is really meant, what has happened? "And then, ten years this side of forty-nine, I suddenly realized that I had prematurely cracked." The cracked plate, the burnt-out case, the reserved, evasive actually, description of some over-whelming emotional crisis. Fitzgerald: "I saw that even my love for those closest to me was become only an attempt to love." Querry: "She was once my mistress. I left her three months ago, poor woman—and that's hypocrisy. I feel no pity."

Fame and emptiness. Fame burns out Querry; it surrounds him with horrors who draw near to touch or to fall in love. "Fame is a powerful aphrodisiac." Publicity, the bed sore of the fame-sick, inflicts its pains. Querry has abandoned his career and gone to a leprosy hospital in the Congo. He is at the end of the road; the boat goes no further; his vocation for

---

From *A View of My Own: Essays on Literature and Society.* © 1961 by Elizabeth Hardwick. Ecco Press, 1982.

building and for loving women has given out; he is empty, desperately and courageously "dead." But his fame runs along after him; he is discovered; he is exposed by a journalist; he is pursued by a European manufacturer of margarine, Rycker, who feels for the famous man the mad, easily resentful but somehow grotesquely transfigured, love made of Querry's success and their shared Catholicism. The famous architect and lover is now, in some sense, impotent. ("He told me once that all his life he had only made use of women, but I think he saw himself in the hardest possible light. I even wondered sometimes whether he suffered from a kind of frigidity.") Rycker kills the object of his over-weening curiosity, Querry, because of an imaginary infidelity. "Absurd," Querry said, "this is absurd or else."

There is an absence of particularity, of the details of experience, in Querry's crack-up, just as there is in Fitzgerald. We reach the end of a great and adored man and accept the despair without any real idea of how it came to be. Curtness, coolness, even carelessness mark the mode of expression. Fitzgerald: "Sometimes, though, the cracked plate has to be retained in the pantry, has to be kept in service as a household necessity. It can never again be warmed on the stove nor shuffled with the other plates in the dishpan; it will not be brought out for company, but it will do to hold crackers late at night or to go into the ice box under left-overs." Querry in disgust: "The darkness was noisy with frogs, and for a long while after his host had said good night and gone, they seemed to croak with Rycker's hollow phrases: Grace: sentiment: duty: love, love, love." Self-condemnation, indifferent, impersonal, given out as a Confession, a general statement of sinfulness, without names or places. Art has failed to bring peace; success does not bring happiness to wives, mistresses or children.

From *Death in Venice:* Art "engraves adventures of the spirit and the mind in the faces of her votaries; let them lead outwardly a life of the most cloistered calm, she will in the end produce in them a fastidiousness, an over-refinement, a nervous fever and exhaustion, such as a career of extravagant passions and pleasures can hardly show." This is a price, perhaps, but a noble, classic fate—far from the sardonic ash-heap of Greene. Or compare Mailer's *Advertisements,* a confession in which I, at least, do not find the voice of personal suffering and so assume it was not intended. The alcoholic reserve of Fitzgerald and the manic expressiveness of Mailer show the twenty years or more that separate the personal documents. For Mailer more and more experience, more and more fame—the Congo as an assignment, perhaps, not as a retreat. "Publicity can be an acid test for virtue," Greene says. Poor Hemingway, honorifically carried to his grave by those wooden angels, the restaurant owner Toots Shor and the gossip columnist Leonard Lyons.

In *The Heart of the Matter* the weary hero faced damnation because of his unconquerable pity for the women whom destiny, capriciously, or due to his own wanting, left in his care. Pity is way beyond Querry. He doesn't want to pretend any longer; it is all meaningless. Fornication is a burden and love is impossible. And yet, what is it about? How to account for the flight, the coldness, the refusal? We have Querry's "aridity" seen by the priests at the leper colony, but we do not have the love affairs or the life of the great architect that make the extraordinary final emptiness important. We see the soul at a point of theological instability, and there only.

Greene has a unique gift for plot and a miraculous way of finding a clever objective correlative for his spiritual perplexities. Loss of faith in art and love equals the "cure" of the leper, mutilated, but at last without pain. The humid tropical atmosphere, the tsetse flies, the intense *colons*, with their apologies and their arrogance, the strained, disputatious priests, interestingly pockmarked with weaknesses: this is the properly exotic and threatening setting for the Greene dialogue. *A Burnt-Out Case* seemed a partial failure to V. S. Pritchett in his *New Statesman* review. He felt the influence of the stage had been unfortunate and worked less well than an earlier absorption of film technique. Yet he is not entirely dissatisfied and decides that Querry, the hero, succeeds as a vehicle for certain ideas if not as a "man." Pritchett calls Graham Greene, "the most piercing and important of our novelists now."

Frank Kermode in a brilliant article in *Encounter* is unhappy about *A Burnt-Out Case*. He finds it "so far below one's expectation that the questions arise, was the expectation reasonable and has there been any previous indication that a failure of this kind was a possibility?" In Kermode's view *The End of the Affair* is Greene's best novel because, to simplify, here the author more openly and with greater seriousness faces his case against God.

Querry, a builder of Catholic churches, is only, the novel tells us, "a legal Catholic." He doesn't pray, he loathes being dragged into other people's lives by the ropes of his religion and his fame; he doesn't want his sins to be made interesting as priests in novels like to do with villains; he resents having his vices stubbornly interpreted as incipient virtues. Father Thomas frantically insists upon accepting Querry's devastated spirit. "Don't you see that you've been given the grace of aridity? Perhaps even now you are walking in the footsteps of St. John of the Cross, the *noche oscura*." In trying to come to some sort of judgment about Greene as a novelist one would have to ask himself whether a significant picture of modern life in the last thirty years could be made from doctrinal puzzles, seminarian wit and paradox, private jokes, Roman Catholic exclusiveness. The characters take their sexual guilt and stand at the edge of damnation discussing possibilities for fresh theological interpretations. They are weary and romantic and fascinated by suffering and they look upon themselves and their feelings in a peculiarly intense Catholic-convert way, a sort of intellectual, clannish, delighted sectarianism. The question is not, in the great Russian manner, how one can live without God, or with God; the question is how one can exist as a moral, or immoral, man without running into vexing complications with the local priest. Marriage, love, sex, pride, art, no matter where you turn things are not quite as the Church would have it and to function at all one has to break rules or offer new versions of the old.

Of course Greene is fascinated by sin and heresy; it could not be otherwise. His terse novels, with their clear, firm themes and symbolic situations, are acted out by men with beautifully apt gifts for language, men raised on Cardinal Newman and Ronald Knox. His world is anti-psychological; the world of psychoanalytical motivation does not exist; its questions are never raised, its interpretations never suggested. Class, childhood, history are irrelevant, too. These are indeed peculiar novels. The omission of so much life and meaning, of the drama of social and psychological existence would seem to be ultimately limiting. There is a sense of disfiguration, baffling sometimes, and yet always intellectually exciting. Everything is sharper and more brilliant than the effects of other writers. God is a sort of sub-plot and the capricious way He treats Roman Catholics is a suspenseful background to love and boredom and pity. It is most perplexing.

How often Greene sees the living thing as a dead or trivial object, an article of manufacture. "A smile like a licorice stick"; "the pouches under his eyes were like purses that contained the smuggled memories of a disappointing life"; "he was like the kind of plant people put in bathrooms, reared on humidity, shooting too high. He had a small black moustache like a smear of city soot and his face was narrow and flat and endless, like an illustration of the law that two parallel lines never meet."

Licorice sticks, purses filled with snakes, leggy bathroom plants are lined up for the argument, the great debate over a whisky and soda at some peaceful, intellectual Priory. And meanwhile it is really to church that Sarah (*The End of the Affair*) is going and not to meet her lover. God laughs maliciously. On this stage, with its oddly clear and yet humanly peculiar themes, with its weary, engaging purity of design, these brilliant, original works take place, each one as arresting as the other, Catholic-convert dramas of sex and renunciation, belief and defiance.

FREDERICK R. KARL

Graham Greene's Demonical Heroes

It has become a commonplace of literary criticism that the hero in major western fiction has more or less vanished, or, at least, become bourgeois, diminished in stature, somewhat trite in his demands upon life. Often, the hero is characterized as an anti-hero, a figure like the tragic-comic Bloom of *Ulysses,* the self-destructive Jim of Conrad's novel or K. of Kafka's, or the fumbling "angry young man" of Kingsley Amis or John Wain. The background for the anti-hero is of course closely connected to changes in the literary as well as political, religious, and social character of the western world and, therefore, precedes by many years the work of the twentieth-century authors in whom the phenomenon is most apparent. One finds such changes, for example, beginning in France during the reaction against romanticism on the part of the realists, Stendhal, Flaubert, Maupassant, and (later) Zola, a reaction which brought with it inevitable disdain for the romantic hero with his simple purity, natural goodness of heart and action, and basically Christian morality, a hero who was an aristocratic Christian knight in modern dress. The realist-naturalist novelists, interested as they often were in the seamier aspects of life, could not help but reject the superficial façade of gentility with which a romantic writer surrounded his protagonist. Then, precisely as these nineteenth-century realists probed from the outside to destroy most heroic notions, so, later, twentieth-century writers were to probe from within with much the same effect. Thus, in France,

---

From *The Contemporary English Novel.* Farrar, Straus & Giroux, 1962.

Proust, Gide, Céline, Camus, Sartre, and several others have followed where Stendhal and Flaubert began.

In England, the anti-heroic type is found—curiously, one is tempted to say—within the works of Dickens, who, despite his "soft" young men and women, often qualified their romantic success with a sense of corrupt failure. We have only to compare Pip in *Great Expectations* with the typical heroes of the then very popular and now forgotten romantic novels which appeared in such great numbers in the second half of the century. Or else, compare the much chastened heroes of Thackeray and Meredith or the heroines of George Eliot with their romantic contemporaries, and then we see where the tradition begins to gain force. In Meredith, for instance, the idea generated its own kind of novel in which the ego of the central character proves self-destructive, for the "hero" (now necessarily placed within inverted commas) can no longer get back into the society which he wants to enter, and now, broken or dead, he is almost completely ineffectual. One thinks of Richard Feverel, Sir Willoughby Patterne, Nevil Beauchamp. Then, a few decades later, with the turn of the twentieth century and the introduction of psychological phenomenon into English fiction, novelists like Conrad, Joyce, and Forster helped put the hero into an early grave. Conrad, with his self-destructive protagonists, persecuted his heroes while he probed their central corruption. Joyce created an egoistic Stephen Dedalus, whose self-centeredness precluded his being anyone's hero but his own. And Forster poked at the corners of the human character, unearthing all kinds of contradictions, odds and ends of behavior which showed with finality that the romantic hero had perished as a serious literary creation. Further, D. H. Lawrence and Virginia Woolf, despite their large differences, here agreed that character must be created anew and that all the old figures, including the superficially charming romantic hero, must be superseded by an inner vision. And this vision is more or less the one that has predominated in the significant English novels of this century. Tragedy is now that of the "fallen democrat," the "struggling bourgeois," the "awkward outsider," all of whom, in the absence of a believable God, try to believe in themselves.

In attempting to recover the "hero" for a democratic age, Graham Greene has taken the "fallen democrat" peculiar to our time and tried to raise him through suffering and pain to more heroic stature. Having assumed that the romantic hero is surely dead, Greene still believes that man can be heroic, although in his terms heroism takes on a different hue from that in previous times. Greene has reached back beyond the superficial romantic hero of the nineteenth century to the Greek concept of tragedy, at the same time remembering that Greek tragedy in itself must be modified to suit a basically irreligious, democratic age. Greene feels he must allow for the "fall" that is central to Aristotle's view of the tragic hero; but here that "fall" is man's demonical descent from grace, and his attempt to embrace faith in a seemingly godless universe is the measure of his heroism.

For Greene, the essential human tragedy, implicit in the gap between what man wants and what, because of personal limitations, he is able to attain, is ironic. The latter, his capacity, mocks the former, his desire. Caught between the two, man must evidently fail unless he has a vision of something beyond himself. For him to concentrate solely on his own limitations is to demonstrate indifference to anything that might be greater. In brief, the self-satisfied or indifferent individual precludes his own tragic role, for he places himself beyond the reach of a powerful force, a force, incidentally, that may lead to severe unhappiness as well as to limited happiness. However, if he recognizes an outside transcendental force, the individual is caught by a phenomenon more powerful than himself, and he reacts; he feels inadequate; he becomes a potentially tragic hero.

Greene has recast the Greek hero, accordingly, to suit a Christian framework, at the same time qualifying the term "hero" itself. The Greene hero, in this way like that of the Greek dramatists, is religious; that is, he operates according to the religious beliefs of his times and gains much of his force and substance, both negative and positive, from surrounding religious ideas. In our day, however, the religious framework within which the Greek dramatists worked is non-existent or, at best, marginal; so that the novelist must "create" both the surroundings and the hero. Thus, while the Greek tragedian could take the religious values of his age for granted and write confidently within them, Greene has had to make these values themselves seem plausible to an audience accustomed to a more secular life and literature. His purpose, evidently, is to recover tragedy in a democratic world, to re-create the Christian "hero," and to make credible the religious world which the Greek dramatist accepted as fact. Greene's mission in his major novels, then, is to write Greek tragedy without forsaking a Christian God.

Because Greene believes that from impurity will come purity, from demonism saintliness, from unbelief belief, from vice virtue, his "heroes" often seem closer to demons than to saints. Nearly every serious Greene protagonist, despite external expedience and even personal degradation, has a vision of saintliness, while his inner conflict, often not apparent to him, results from his inability to live up to his ideal. In these terms Greene places the tension between pride and moderation, analogous to the conflict of the Greek tragic hero. Like Oedipus, whose pride has overwhelmed his sense of reasonableness, Scobie (*The Heart of the Matter*, 1948), Pinkie (*Brighton*

Rock, 1938), and the whiskey-priest (*The Power and the Glory*, 1940), for example, all recognize how far short they have fallen of the ideal, how mortal they really are. In *The Confidential Agent* (1939), one of his entertainments, Greene retells the *Song of Roland* to illustrate explicitly this theme of false heroism and pride which deceive men into thinking themselves gods.

The Berne MS of the *Song of Roland*, discovered and annotated by Agent D., a disillusioned "hero" himself, destroys the romantic heroic picture of Roland and puts in his stead an Oliver who is realistic and who is the real "hero" simply because he avoids heroics of an obvious sort. As D. points out:

> "That's the importance of the Berne MS. It re-establishes Oliver. It makes the story tragedy, not just heroics. Because in the Oxford version Oliver is reconciled, he gives Roland his death-blow by accident, his eyes blinded by wounds. The story, you see, has been tidied up to suit. . . . But in the Berne version, he strikes his friend down with full knowledge—because of what he has done to his men: all the wasted lives. He dies hating the man he loves—the big boasting courageous fool who was more concerned with his own glory than with the victory of his faith. But you can see how that version didn't appeal—in the castles—at the banquets, among the dogs and reeds and beakers; the jongleurs had to adapt it to meet the tastes of the medieval nobles, who were quite capable of being Rolands in a small way—it only needs conceit and a strong arm—but couldn't understand what Oliver was at."

By downgrading heroic roles in general and unthinking heroes in particular, Greene, like the author of the Berne MS, leaves room for the humility that is clearly part of a tragic vision. Roland, the so-called hero of the Oxford MS, believing that he and only he can conquer, thinks he is God, while Oliver, the "real hero" of the Berne MS, knows that he isn't. Thus Roland, like Oedipus in his tragedy, plays God and becomes a proud fool, while Oliver, allowing God's intervention, retains the strength of the humble. This is almost a "parable" of Greene's claim that only through humbling oneself before "God" can one become truly heroic. If one disbelieves in his own perfectibility—the "false hero" of course believes in just this—he then allows for the ingress of sin that makes him need God. The imperfect man, the one closest to the devil, is, for Greene, precisely the one who is in need of God, and although Agent D., in *The Confidential Agent*, is agnostic, he is surely close to God in his humble sense of failure.

We see, then, in nearly all of Greene's work that what is true of Agent D. also holds for Scobie, the whiskey-priest, Bendrix (*The End of the Affair*, 1957), Minty (*England Made Me*, 1935), Francis Andrews (*The Man Within*, 1929), Querry (*A Burnt-Out Case*, 1961), even Pinkie. The failure, the devilish man, the seeming anti-hero is somehow, unconsciously, approaching God; for in failure, not success, we fathom our sins and recognize our faults. We see again that Oliver and not Roland is the real "hero." Greene's belief that the failure is nearer God than the success is of course close to the Greek idea of hubris: in this view, the successful, boasting man, full of overweening pride, challenges the order of the universe by considering himself greater than the gods, and at this point, when he attempts to expand from man-size to god-size, at the very apex of pride and vanity, he is struck down. Thus, also within the Christian world, God operates, although He retains sympathy and pity for the failure, for the one struck down. In fact, He reserves his strength and force, Greene often seems to be saying, almost exclusively for the ones who approach the devil. The lovers of God do not necessarily find Him through their belief. He is more likely to be discovered by the tortured deniers. Thus, those who hate may be closer to God than those who love; those who deny closer than those who believe; those who despair closer than those who are elated; those who kill closer than those who save or try to save; those who commit suicide closer than those who fear to; those who ponder despair closer than those who accept dogma. In every instance, Greene feels that God seeks out the ones who would deny Him, for they are probing the very roots of His existence, and with this, God can sympathize. God is, in Greene's terms, reborn only in those who question Him, and dies within those who acquiesce unquestioningly to His supremacy.

Accordingly, the major contrast in several of Greene's novels occurs between the conventional believers, who live according to the Church's dictates, and the conventional unbelievers, who flout belief of any sort. And yet, as we see, Greene avoids the easy solution that the believer will be saved and the unbeliever damned; in fact, he turns the stereotyped formula inside out. His unbelievers wallow in a kind of dumb despair that would seem to preclude their salvation. Obsessed as they are with their transgressions, they often fail to recognize that they are not gods and that God has powers which they cannot understand. Nevertheless, in this scheme, Scobie, who has sinned mortally by taking communion without prior absolution and who commits suicide—the final and unredemptive act of despair—can be saved by God's grace if He should so wish; nothing Scobie has done precludes the possibility.

Scobie of *The Heart of the Matter*, as well as the whiskey-priest of *The*

Power and the Glory, is undergoing that kind of reevaluation of self in which he becomes a focus of failure, and failure itself and love of failure become, as it were, a way of life. Unsuccessful in his career, not in love with his wife who cannot share his interests or even come close to understanding him, lacking money, respect, and often dignity, dissatisfied with his religion (he is a convert), Scobie, now isolated and alone, is approaching that state of acedia which places him outside the ken of other men and which even denies the efficacy of God's grace. Still faithful to his ideal of honesty and integrity, Scobie gives up hope. The only thing that can bring him back momentarily to a community of men is his affair with Helen, who, having lost her husband in a shipwreck and drifted in the open sea for forty days while waiting to be saved, comes to him as a piece of flotsam. She is, like Scobie, a derelict, and only with her can he find some kind of love—he can, in his condition, turn only to another failure. Through love for a failure (as God will perhaps love him), Scobie has a temporary desire for life, although this too passes when his wife, the symbol of all his past deficiencies, returns to him.

Like a Greek protagonist, Scobie is fixed within his character, unable to resist what he is and what he is becoming. Once again analogous to the Greek dramatist, Greene finds nothing easy in life, nothing flexible or soft; for as man has put himself into his situation, so only man, with the possible aid of belief if it is forthcoming, can extract himself. Although "miracles" do occur in a Greene novel, they never "save" a character; only suffering, inner conflict, soul-searching tension, recognition of self—all the qualities a Dostoyevskian hero must acquire, and here, as elsewhere, we see the great influence the Russian writer had on Greene—can help a Greene character by making him dissatisfied with the devil.

Greene has, as it were, revised the Christian novel: if the prototype of the Christian quest in Bunyan's *Pilgrim's Progress*—the quest of the good man for virtue, for the Heavenly City of God—then Greene has indeed changed the procedure. In Greene's work, the quest is undertaken by a sinner who stumbles along the way to the Heavenly City, almost forsaking God and embracing the devil in his crude inability to fulfill what God requires. Greene is concerned, in a way, with how the Christian underground and marginal man can be saved, how the poor in spirit, the weak in will, the proud in soul can be saved; the rest, he suggests, can take care of themselves.

God's force here, as the power of fate in Greek tragedy, is directed toward those who think they are least subject to it or deserve it. In earthly failure, God sees potential salvation; in vain success, He sees weakness; in satanical pride, He sees the capacity for humility; in indecision and denial,

He sees the possibility of faith. Only indifference, Greene claims, can destroy God. In several ways, then, Greene has turned tradition upside down: rather than accepting his belief, he examines his unbelief and measures its strength. And while the actual "leap" into faith that his protagonists take may not be fully persuasive to the lay reader, nevertheless the conflicts themselves are often cogent, given the nature of a Greene character. Greene asks, among other things: what can God mean to a man who rejects Him? to one who traffics with the devil? Further, what does God mean in a world that seems compounded of evil? Who will prove stronger in the battle for man's will, God or the devil, even though God may bring more pain than the latter? Greene suggests, paradoxically, that in reaching out for the devil, one may well find God intervening; and conversely, in reaching for God, one may indeed find the devil. While the Church may demand conformity of behavior and belief according to fixed dogmas, God, like the devil, operates inexplicably, apart, if necessary, from the Church's body of dogma. In his concern with evil and the demonical hero, we see that Greene is closer to Dostoyevski and Mauriac than to any Anglo-American tradition of the religious novel.

The whiskey-priest of *The Power and the Glory* is the last priest in the state, his fellow priests having been outlawed—killed off or forced to marry in a purge by a local dictator. He can try to escape or he can live a normal married life that mocks his former vocation. He can save his soul or his body. The whiskey-priest reluctantly stays, but he is constantly reminded of the fact that he is not worthy of the role cut out for him: to be, in effect, a martyr. If Christ is his ideal, he sadly fails to live up to this high conception, for he drinks to excess, has fathered a child, and is not even sure he can practice his profession when fear overtakes him; in brief, he is, according to Greene, a devil ready for sainthood. Full of self pride, the whiskey-priest, like a Greek hero, is partially ennobled through suffering, doubt, and self-realization. At every point, the priest is made aware of the depths to which he has fallen, aware that the devil has indeed entered his body and exorcised his God. In denying God, the priest comes close to Him, analogous to the Greek protagonist who comes closest to the powers of fate exactly while flaunting his pride. The very terms of denial contain the seeds of attachment; denial belies indifference, is, indeed, the first step toward acceptance.

Similarly, *Brighton Rock*, whose background seems more suitable for Dante's infernal sufferers or Milton's proud demons than for inhabitants of contemporary England, is full of demonic characters, with Pinkie as a juvenile Satan and his followers as fallen angels. Pinkie himself, a pathological killer, is first cousin to the superman who thinks he can conquer everything in his way. Pinkie's vision is to be an Alexander of crime, to be a man-god; and, like Dostoyevski's Raskolnikov, he conceives of himself as possessing powers which make him superior to those around him. "No more human contacts," he dreams, "other people's emotions washing at the brain—he would be free again: nothing to think about but himself." The only thing that matters in a world that went to pieces the day he saw his grunting parents tossing on their bed is self-satisfaction, self-appeasement: since they abandoned him to indulge their lonely passion, he will, in turn, abandon everyone else. Like the child he really is, he must gratify himself; and he must not be crossed, for he will kill to protect his interests. The chief difference between Pinkie and the "romantic" figures, like Raskolnikov and Julien Sorel, who preceded him, comes from Greene's recognition that the humility, the obedience, the sense of good and evil implicit in a former age, values threaded right into the social fabric, can no longer be taken for granted. Now, anything goes, and in such a society, the Pinkies will exist in ever greater numbers—they will become the norm, not the anomaly.

Even a sense of mortal sin cannot make Pinkie humble, and this force, Greene suggests, is the strongest that can be exerted upon him. Put another way: Pinkie is so far outside normality and so bizarre in his demands upon life that he functions beyond all laws of God and man, and even the law of God, so much stronger in effect upon Pinkie than that of man, is still inconclusive. The Pinkies are to that degree outside the control of human society. This is, according to Greene, a measure of the difficulty. If we wish to control them, we must leave it to God's law, which, while it may seem ineffective, is still the only force strong enough to penetrate someone like the satanical Pinkie.

Raskolnikov, for example, could be reached through love of God, through love of a good woman, and through love of mother country (one way of saying family), but these values predicate a society that can affect a person; the values are still implicit in the society, still latent in the individual. But remove all these values, as Greene does, and the barriers fall. Such is the condition or atmosphere in which we meet Pinkie, or Scobie, Bendrix, Agent D., the whiskey-priest, James Raven (*This Gun for Hire*, 1936), Grünlich (*Stamboul Train*, 1932), Francis Andrews, Harry Lime (*The Third Man*, 1950), and several others: who is responsible? who can place strictures? who can judge? is Pinkie guilty?

Any substantial conclusions are apparently outside the area allowed to man; only God can answer by extending His mercy and salvation, Greene says, to those He feels worthy of it, and He may well extend grace to those who seem to deserve it least. As the priest tells Rose: "You can't conceive, my child, nor can I or anyone—the . . . appalling . . . strangeness of the mercy of God." When Rose mentions that Pinkie was a Catholic and knew that he was doing wrong, that is, explicitly damning himself, the priest answers: "*Corruptio optimi est pessima.*" Then he continues: " 'I mean—a Catholic is more capable of evil than anyone. I think perhaps—because we believe in him—we are more in touch with the devil than other people. But we must hope,' he said mechanically, 'hope and pray.' " He claims that Pinkie's love, no matter what kind it was and no matter how filled with shreds of hatred and revulsion, is an indication of some goodness. Love is necessary; and who can tell what it means, no matter what the intention? Sometimes, one expresses love, as the wicked Frenchman (Charles Peguy) in the priest's little story, by seeking damnation in order to express sympathy with all the damned. This, too, is a kind of salvation in God's eyes. Unlike Milton who was anxious to explain the ways of God to man, Greene is eager to demonstrate that the ways of God must remain inexplicable.

Greene has staked everything on his "demonic hero," who, by turning all accepted values upside down, has come to understand God through knowledge of the devil. These heroes operate within a decay-saturated world, a world as much corrupted as that of Conrad's novels; yet unlike the heroes of the latter, they do not turn inward so much as upward or downward. In their attempt to transcend themselves through a knowledge of both God and the devil, they try to regain some sense of balance in a corrupted universe. In short, they seek God in what appears to be a devil-controlled universe. This is, in a way, their heroism. Yet throughout their martyrdom, they are fully aware of the puniness of their selves, aware of the baseness of their desires in contrast with the transcendency of their hopes. To "leap" the gap between the pride which damns and the humility which saves, they must suffer the pains of conscience; and in their suffering, they come to terms with their individual salvation.

As an attempt to regain a tragic view of the universe through the use of this kind of hero, Greene's novels have their limitations as well as their virtues. Greene believes strongly that, as he wrote, "doubt and denial must be given their chance of self-expression." Yet the "leap" his characters make from earth to heaven is rarely effective, except, perhaps, in *The Power and the Glory*, and there the whiskey-priest *begins* as a man of God. The transcendental apparatus is often in excess of what the figure can bear, for Greene's characters frequently cannot rise to the vision he has of their potential greatness. Unlike the Greek dramatist, Greene cannot draw upon an entire culture. The ideas he is anxious to develop are rarely alive within either the characters or those surrounding them. Therefore, everything becomes contrived: he must present a hero capable of commitment, surround him with the conditions which will make commitment possible, and provide temptations and counters; finally, he must make the reader believe in the "leap" that the hero will make to insure his salvation. And Greene must do all this without the aids that the Greek writer could take for granted. Nothing can be assumed.

Furthermore, we as readers are conditioned, more or less, to a literature in which these "leaps" are rarely taken, and to a life in which the "leap" itself is suspected of being factitious. We accept easily enough, for instance, Kafka's traps for his frustrated heroes, Conrad's crushing of his finest protagonists, Joyce's reduction of his characters to lower-middle class Dubliners, Lawrence's obsessive deification of gamekeepers, Hemingway's emphasis on hunters and bullfighters, matters now implicit in our literary culture; however, when Greene tries to go beyond to create an aristocracy of the spirit, we feel that tragedy now becomes subservient to religion. Yet, it is the serious reader of Kafka, Joyce, Conrad, and Lawrence whom Greene wants to engage, the very reader who will most damagingly question either his assumptions or his results, or more likely both.

If Greene had meant his several "quests for God" as contemporary symbols rather than as real acts of belief, then perhaps the difficulty would be partially removed. Our literary heritage being what it is, it is difficult indeed to accept a tragic vision as long as there is a "religious out." In just this area, Greene perhaps fails to convince. Although the spiritual struggles of his characters are remarkably effective, and although their tensions are similar to those of the greatest characters in literature—yet the "leap" that each takes, by its very nature, reduces the tragic content. The Greek hero had no redress once he had fallen: salvation was nowhere apparent. When salvation appears, tragedy becomes romance, and the rules change; though, obviously, Greene is concerned with the tragic and not the romantic. The fact that his characters obtain actual rewards or that reward is implicit in their existence diminishes tragic power, makes the author seem a meddling intruder. A more secular author like Conrad, for example, has Axel Heyst (*Victory*) recognize his guilt for having abandoned mankind in order to pursue solitude; but while he realizes his destructive attitude, this realization is not enough to save him. His sacrificial death is necessary.

In Greene's world, few are past saving. Even Pinkie, who has reached so far into the lower depths, can be saved because he did love at one time. The Christian attitude explicitly applied to the novel dilutes the tragic vision. Perhaps tragedy in its real sense can exist only in a world stripped of the Christian amenities, one in which heaven, paradise, and salvation are pleasant but meaningless terms; for the tragic man's fate, as Hardy well knew, is determined by his character. Give men even the limited "escape" that Greene permits his characters, and they forsake their tragic roles; no matter how severe their crime, they can still "leap" from their situation.

Greene's use of the "demonical hero" who can attain salvation through God's almost arbitrary use of grace, raises several interesting questions both to the religious and secular reader: what is the use of legal boundaries placed upon man if they are merely temporary and finally meaningless, if God may choose to ignore them in His judgment? is not someone like Ida (in *Brighton Rock*), a non-believer, preferable to someone like Pinkie, a warped believer, even though God may eventually choose to save Pinkie and damn Ida? if the kingdom of God is preferable to the kingdom of Man, is it not true that anything really does go, and that man's conduct, even when it is righteous, is then of little worth? if forgiveness, as Greene indicates, is forthcoming according to God's wishes, which no one may hope to understand, what is to prevent chaos, the frenzy of those who wait for God's judgment and flout Man's law? Is Greene perhaps more interested in saints than in people?

By indicating that God can save where's Man's devices fail, does not Greene claim the very kind of "inside" knowledge of God that he states it is impossible to have? Is there not implicit an underlying arrogance in his message, a lack of humility, especially in his claim that the Catholic more than anyone else is closer to the devil? Further, why should pain lead necessarily to belief?

And yet Greene has probably come closest of all "religious" novelists in English to retaining the terms of tragedy without forsaking a Christian framework. By working with sordidness, a commonplace in major twentieth-century fiction, Greene attempts to make his demonical heroes play the game of his secular contemporaries. Yet the very nature of the enterprise is partially self-defeating, even after one grants his great success in creating drama, tension, suspense, excitement, and intellectual sport. But this is not tragedy. In Greek tragedy the realization of one's wrongdoing was the crisis of one's life. The fall allowed no ascension. In Greene's world, the "fall" still permits redemption; in the universe there are rewards of which man may partake. If something can save the hero, whether he is demonical or not, he is not truly tragic.

In 1938, Greene traveled widely in Mexico and in the following year published *The Lawless Roads*, an account of his Mexican sojourn. In chapters five and six of that book, there occur several paragraphs about a drunken priest who held out against the police for ten years in Tabasco, a small province in the south of Mexico where the clergy had been proscribed.

Greene describes him: "He was a little lost, poor man, a kind of Padre Rey [a married priest]; but who can judge what terror and hardship and isolation may have excused him in the eyes of God?" From the unequivocal, intense religious belief that Greene shows in *The Lawless Roads* comes the paradoxical faith of the priest; the author turns particularities of autobiography into a universalized fiction. While *The Lawless Roads* provides some of the facts and attitudes for the novel, the work of fiction demonstrates an imaginative breadth nowhere found in the travel book.

The Power and the Glory (first published as *The Labyrinthine Ways*) is concerned with the (by now common) theme of isolation. Greene's priest is, here, similar to Conrad's Jim; the chief difference is of course that the priest is actually being chased while Jim imagines Furies that exist only in his own consciousness. But whether the Furies are inside or outside makes little significant difference, for the important element is the character's reaction to them. Step by step, the priest moves away from his former life; all familiar objects—clothes, materials for the mass, slips of paper from the past, even memories themselves—drop away, and like Jim he is stripped to his fears and weaknesses. What identity does a man have when he is deprived of everything he holds essential? Further, what identity does a priest have when he feels that even God's grace has forsaken him, and he is left floating in a spiritual purgatory, neither saved nor damned, simply uncertain of himself and of his relation to God? And, finally, what kinship can such a priest have with his worshipers when he feels he has failed them as much as he has failed himself and his God?

Greene's novel of the whiskey-priest pursues a theme similar to that of his other major novels and many of his entertainments, although its intensity here marks this as perhaps his finest book. Like Scobie, the priest is closest to God when sinning. To understand deity, Greene suggests, one must, like Job, always be tempted; the orthodox believer deprived of God's indulgence remains on the periphery of true faith. The true believer reaches out for the devil and instead finds God. Despite the commission of a mortal sin, he may find that God forgives him. Apparently more interested in evil than in good, Greene presents individuals, like Dostoyevski's Ivan or some of Mauriac's "heroes," whose spirits become battlegrounds between the forces of God and the devil. Greene suggests the Manichean heresy: good and evil fight over man continually, and we are never sure who wins, for the ways of God, by their very nature, are inscrutable.

Greene's God is an enigmatical being who extends grace in ways that man can never understand, and when the priest offers this as his faith, the lieutenant justifiably thinks the priest is deceiving him. As one of the several parallels and opposites to the priest, the lieutenant exemplifies the political world, the commissar who has little use for the yogi. The battle between the priest and the lieutenant is a battle for the minds of men, as much as God and the devil battle for the mind of Ivan Karamazov. The lieutenant offers a new kind of church, one stripped of faith, superstition, and hope, one based solely on the material needs of the people. This is a church of the world, and the lieutenant is its ascetic priest.

In his asceticism, the lieutenant (unnamed, as the priest is unnamed) apes what he thinks should be the virtues of those he opposes. He simply transfers the values of the clerical orders to his own: no indulgence in sensory pleasure, no swerving from the path of righteousness, no guilt about the commission of a bad act in order to insure a future good, no qualms about effacing self in favor of the public welfare. In his doctrinaire political and economic beliefs, he challenges the church on its own grounds: the means justify the ends, and the battle is to the death. The lieutenant, in his priestly role, accepts everything the church stands for except the altar.

The priest, on the other hand, accepts little else but the altar. Greene leads us to believe that he was never a very devout priest, for he suffered from pride in the days when he was honored with good dinners and fine wines. He grew fat, and he expected obeisance as his right. He aligned himself with traditional power against the peasant. The lieutenant, however, will kill in order to help the peasants, often against themselves; and he is willing to shoot hostages if necessary in order to discover the hiding place of the last priest in the province. The lieutenant, thus, finds himself injuring those he has sworn to help; while the priest finds himself injuring the God he has sworn to love.

As a man of the people, the lieutenant is willing to die to effect his ideas—justice and equality for the peasants. As a man of God, the priest is afraid for his life and unsure about being a martyr to the church. Years of isolation have worn him down, so that he is unable and unwilling to call upon reserves. Consequently, the roles of the two men have been reversed. The lieutenant will sacrifice himself for his ideal—to free his people, despite themselves, from superstitions and the oppression of the church; the priest is also aware of an ideal but is unable to sacrifice himself for it. The lieutenant, the devil's agent, is strong in his desire to destroy God's image on earth, and the priest, God's representative, is weak in defending God's image. The priest constantly warns his admirers as well as the lieutenant not to judge the church and God by his own example, for he is a bad priest, but nevertheless, he suggests, the best the province has at the moment—in fact, the only one.

Yet God endures in the hearts of the people despite the militant activity against Him, and this persistence of course "proves" Greene's point. For just as God endures in the people's hearts, sullied though He may be by the visible church, so does He endure in the priest's heart, defiled though He may be there. Both the priest and the lieutenant are striving for sainthood, paradoxically, without either asceticism for the priest or humanitarianism for the lieutenant. But only the priest—because he is inevitably humbled by God—realizes how difficult it is to be a saint. The lieutenant, in his do-good arrogance, can never recognize this point. Thus, fundamentally, they must be different.

The lieutenant's world is predicated on the assumption that good men will always be forthcoming to perpetuate his ideal; but the priest suggests that there is no guarantee, for only belief can insure the humility that might prevent the persecution of the people in the name of enlightenment. This is the same point Conrad made in *Nostromo*—a novel, incidentally, that hangs heavily over *The Power and the Glory:* what will happen after Charles Gould's death when a man less dedicated to the silver mine takes over in the name of self-interest? What protections are there, then? There is, obviously, no possible answer. The priest says to the lieutenant: " 'It's no good your working for your end unless you're a good man yourself. And there won't always be good men in your party. Then you'll have all the old starvation, beating, getting rich anyhow.' "

When the lieutenant asks the priest's motives in staying when everyone else left, the latter replies using the same kind of paradox with which Jesus answered his questioners. The priest admits his deadly pride, and says that like the angels he fell because he conceived of himself as godlike. And he argues, well-schooled, it seems, in Greene's peculiar theology, that precisely because it was dangerous and difficult, he remained out of pride, and not to further God's interest. He denies following God's wishes and trying to become a martyr and saint. Greene reminds us that one does not necessarily serve God by accepting danger in His name, for God's grace can operate incomprehensibly. Perhaps, then, only the weak, the criminal, the evil, the proud are saved; damnation awaits the pious, the humble, and the devout.

Had Greene left the priest at this point, involved in his indecisions, then the novel would have been compelling. As long as the priest and the lieutenant oppose each other, all the ironies and paradoxes of their conflict are dramatically forceful. Once the priest convinces the lieutenant of his sincerity and the fickleness of God's ways, the novel declines into a tract, and the character of the lieutenant loses sharpness. There is much ineffective sentiment in the priest's recognition of the lieutenant as a good fellow and in the lieutenant's realization that the priest is also interested in the peasants. The two cross each other's paths as brothers, Greene indicates here, one looking after the spirit, the other after the body; and sadly, one must die—Cain must kill Abel. At this point the novel becomes effusive, and the final section devoted to the saving of Luis, who had first shown loyalty to the lieutenant and then to the priest, is as false as the priest's former agony was real. Only the character in conflict without any chance of salvation can provide the tragic tone that this novel requires, unless it is to sink into bathos and melodrama. Greene evidently became seduced by doctrine, and, unwilling to desert his paradox, marred with specious arguments the dramatic tension of the earlier parts of the novel. For the priest held in suspension is a believable character; as soon as he finds God by finding himself, however, he is less effective dramatically than spiritually. With the priest's ultimate salvation, which only a believer can accept, the novel becomes meaningless as a work of art.

In many ways, nevertheless, despite its flaws, *The Power and the Glory* is a political-religious novel in the manner of *The Brothers Karamazov* and *The Magic Mountain*. The surface detail, as in every political novel, masks the interplay of antinomies: the political versus the religious, the dictator versus the saint. Greene twists the opposition from its usual course by making a whiskey-priest with an illegitimate child God's representative on earth; and even more than merely representative, the sole representative in the entire state, God's last man to struggle against His earthly enemies. This is indeed a frail Jesus among the sinners, a debilitated Jesus who must do God's bidding when he is unsure of what he bids for, an anguished Jesus who is as much magnetized by the world he opposes as by God's will. The use of the whiskey-priest to represent the best that faith has to offer conveys both the strengths and weaknesses of the novel. Perhaps only in Scobie of *The Heart of the Matter* was Greene able to present a weak man with so much of a burden, the burden of sin and grace and heaven and hell. The problem, however, is more fierce with the priest than even with Scobie: for Greene is asking how a man dedicated to God must live in the world under circumstances in which God's aid is tenuous.

Like most powerful novels of the individual and the surroundings he lives in, *The Power and the Glory* is loosely existential, in much the same way as the work of Mauriac and Dostoyevski. In all three, their Christian existentialism does not preclude a secular view from becoming attractive, and the existential quality of their novels often takes the character of a tension between those opposing values. In brief, how does one live, priest or not, when faith tells one thing while experience tells another? how does one live when heart and mind are split, and neither can follow the other? finally, how can one live when vacillation and weakness are more apparent than the strength one needs to survive? Scobie and the whiskey-priest both recognize that the only way to achieve salvation is by attaining martyrdom or sainthood, or both. Scobie tries to reach his through suicide, an unforgivable sin, and the priest through offering Catholic blessings to a dying American gangster, who refuses them.

It is a further part of Greene's irony that his priest should risk everything over an American criminal who is dying in the province and needs absolution (for what?). There is of course only a small difference between them, and when the priest offers conditional absolution to the criminal, he proffers what he hopes God will offer him: at least conditional absolution. Greene writes: "At the best, it was only one criminal trying to aid the escape of another—whichever way you looked, there wasn't much merit in either of them." Like Jim's relationship with Gentleman Brown in the Patusan section of *Lord Jim*, the connection between the murderous American and the Mexican priest disallows righteousness on the part of a man with a past. Like Jim, the priest recognizes that his past frailty disarms him, and that he can offer only the minimum of what God allows. To confess people, to offer them moral solace, even to give absolution—all these are mockeries when given by a bad priest. The criminal who is hounded by the authorities is a vague existential parallel to the priest who is also hounded by the authorities. It is not fortuitous that Greene has the priest captured while he is trying to save the one man who would seem farthest from God's salvation. The priest boasts that as long as there is a single man damned in the state, then he too will be damned. To save the man least able to save himself is a mark of his devotion, and for him to save a fellow criminal is a mark of God's irony in a universe that remains inscrutable.

As the priest moves further from his original identity, as he tries, with increasing difficulty, to reconcile the pride that damns with the humility that saves, as he almost literally is chased by the "hound of heaven and earth," he gradually finds out what he is. This element of knowing oneself, which usually comes from within a Greene character under the stress of severe external events, takes the form of repentance that God requires, and is similar in its way to the recognition that the Greek dramatist required. The chase or something akin to it forces an inner response previously ignored by the character. Only under stress does the priest recognize what a proud and vain man he was in the past when he courted good meals, comfortable quarters, and slaked his own thirst rather than that of lost souls. Only under stress does he see how far short of God's perfection he has fallen. And only under stress does he feel for mankind the kind of pity that is allied to charity. The violence of many of Greene's novels is perhaps predicated on this belief: that only violence or stress or chaotic conditions can upset a man's complacency and create out of his former indifference the kind of belief necessary for his salvation.

As I mentioned above, this attitude is not dissimilar to a tragic one; indeed it would be compellingly tragic if not for ultimate salvation which eases over the crises of real tragedy. The stress of the chase here is the stress of a disclosure in a Greek play; and after this recognition of what he is, the character steps out a new person, stripped of indifference and complacency. This new person is usually completely crushed, but we are led to believe that he is preferable to the former being who lived by illusions. The "resurrected" man, while virtually destroyed, must gather the shreds of his now unfamiliar life and try to survive through self-knowledge; he can no longer disguise what he is and gain strength by virtue of his disguise. He must live with the truth about himself even if it destroys him. The Greek dramatist stopped at this point, and the tragic element was obvious. Greene goes one step further and offers God's salvation to the man resurrected by his recognition of what he is.

At this point, the secular reader is troubled as the novels lose cogency as literature. The force of narrative and character, even for the secular reader, was obvious. The intimation, however, that a miracle has perhaps occurred, that a damned man may be saved, and that God's grace can operate in ways unknown to man and therefore must remain inexplicable are perhaps the necessities of faith but barely the stuff of novels filled with dramatic irony. Devotional, religious, godly, all these things a novel concerned with salvation may be, but when they predominate to the exclusion of all else, then they enfeeble the drama. In attempting to reconcile Christian romanticism with the starkness of Greek tragedy, Greene has tried to write cosmic novels in which the author asks many of the significant questions. That Greene has attempted so much and achieved the power of nearly first-rate novels is not to be denied; but to claim more for them is to read in the religious hopes of the reader.

One only raises these disclaimers because Greene does try to provide some final solution, tenuous and diluted as he recognizes it must be in the modern world. The priest answers the lieutenant that it is not advisable to give the poor man power, because then he stands less chance of gaining heaven. "It's better to let him die in dirt and wake in heaven—so long as we don't push his face in the dirt." Greene offers the traditional paradox of religious humanitarianism—help people who need it but not too much, for they may lose their souls with prosperity: an answer that is obviously insufficient to the secular reader and to the lieutenant whose own brand of expedience is insufficient as well. The novel's entire force is vitiated by the priest's verbalization of his ideas, for how trite they are in juxtaposition to his personal agonies. This is a novel about just that feeling—agony—and when it becomes explanatory, discursive, argumentative, it loses its meaning, which is simply that men find it difficult not only to live up to their ideals but to have ideals at all.

MIRIAM ALLOTT

The Moral Situation in The Quiet American

When *The Quiet American* appeared in 1955 it was described on the jacket as "a modern variant on a theme which in the last century attracted Mark Twain and other writers: a study of New World hope and innocence set in an old world of violence," a statement which places it in a literary tradition with which it has some important elements in common. We are likely to do it more justice, I suggest, if we look at it in the context of sophisticated moral analysis of the kind associated with some later nineteenth century English and American fiction than if we begin by relating it to certain types of contemporary existentialist thinking. In its concern with the nature of effective moral action, its feeling for the anomalies which surround most human attempts to achieve this, and its assertion nevertheless of certain enduring human values, it reminds us particularly of James and Conrad (both writers with whom Greene is especially familiar). At the same time, in spite of its non-Catholic central characters, it gives a fresh focus to themes which Greene explores in his "Catholic" novels and, as we might expect, it shows a close emotional and intellectual kinship with these books. For a "correct reading" of this novel all these factors ought to be considered.

The notion that active intelligence rather than simple good intentions is necessary for the successful ordering of human relationships barely emerges as an explicit theme in the English novel until George Eliot; and even here the sober vision which this theme encourages is not yet of the kind to instill serious misgivings about the moral consonance of ends and means. Although

From *Graham Greene: Some Critical Considerations*, edited by Robert O. Evans.

George Eliot feels that "heroic Promethean effort" is required to achieve ultimate moral good, she places the effort within the limits of human ability and tries to free it from those limitations of temperament to which she is otherwise particularly sensitive. It is clearly no part of her purpose to unsettle her Victorian readers by suggesting that action directed towards "ultimate moral good" can be contaminated by the evil which it is designed to overcome. A more unflinching reading of experience is offered by her successors in the next generation, who confront more squarely than she does the fact that in an imperfect world choice lies between greater and lesser evil rather than between clear right and wrong. Conrad puts forward his "few simple ideas" concerning fidelity and honour, and then shows in his characters' fated lives, and with the help of Marlow's brooding commentaries, that a code of behaviour based on such ideas is at best no more than a fragile defence. James takes the argument several stages further in his own analysis of the moral life. In characters such as Isabel Archer, Maggie Verver, and Milly Theale, innocence is equated with immaturity, and it is through their experience of betrayal and treachery that these people arrive at a fuller moral vision and come at last to understand the situation into which they have been drawn as much by their own limitations as by their adversaries' self-will and ambitious cunning. Determining now to retrieve this situation, they take up the instruments whose use they have just learned. So Maggie resorts to deceit in order to counteract the deception practised on herself and her father by the Prince and Charlotte, and Milly Theale relies on the "cunning of the serpent" rather than the "innocence of the dove" to make her way through the labyrinth which Kate and Merton, Lord Mark, and Mrs. Lowder, have prepared for her (it is this "cunning" which ultimately helps to bring about Merton Densher's moral awakening and his final separation from Kate).

Graham Greene's handling of his central characters in *The Quiet American* displays a similarly ironical criticism of life, the main difference being that Pyle's naive good intentions and their disastrous consequences carry James's theme of simple good faith divorced from wisdom into a wider area of social reference, while Fowler's behaviour extends the relevance of James's statement about the corrupting effects of experience to a more urgent and far-reaching "international situation" than any which he could foresee. Some prominent nonexistentialist French writers also share Greene's concern about the high price in personal integrity which may be paid by anyone aiming at efficient moral action for the general good, and they explore in a comparable way the ambiguous relationship between "intelligence" and "goodness." Albert Camus, who firmly opposes Sartre's existentialist beliefs, reminds us in *La Peste* that those who dedicate themselves to the conquest of violence find it hard to escape infection by this "pestilence." Again, in Anouilh's *Antigone*, we find Creon depending on violence and trickery to restore order in his troubled kingdom; his destruction of Antigone is forced on him because, in the society which he must hold together by compromise, backstairs intrigue, and the ruthless suppression of criticism, her inflexible—and in this case noble—innocence can only make for disaster.

Graham Greene's kindred themes point to the contemporary relevance of much of his thinking, but the reader of *The Quiet American* is bound, I suppose, to be more immediately struck by its Jamesian affinities, which are especially noticeable in its dramatization of what is primarily an Anglo-American "international situation"; its quasi-metaphorical juxtaposition of representatives from the "New" and the "Old" worlds; and its probing concern both with the motivation of treachery and betrayal and with the nature of an innocence which is dangerous because ignorant. There is a further similarity in the close interdependence of its tragic and its comic elements. It is after he has exhausted the more direct possibilities for social comedy in his "international situation" that we see James beginning to explore differences between the "New" and the "Old," less as a Balzacian social historian than as a moralist for whom the two worlds are convenient illustrations for universally opposed systems of value. The people who find themselves at odds with each other in *The Golden Bowl* or *The Wings of the Dove* illustrate general moral dilemmas of a kind with which contemporary sensibility is still deeply engaged. Yet at the same time that James locks together his victims and victimizers, his betrayed and betrayers, in their mutually destructive embrace he still manages to surround them with a strong flavour of irony. Similarly Pyle and Fowler, the two principal figures in *The Quiet American* who represent the New and the Old worlds, sometimes appear to stand for conflicting systems of value which cut across the artificial boundaries of nationality and race; at the same time they also succeed in conveying their author's strong feeling for comic incongruity. Pyle and Fowler at cross purposes are often as entertaining as, let us say, Sarah Pocock and Madame de Vionnet in that historic confrontation at the Paris hotel; and in association with the delightful and uncomprehending Phuong, whom they both love, they also demonstrate their author's skill in mingling the funny and the sad, a quality which gives special distinction to some of James's most intelligent achievements from the 1890s onwards.

This ironical temper also links Graham Greene with earlier writers than James, a point which he emphasizes himself by his choice of passages from Byron and Clough as epigraphs for his story. The lines from Byron occur in *Don Juan*, canto 1, stanza 132.

> This is the patent age of new inventions
> For killing bodies and for saving souls,
> All propagated with the best intentions.

Like the description of armies attacking from the air in *Rasselas*, the passage can arouse amusement and surprise in a modern reader, who sees in it a longer reach of irony than the author originally intended. However, a little more may be said about its appearance in this new context without straining its significance too far. As it happens, it follows immediately after a stanza in which Byron indulges in some high-spirited satirical junketing at the expense of America. Along with even more libellous statements, Byron suggests that it might be a good thing if the population of America were to be thinned

> With war, or plague, or famine—any way,
> So that civilization they may learn.

It is hard to ignore the bearing of this remark on Greene's presentation of Alden Pyle, which is also in keeping, both in theme and tone, with Byron's frequent emphasis in his satirical verse on the connection between "good intentions" and, so to speak, the road to hell. In *The Quiet American* Alden Pyle, setting out equipped with simple humanitarian "good intentions" and a totally untutored moral intelligence, ends up helping General Thé to bomb civilians with explosive bicycle pumps, one of the age's newest "inventions for killing bodies." The epigraph from Byron thus underlines Greene's sardonic commentary on a combination of qualities now distressingly prevalent: i.e., the high development of technical skill combined with the low development of moral intelligence, so that the skill too often gets used for "killing bodies" instead of helping to make them good and happy. Alden Pyle, then, has to carry the burden of representing this combination of qualities, while Fowler, as the knowing observer who is intelligent enough to see the menace in Pyle but refrains from taking preventive action until it is almost too late, illustrates the more complex aspects of Greene's argument about moral responsibility. "Innocence is a kind of insanity," Fowler says, thinking of the way in which Pyle is "impregnably armoured" against knowing his own power for harm "by his good intentions and his ignorance." Like the spokesman of *Don Juan*, Fowler inhabits a mental region which is situated at some distance from Pyle's "psychological world of great simplicity," where one heroically asks trusting questions of one's rival in love. "You'd play straight with me, Thomas, wouldn't you?" Pyle asks, but Thomas Fowler knows that human behaviour, whether in love or war, demands more complex formulations than this. In the consequent disenchantment of its tone his narrative has in fact much in common with Byron's wry amusement, his distrust of cant, and his admiration for the civilization of the Old World as against that of the New.

What it does not have, however, is Byron's vigour. Here one sees the relevance of the quotation from Clough which appears above the lines from Byron at the beginning of the book. The passage is taken from *Amours de Voyage* (canto 2, stanza 11) and the spokesman this time is a young man, Claude, who suffers from that paralysis of the will and the emotions which is a continuing theme in nineteenth century European literature and which owes so much to the "other" Byron—the Byron, that is, of the verse tales and *Childe Harold.* It unites Russian Hamlet-figures, like the heroes in Pushkin and Lermontov, with Flaubert's Frédéric Moreau, and it even emerges as late as "The Beast in the Jungle," Henry James's short story about the man whose destiny it is to be someone "to whom nothing on earth was to happen." But the major factor in Claude's predicament is the sort of scepticism which we associate particularly with the movement of ideas in mid-nineteenth century England. His creator is an expert on the crippling effects of this kind of doubt and is also skilled in aiming his best ironical effects at his own indecisiveness. It is almost certain that Greene intends us to place Fowler in this context and see him as a "doubting Thomas," who is endowed with moral sensibility and yet fears, or is too lazy, to act, these characteristics meanwhile providing constantly renewed resources for the free play of his own ironic sense. Clough's hero does not like "being moved," we are told in the lines which Greene quotes:

> I do not like being moved; for the will is
> excited; and action
> Is a most dangerous thing; I tremble for
> something factitious,
> Some malpractice of heart and illegitimate
> process;
> We're so prone to these things, with our
> terrible notions of duty.

Fowler does not "like being moved" either, and he goes out of his way to assert his lack of involvement. "You can rule me out," he says early in the story, though it is already apparent that he is protesting too much:

> "I'm not involved. Not involved," I repeated. It had been an article of my creed. The human condition being what it was, let

> them love, let them murder, I would not be involved. My fellow journalists called themselves correspondents; I preferred the title of reporter. I wrote what I saw; I took no action—even opinion is a kind of action.

For all his assumed air of disengagement, however, Fowler cannot permanently refrain from action. Face to face at last with "the malpractice of heart and illegitimate process" which Pyle is led into by his "terrible notions of duty," he finds that he too has his "notions of duty" and must act upon them. One of the various ironical implications here is that these "notions of duty" again lead to "an illegitimate process." The tragicomic temper of this writing sees to it that Fowler's decision to act, which is founded on a sense of moral outrage and the desire to prevent further violence and suffering, should nevertheless result in betrayal, murder and—as the result of yet another ironical twist to the plot—considerable material advantage to himself. As we pursue the windings of the story it also becomes apparent that the author's tragicomic method acts as a necessary distancing device for certain strongly obsessive emotions.

Here it is necessary to take into account Fowler's relationship with Phuong, for one's judgment of the book depends to a great extent on what is make of this part of it. In the first four lines of the stanza from Clough's poem (Greene gives only the last four) Claude tells us,

> There are two different kinds, I believe, of
> human attraction.
> One which simply disturbs, unsettles, and makes
> you uneasy,
> And another that poises, retains, and fixes
> and holds you.
> I have no doubt, for myself, in giving my voice
> for the latter.

Fowler "gives his voice" for it too. Phuong—who is charmingly drawn: the elegance and economy of the style are nicely adjusted to the subject—represents the attraction which "poises, retains, and fixes and holds. . . ." She is totally different from "the girl in the red dressing-gown" of Fowler's earlier love affair. Sometimes, he tells Pyle, she seems "invisible like peace," while the girl of the old affair stands for the other kind of human attraction which "disturbs, unsettles, and makes you uneasy."

> "I was terrified of losing her. . . . I couldn't bear the uncertainty any longer. I ran towards the finish, just like a coward

> runs towards the enemy and wins a medal. . . . Then I came east."
>
> "And found Phuong?"
>
> "Yes."
>
> "But don't you find the same thing with Phuong?"
>
> "Not the same. You see, the other one loved me. I was afraid of losing love. Now I'm only afraid of losing Phuong."

For a reader interpreting the book in existentialist terms it is naturally hard to believe that Fowler "loves" Phuong. "Fowler lives with Phuong because she prepares his opium pipe and satiates his sexual appetites" is one of the views expressed in the essay referred to [elsewhere]; but this is a simplification which may lead to our misjudging both the quality of Fowler's feelings for Phuong and the function of Phuong herself in the structure of the story. Through her, and through the reactions which she arouses in Fowler, the author succeeds in making us see how inevitable Fowler's ultimate commitment really is. Fowler, we realise, acts as he does because he has never, in any real sense, managed to remain uninvolved. His feelings for Phuong help to explain why. They are complex and, if we may judge by the general effect of his novels, they are also fairly typical of Greene's own feelings about humanity. They mingle tenderness, selfishness, compassion, pain, respect for human dignity, and a bitter sense of the limitations of human faith and love. A passage like the following, even though it is supposed to voice the thoughts of a non-believer, could have been written by no one but this particular novelist.

> Why should I want to die when Phuong slept beside me every night? But I knew the answer to that question. From childhood I had never believed in permanence, and yet I had longed for it. Always I was afraid of losing happiness. This month, next year, Phuong would leave me. If not next year, in three years. Death was the only absolute value in my world. Lose life and one would lose nothing again for ever. I envied those who could believe in a God and I distrusted them. I felt they were keeping their courage up with a fable of the changeless and the permanent. Death was far more certain than God, and with death there would be no longer the daily possibility of love dying.

A strong ingredient in these complex feelings is pity, an emotion which afflicts Greene's characters like a disease. Fowler's clipped reporting does not disguise from us—though it may do so from the imperceptive Pyle—

the intensity with which this feeling can work in him. It is present when he recalls the vulnerability of Phuong as he saw her first, dancing with lightness and precision on her "eighteen-year-old feet" and living on simple dreams about security and happiness; when he seeks emotional relief by describing the grey drained bodies of men caught in a crossfire and filling the canal at Phat Diem as "an Irish stew containing too much meat"; and when he thinks of the peasant woman holding in her lap and covering "with a kind of modesty" what is left of her baby after General Thé's bombs have exploded in the square.

It is this suppressed but inextinguishable emotion which binds Fowler indissolubly to his fellow creatures and makes it impossible for him to remain not involved. It is this, too, which finally separates him from Alden Pyle, whose "York Harding" liberalism encourages belief in large clean abstractions like Freedom and Honour which exist on a plane safely out of sight of "the fury and the mire of human veins." It is true that this belief can promote Pyle's daring cloak-and-dagger enterprise in saving his rival's life under fire because this "is the right thing to do," an act of heroism which stands beyond criticism. And yet nothing in the belief is capable of bringing home to its possessor the enormity of what has happened when General Thé's bombs go off in the square. "I dealt with him severely," Pyle says afterwards, and he speaks "like the captain of a school-team who has found one of his boys breaking his training." His continued association with Thé does not present itself to him as needing any kind of moral justification. The General is "the only hope we have" in the struggle for power, and the Vietnamese he sees as too childlike and uncomplicated to nurse any resentment against the violence which he and Thé will continue to inflict on them so long as the struggle for power goes on. It is just after Pyle has uttered these shattering statements that Fowler finally commits himself. He moves to the window and gives to the waiting trishaw driver the signal that Pyle must die. "Sooner or later," he has been told earlier by Heng, a man who will help to bring this death about, "one has to take sides. If one is to remain human." In spite of his hatred of political action, he joins at last in Pyle's cloak-and-dagger game, ranging himself in the name of humanity beside Heng and his undercover gang against Pyle and *his* fellow-plotters.

It is at this point, I think, that one becomes aware of the thematic continuity linking this book with Greene's "Catholic" novels, where the author is occupied with the allied problems of pain and of how far man is justified in risking damnation for the sake of relieving the suffering of his fellow creatures. These stories are haunted by memories of "the curé d'Ars admitting to his mind all the impurity of a province, Péguy challenging God in the cause of the damned." It is Péguy of whom the priest speaks in *Brighton Rock* when he seeks to console Rose after Pinkie's death.

> He was a good man, a holy man, and he lived in sin all through his life, because he couldn't bear the idea that any soul should suffer damnation. . . . He never took the sacraments, he never married his wife in church. I don't know, my child, but some people think he was—well, a saint.

Scobie, in *The Heart of the Matter*, risks damnation by committing suicide to save his wife and mistress from further suffering, and the whiskey-priest in *The Power and the Glory*, praying for the salvation of his corrupted child, beseeches God, "Give me any kind of death—without contrition, in a state of sin—only save this child." Like Ivan Karamazov, who challenges Alyosha on the subject of divine justice and can find no justification for innocent suffering, these people find no escape from the ravages of their sense of pity. The extra turn of the screw in their case is their full consciousness of the spiritual peril into which they have been led by their compassion.

This theological dilemma is absent in *The Quiet American*, but the moral and emotional predicament is essentially unchanged: indeed since the author is now depicting man without God, it is possibly even more urgent in its presentation. We sense this urgency when we realise that Scobie's feelings about suffering lead him to incur the risk, but not the certainty, of damnation, while the effect of comparable feelings in Fowler is to make him take on a burden of guilt from which he cannot be set free. For Scobie and his Catholic fellow-sinners there is always the hope of grace; the point of light may appear at the end of the tunnel, the glimmer of dawn may rise in the night sky, the hand of God may reach out to stay their free fall from "the stirrup to the ground." For Fowler, enacting his Judas role, there is guilt and a happiness stained with remorse. A certain emotional resonance in Greene's treatment of this situation calls to mind Tarrou's question towards the close of *La Peste:* "Can one be a saint without God?—that's the problem, in fact the only problem, I'm up against today." Obviously we cannot say of Fowler, as the priest in *Brighton Rock* says of Péguy, that he may be "well, a saint." And yet it is also obvious that among the characteristics which Fowler shares with these Catholics who challenge God in the cause of suffering is his willingness to take the responsibility of wrong-doing for the sake of diminishing human pain.

He also shares with these Catholic characters the longing for peace which is one of the consequences of their burden of pity, especially their pity for the suffering of children. Like Scobie at the bedside of the shipwrecked child and the whiskey-priest praying for his daughter—and like Father Paneloux in *La Peste* watching a child's protracted death from plague or Ivan Karamazov torturing himself with stories about cruelty to children—Fowler experiences with the growth of this anguish the growth also of an angry despair. All victims of suffering—the men in the canal at Phat Diem, the young soldiers in the watch-tower—arouse these feelings in him. But it is memories of the child in the ditch ("one shouldn't fight a war with children . . . a little curled body in a ditch came back to my mind") and of the mangled baby in the Saigon square, which trigger off his decision to take measures against Pyle. His desire for peace is accentuated by these feelings about human suffering, and its existence is in itself a measure of how deeply, after all, he has always been "involved." He identifies Phuong with "peace" and loves her for her stillness and serenity, while death seems to him to be "the only absolute value" because it puts a stop to despair. "There can be no peace without hope," thinks Rieux in *La Peste*, as he meditates on the death of Tarrou, the man who had wondered whether one could be "a saint without God."

> Tarrou had lived a life riddled with contradictions and had never known hope's solace. Did that explain his aspirations towards saintliness, his quest of peace by service in the course of others?
> (part 4, chap. 3)

Fowler's life, too, though lived at a lower emotional temperature, is "riddled with contradictions" and he has "never known hope's solace," while "service in the cause of others" does not bring him peace any more than it really does to Tarrou. On the contrary it gives him cause to long for it all the more. Peace remains the *princesse lointaine* of his dreams, and his author may well intend this longing to be felt as an expression of the love of God. The desire for peace seems to pursue Fowler as the nameless "something" pursues Pinkie in his last despairing drive through the dark. Like Tarrou, Fowler appears to be one of those people who, as Rieux puts it, "desired reunion with something they couldn't have defined, but which seemed to them the only desirable thing on earth. For want of a better name, they sometimes called it peace" (*La Peste*, part 4, chap. 4).

Fowler himself finds another explanation for his longing, seeing it simply as the manifestation of his own selfish egotism. When Pyle at the risk of his own life brings members of the patrol to his rescue, Fowler refuses their aid until they have attended to the young soldier whose moaning (it is now stilled because he is dead) had filled him with a sense of anguish and guilt harder to bear than the pain of his wounded leg. He totally repudiates Pyle's admiring interpretation of this behaviour. Pyle sees him, one understands, as another Sidney at Zutphen, but Fowler merely remarks that he "cannot be at ease (and to be at ease is my chief wish) if someone else is in pain, visibly or audibly or tactually." He goes on: "Sometimes this is mistaken by the innocent for unselfishness, when all I am doing is sacrificing a small good—in this case postponement in attending to my hurt—for the sake of a far greater good, a peace of mind when I need only think of myself." There is, of course, some truth in this, for Fowler, as I have said, is by no means a saintly figure: largely, he illustrates the ordinary self-regarding emotions of the *homme moyen sensuel.* Yet the revelation that his peace is contingent upon the peace of others only succeeds in further emphasising how inescapably involved he is in the human situation. Moreover his remark about "sacrificing a small good . . . for the sake of a far greater good" acquires an impressive irony when it is applied to his betrayal of Pyle. The possibility of repose recedes even further into the distance once he has sent to his death the man who is at once the preserver of his life and his rival in love. In the earlier part of his story he explains that the human situation "being what it is" he has never been able to experience the "peace of mind when I need only think of myself" (it is only in his opium-sleep that he manages to approach this state): in the later part of his story he indicates that his own actions have done little to bring the experience any nearer.

It is also in this later part of the story, as we should expect, that the possible religious significance of his longing for peace presses itself more noticeably on our attention. It is especially apparent in his final interview with Vigot, the intelligent Roman Catholic police officer at the Sureté, who keeps his copy of Pascal at his side like a manual for living. Vigot is in charge of the investigations into Pyle's death, and the verbal fencing which characterizes his exchanges with Fowler, although far less elaborate, is not unlike the dialectical duelling which takes place between Raskolnikov and the examining magistrate in *Crime and Punishment.* Fowler certainly shares with Raskolnikov a compulsive desire to unburden his conscience. The similarity in their situations also draws attention to the enormous contrast between Raskolnikov's intensity of feeling and Fowler's cooler response. He does not give himself away, but he comes near to it in the interview which at last closes his association with Vigot.

> "I've got nothing to tell you. Nothing at all."
>
> "Then I'll be going," he said. "I don't suppose I'll trouble you again."
>
> At the door he turned as though he were unwilling to abandon hope—his hope or mine.

> "That was a strange picture for you to go and see that night. I wouldn't have thought you cared for costume drama. What was it? *Robin Hood?*"
>
> "*Scaramouche*, I think. I had to kill time. And I needed distraction."
>
> "Distraction?"
>
> "We all have our private worries, Vigot," I carefully explained.
>
> It was strange how disturbed I had been by Vigot's visit. It was as though a poet had brought me his work to criticise and through some careless action I had destroyed it. I was a man without a vocation . . . but I could recognize a vocation in another. Now that Vigot had gone to close his uncompleted file, I wished I had the courage to call him back and say, "You are right. I did see Pyle the night he died."

The dialogue here has the allusive understatement which serves its authors well in his plays. Even the film-titles carry their ironic overtures. The make-believe world of *Robin Hood*, where a gay and gallant solution is found for the problem of wrong and injustice, and the mischief-making buffoonery of *Scaramouche*—Fowler provides himself with an alibi for the last hours of Pyle's life by sitting through this film—underline the contrast between sober reality and the boy's adventure-story world in which Pyle had so touchingly and yet so dangerously believed. There is a similar telling allusiveness in Fowler's throwaway remark about "hope." In the unwillingness on Vigot's side "to abandon hope—his hope or mine," especially when it is taken in conjunction with the references to Vigot's "vocation" and Fowler's desire to confess, one sees the police officer assuming at this point in the story the function in Greene's Catholic novels which is often fulfilled by his priests. The reader is surely intended to remember here Fowler's earlier conversation with the Catholic priest whom he encounters at the top of the church tower in Phat Diem.

> He said, "Did you come up here to find me?"
>
> "No. I wanted to get my bearings."
>
> "I asked you because I had a man up here last night. He wanted to go to confession. He had got a little frightened, you see, with what he had seen along the canal. One couldn't blame him."
>
> "It's bad along there?"
>
> "The parachutists caught them in a cross-fire. Poor souls. I thought perhaps you were feeling the same."
>
> "I'm not a Roman Catholic. I don't think you would even call me a Christian."

> "It's strange what fear does to a man."
> "It would never do that to me. If I believed in any God at all, I should still hate the idea of confession. Kneeling in one of your boxes. Exposing myself to another man. You must excuse me, Father, but to me it seems morbid—unmanly even."
> "Oh," he said lightly, "I expect you are a good man. I don't suppose you've ever had much to regret."

The unconscious irony of the priest's reply is brought home to the reader when Fowler, now with something momentous to regret, wishes he has the courage to obey his impulse, recall Vigot and confess the truth.

Although this wish is not fulfilled, it seems on the face of it that Fowler's story will nevertheless have "the happy ending" which Phuong has tried so hard all along not to seem to want: his job is secure; his divorce will come through; he will be able to marry Phuong; she will stay with him now that Pyle is dead. But the shadow of Pyle remains. Even when the wonderful telegram arrives and Phuong knows that she is to have the security which she had earlier sought with Pyle, the shadow is still there. Pyle's copy of York Harding's *The Role of the West*—another title obviously chosen for its ironical effect—stands out from Fowler's bookshelves

> like a cabinet portrait—of a young man with a crew cut and a black dog at his heels. I could harm no one any more. I said to Phuong, "Do you miss him much?"
> "Who?"
> "Pyle." Strange how even now, even to her, it was impossible to use his first name.
> "Can I go please? My sister will be so excited."
> "You spoke his name once in your sleep."
> "I never remember my dreams."
> "There was so much you could have done together. He was young."
> "You are not old."
> "The skyscrapers. The Empire State Building."
> She said with a small hesitation, "I want to see the Cheddar Gorge."

These nicely adjusted lines of dialogue at the close of the novel, their hinted regrets signalizing new areas of sensitivity in the relationship between Fowler and Phuong (" 'It's like it used to be,' I lied, 'a year ago' ") show Fowler ruefully admitting that the memory of Pyle will be difficult to discard. As we see him last, Pyle is still on his mind.

> I thought of the first day and Pyle sitting beside me at the Continental, with his eye on the soda-fountain across the way. Everything had gone right with me since he had died, but how I wished there existed someone to whom I could say that I was sorry.

Pyle may not always stay in his mind, one feels, but what has mattered in Fowler's story is that he is capable of feeling this pity and sorrow for the lost young man; that as an ordinary, nonpolitical, moderately selfish, but intelligent human being he is moved to act against violence and stupidity; and that he is impelled towards such action above all by his insight into human suffering, especially the suffering caused by war and political conflict.

It is easy to mistake the nature of Greene's achievement in this novel, partly because its extreme economy disguises both the range and quality of its feeling and the reach of its ideas. Perhaps it is also true to say that it illustrates how far this author's obsessive themes make for weakness as well as strength. Pity is one of the most urgent of these themes and it is a dangerous one for any artist to handle. It requires stringent distancing devices, and although the author's careful understatement and the operation of his irony go a long way towards supplying these, there are times when one feels that he may be near to an unbalancing subjectivity. All the same, the theme enables him to present with necessary dramatic intensity issues which it would be perilous to ignore. He succeeds in reminding us that we need Pyle's courage and none of his ignorance, Fowler's moral intelligence and none of his indecisiveness, if we are to find a way out of the alarming difficulties which as nations and individuals we are most of us nowadays required to face. He takes us a long distance, I feel, from the moral position implied in a good deal of modern existentialist writing.

A. A. DEVITIS

Religious Aspects in the Novels of Graham Greene

Anyone approaching the work of Graham Greene is immediately confronted by a number of literary, scholarly, and, perhaps, theological problems; for Greene's career since the publication in 1929 of his first novel, *The Man Within*, has led him into many aspects of creative and imaginative literature. As well as his serious novels, he has written thrillers (which he calls "entertainments"), plays, motion picture scripts, essays, and several dozen short stories; more recently he has edited books for The Bodley Head Press. He has, besides, written countless reviews of novels and motion pictures for the *Spectator* and the *Times* but these enterprises date to his early career in the field of letters. In this category can be placed those pieces that appear from time to time in various magazines and journals from remote areas of the globe—from Indo-China, Cuba, and Haiti, places that frequently serve as locales for both his novels and his entertainments. Still, Greene is best known for his spy stories, such as *The Ministry of Fear* and *The Third Man*, and for his serious "novels," books that deal with "religious" problems.

According to many of his critics, Greene is a divided novelist who frequently doesn't know exactly where to place his emphasis—on action and suspense, as in the entertainments; or on characterization and philosophical speculation, as in the novels. To many of his readers, his religious, philosophical, and literary preoccupations range from Manicheism to latter-day Existentialism. Others see him simply as a writer whose Roman Catholicism

---

From *The Shapeless God: Essays on Modern Fiction*, edited by Harry J. Mooney, Jr., and Thomas F. Staley.

is a device that allows him to comment on and perhaps even to play fast and loose with his one true love, the Church itself.

Perhaps there is a great deal of truth in this last assertion: the majority of his novels deal with people who happen to be Roman Catholics, people caught up in emotional dilemmas that give rise to theological speculations of the most beguiling kind. Frequently the solutions Greene implies for these very human problems do not seem consistent with the teachings of his church; and to that church he must stand as something of an enigma. But when one considers the general movement of Ecumenism, Greene's search for some sort of tolerance and understanding within the confines of his faith does not seem so very far from the new feeling the Catholic Church has been promulgating. The fact is that since his first novel Greene's career has involved him in an ever-widening circle of interests and beliefs that have taken him farther and farther from dogmatic Roman Catholicism toward a wider-ranging humanism; and it is this tendency towards humanism which places him strictly within the tradition of English letters, and marks at the same time his place as the most compelling and the best of modern novelists.

I

In 1938 appeared *Brighton Rock*, a novel that read much like a detective story, but one that upon reflection hardly seemed a detective story at all. In addition to the obvious paraphernalia of the thriller—the chase, the melodramatic contrivances, the sensational murders—that Greene had made use of in *The Ministry of Fear* and *This Gun for Hire*, Greene presented an obvious allegory. The protagonist, an antihero named Pinkie Brown, was handled with a sophistication rare since Conrad, and the antagonist, a blowsy blonde named Ida Arnold, proved a bewildering as well as bewildered pursuer of the seventeen-year-old racketeer. That there must have been some confusion in Greene's mind about the kind of book he had written is apparent from his first calling *Brighton Rock* an "entertainment," and only later a "novel."

What is apparent now is that *Brighton Rock* was actually an attempt on Greene's part to explain the nature of right and wrong and good and evil in the world of ordinary men and women—good-hearted, generous, fine-feeling people like Ida Arnold. Still and all, people like Ida Arnold found themselves confused and bewildered when entering a world of good and evil, a world in which the values taught and insisted on were those of the Roman Catholic Church. Consequently, one of the most beguiling aspects of the novel is the subtle yet relentless way in which Greene managed to shift his reader's interest away from right and wrong—morally easy Ida—to good and evil—

the Roman Catholic girl Rose and the boy Pinkie. As the focus shifted, the reader's affection for Ida diminished, and her undeniable humanity, at first so captivating, became tedious and then even unreal. The allegorical importunities of the theme began to dominate the narrative as the reader understood that Ida was merely a catalyst, the agent that precipitated a reaction that must have occurred in any event.

Within the allegory, Ida's concepts, right and wrong, are secondary to considerations of good and evil. Yet *Brighton Rock* is also a detective story, and within that pattern Ida Arnold exemplifies human nature and human justice—she is like a stick of Brighton rock candy: wherever one bites into it, it spells "Brighton." Ida is, however, an alien in the spiritual drama; she likens herself to a traveler in a foreign country who has neither phrase nor guidebook to help her find her way. She is "a stickler where right's concerned," a competent pursuer of human justice, an avenging spirit, but an alien in a spiritual dilemma. She represents humanity; she is the vitality of most people, and the highest praise she can pay to any activity is that for her it is "fun." The reader sees her at first as friendly, good-natured, morally easy; but as the action progresses her "humanity" seems somehow to diminish as the reality of good and evil, a consideration Ida is not competent to understand, becomes infinitely more meaningful.

In turning to the girl Rose, the reader soon appreciates Greene's frightening comment made on Ida's world of right and wrong, this world of the everyday; for Rose is returned to the worst horror of all, a life without hope. On the recording that Pinkie had made for her she learns what her emotions have kept her incapable of appreciating—that Pinkie despised her and that her chief attraction to him had been her goodness, which he was determined to destroy. At the end of the novel Rose knows that she is pregnant with Pinkie's child; the reader is left to draw the conclusion that her marriage to Pinkie has been the union of heaven and hell. These, briefly noted, are the allegorical importunities of the theme; but the fact that the novel is also a detective story, and a brilliant one at that, should not be overlooked. *Brighton Rock* in 1938 begins for Greene a pattern of interest culminating with *The End of the Affair* in 1951. In the novels written between these dates Greene defines and clarifies his "religious" preoccupations without ever becoming a dogmatist or a religious teacher.

In an essay on the religious aspect of the writing of Henry James, included in *The Lost Childhood*, Greene writes, "The novelist depends preponderantly on his personal experience, the philosopher on correlating the experience of others, and the novelist's philosophy will always be a little lopsided." To this statement might be added a comment from *In Search of a*

Character (1961): "I would claim not to be a writer of Catholic novels, but a novelist who in four or five books took characters with Catholic ideas for his material. Nonetheless for years . . . I found myself haunted by people who wanted help with spiritual problems that I was incapable of giving." It would seem then that the sensible approach to a study of the artistry of Graham Greene is to take him at his own word. He is not a "Catholic writer," considering the classification in its narrowest sense; he is not a novelist like G. K. Chesterton or Helen White, who writes remarkably astute novels for Catholic girls. He is, as he says himself, a novelist who uses as his characters people who happen to be Roman Catholics. The sensible way to approach Greene's craft is to read what he writes about his use of Roman Catholicism as background for characters and plots in *Why Do I Write?*:

> If I may be personal, I belong to a group, the Catholic Church, which would present me with grave problems as a writer were I not saved by my disloyalty. If my conscience were as acute as M. Mauriac's showed itself to be in his essay *God and Mammon*, I could not write a line. There are leaders of the Church who regard literature as a means to an end, edification. I am not arguing that literature is amoral, but that it presents a different moral, and the personal morality of an individual is seldom identical with the morality of the group to which he belongs. You remember the black and white squares of Bishop Blougram's chess board. As a novelist, I must be allowed to write from the point of view of the black square as well as of the white: doubt and even denial must be given their chance of self-expression, or how is one freer than the Leningrad group?

The Power and the Glory (1940), grew out of a trip Greene took through the Mexican provinces of Tabasco and Chiapas in the late thirties. Here again Roman Catholicism is used as background, and again it is allegory that lends the events of the narrative an excitement above and beyond the simple adventure of flight and pursuit. The whiskey-priest in the Mexican novel is a reluctant recipient of grace, and to many readers this fact immediately transforms the novel into a Catholic document of such mysterious overtones that only the initiate can understand and appreciate it.

Greene's whiskey-priest is opposed by the lieutenant of the new order, the socialist state; neither protagonist nor antagonist is named, in keeping with the main theme of the novel, which is quite simply the portrayal of the meaning and value of the code handed down by Christianity since its inspiration by and in the New Testament. Yet in the final pages of the novel the priest becomes not so much a champion of Roman Catholicism or Christianity as a champion of the individual: in his dramatic debate with the lieutenant toward the end of the narrative he points out in his simple manner the real dignity of his humanity, something the lieutenant has been only reluctantly aware of.

The immediate frame of reference in *The Power and the Glory* is specifically the protagonist's Roman Catholicism, yet the ultimate referent is the humanistic ideal. The whiskey-priest is one who administers the sacraments of his church while in the state of mortal sin; he evades the police of the new state as he evades God, all the while sustaining his courage with drink. The theme of flight and pursuit is thus doubly pointed. In his characterization of the priest Greene consciously works within the anatomy of sainthood, a theme which was to preoccupy him in various ways until the publication of *The End of the Affair*.

In the Mexican novel Greene takes the weak priest who must drink to preserve his courage and through him portrays the thesis that the evil man discovers in himself is an index to his love of God. As a young man the unnamed priest had been good in the narrow and conventional sense. Concerned with sodalities and baptisms, he had been guilty of only venial sins; but he had felt love for no one except himself. Since the outlawing of Roman Catholicism in his province he has fallen to drink—and in a lonely hour fathered a child. It is his acquaintance with evil that allows him to learn about the resources of his religion. Closed in tight in a prison cell, aware with a precocious intensity of the foulness and stench of human misery, he recognizes the reality of evil and, conversely, feels the presence of God: "This place was very like the world; overcrowded with lust and crime and unhappy love; it stank to heaven; but he realized that after all it was possible to find peace there, when you knew for certain that the time was short."

In *Brighton Rock* Greene had sketched the theme of power in the relationship between Pinkie and his adopted father, Kite. In *The Power and the Glory* Greene develops his thesis in terms of the ironical similarities set up between the unnamed priest and lieutenant. It is through this representative of the new order that Greene portrays the vitality and strange beauty of power, subtly relating the cult of power to an ultimate consideration of evil. The battle of individual choice for good or evil is fought in the soul of the priest, who comes to represent individual protest against the degrading urges of power politics. In *The Lawless Roads* of 1939 Greene wrote: "Perhaps the only body in the world today which consistently—and sometimes successfully—opposes the totalitarian state is the Catholic Church."

The Power and the Glory, despite the fact that it apologizes in a very real way for the author's faith, nevertheless transcends its narrowly Roman Catholic theme. George Woodcock's observation in *The Writer and Politics* is in this respect cogent:

> [W]hile the police lieutenant remains the representative of a collective idea, the servant of the State, the presence of the Church becomes steadily more distant and shadowy, and the priest seems to stand out more solidly as an individual, without tangible connections or allegiances, fighting a guerilla war for an idea which he considers right. Instead of being the representative of Catholicism, he becomes more and more the type of human person fighting against the unifying urges of a power society, and triumphing even in defeat and destruction, because in this battle there are no fronts and the messages are passed on by examples to other individuals who continue as rebellious elements in the total State. This is an underground which is never eliminated, because it has no central committee and no headquarters, except in the heart of each man who feels the need for freedom.

As the whiskey-priest confronts the lieutenant and points out the evil of the organized violence he espouses, the Catholic Church fades more and more into the background; and as this happens the priest becomes more and more Everyman, seeking the ways and means to his own salvation and indicating at the same time the quality and nature of his convictions. In the character of the priest, Greene creates an important figure in contemporary mythology.

The Heart of the Matter, written in 1948, is the next major novel to develop and exploit religious considerations. Again there are allegorical importunities, but they are neither as obvious nor as insistent as they were in *Brighton Rock* and *The Power and the Glory*. In *The Heart of the Matter* the theme of pity, sketched in both the preceding novels, is given full expression by means of the central character, Major Scobie. Once again, this time in the careful characterization of the protagonist, the reader finds Greene working with myth: like the whiskey-priest Scobie escapes the immediate confines of the novel's situation and plot and becomes a character capable of exciting the curiosity, the imagination, and the humanity of the reader. The idea of Scobie remains with the reader long after he has forgotten about the intrigues of the melodramatic action.

Greene had successfully worked within the anatomy of pity in *The Ministry of Fear*, the entertainment that immediately preceded *The Heart of the Matter*; but the theme had not been distinctly related to a religious content.

In both *The Ministry of Fear* and *The Heart of the Matter* pity is shown to be a force that dominates the personality and the actions of the protagonist, making him subject to the suffering of the world, the victim of the unhappy and the discontented. This pity is diagnosed as a sort of egotism, insisting as it does that the individual assume responsibility for his fellow man without consulting the referents of religion or philosophy. Hence pity is shown to be an excess, and Greene comments indirectly on the value of a religious or philosophical orientation that accounts for suffering. The aspect of pride can be neither overly insisted upon nor ignored: Scobie's responsibility and concern for unhappiness characterize him in such a way that he deludes himself, and perhaps the undiscriminating reader, into thinking that he is essentially humble. And this is the paradox upon which the characterization is built: Greene challenges the reader to discover the error of Scobie's thought, while at the same time he makes Scobie so human and so understandable that his error appears to be noble, as Prometheus's stealing of fire from the gods appears noble to mankind. What Greene achieves, then, is the creation of a man whose character flaw reaches tragic proportions.

The beguiling problem of whether or not Major Scobie is saved according to the teachings of his Church has aroused much speculation. Scobie's struggle with himself and with his Roman Catholic God forms the basis of the conflict: it is Scobie's pity that forces him to suicide. But to abstract from the character's actions Green's philosophy or personal belief is absurd, for the novel has been constructed with an artistic consideration in mind, not a philosophical or a religious one. Both Arthur Rowe and Henry Scobie are moved by suffering, misery, and ugliness. Unlike Rowe, whose preoccupation with pity is put down to a childhood loss of innocence, Scobie is possessed of a love of God that orients his actions and determines his suicide. The individual struggle is made the first consideration of the novel; as the character develops, the Roman Catholic Church fades more and more into the background, becoming a portion of the Necessity that propels Scobie on his quest for identity and recognition.

As the action of the novel progresses, Scobie's pity and his sense of responsibility are described as images of his love of God. But Scobie's personal God is one of infinite mercy and forgiveness. As Scobie, a police officer in West Africa, goes off to investigate the suicide of a young district commander, he feels in his heart that his God will not exact damnation from one so young, so unformed. Father Clay, the district priest, attempts to reason with Scobie, but is interrupted: "Even the Church can't teach me that God doesn't pity the young." Scobie prefers the God who died for sinners over the God of justice and retribution; he chooses the God who allowed Himself to be crucified to prevent unhappiness over the God of justice. Scobie, then, trusts his own instincts concerning mercy and forgiveness above the written law. This is pride, but a pride compounded of a keen awareness and appreciation of unhappiness. For, paradoxically, it is his pride that makes Scobie humble; his intolerance of suffering is the index of his emotion. Indeed, the opposites seem irreconcilable, for Scobie accepts personally the responsibility for sin. But so had Christ. Scobie mistakenly sees himself in relation to Christ, who died to save mankind from the blight of the first sin.

Scobie is aware of this precarious logic, recognizing the possibility that the sense of pity he cherishes is an excess; but he knows equally well that he cannot avoid the call of misery and unhappiness. He reasons that with death, responsibility ends. "There's nothing more we can do about it," he says. "We can rest in peace."

Scobie's humility is evidenced by his willingness to accept the teachings of the Catholic Church for himself even though both his pride and his pity refuse to allow him to accept these same harsh strictures for others. He knows that if he kills himself to keep from hurting both his wife and his mistress (again he is mistaken, for his experience has shown him that no one person can arrange the happiness of another), he damns himself for all eternity. He does not so much fear hellfire as he does the permanent sense of loss of God that the Church teaches as a condition of hell. To be deprived of the God he loves is the worst torment of all for Scobie, yet he chooses this over giving more hurt to Louise and Helen. Sentimentally he sees himself as Christ committing suicide for mankind.

The Heart of the Matter takes its epigraph from Péguy: "The sinner is at the very heart of Christianity. No one is as competent as the sinner in matters of Christianity. No one, unless it is the saint." In *The Heart of the Matter* Scobie's competence in matters of his religion is shown all too clearly. His love, consistent with his pity, becomes indicative of a universal love. In the process of learning the substance of his religion he realizes the immensity of human love; he places himself alongside God and insists on dealing personally with matters of happiness. Both his pride and his humility, seen as opposite sides of the same coin, conspire against him. Paradoxically, since he refuses to trust the God he loves, he becomes at once Christ and Judas. He dies for man, but in doing so he betrays God.

Ultimately Scobie is a hero of tragic proportions. He knows his antagonist, recognizes his strength. What Scobie cannot accept is an orthodox conception of a God who seems indifferent to the agony of those He has created. He cannot conceive of a God who has not the same sense of pity as himself, and cannot trust a God who allows misery and unhappiness. Scobie is at once a scapegoat and a traitor, and his pity, mistaken though it may be in its applications, becomes his tragic flaw. Whether or not he is damned is unimportant in the consideration of his heroism or the novel's artistry. But Greene invites speculation and comment: the reader's concern for Scobie is, paradoxically, the most telling aspect of Green's artistry; for Scobie's humanity is what most readers retain from the pages of the novel.

In *The End of the Affair* (1951) Greene creates a situation in which God becomes the lover of the heroine, Sarah Miles. At the expense of incident and action, the aspects of his art which had stood him in best stead in the earlier pieces, he develops the theme that human love, even abandonment to passion, is an index to divine love.

Greene's narrative is set in the midst of contemporary events. Yet his minimizing the allegorical dimension and restricting the action of the novel to a bomb-torn city somehow detracts from the veracity of the presentation: the real world does not here appear as compelling as the symbolically conceived world of Brighton, Mexico, or West Africa.

Sarah Miles becomes a saint and Greene goes so far as to ascribe miracles to her. What the reader could have accepted in the earlier novels as compelling truth becomes in *The End of the Affair* embarrassing insistence on the author's part that his theme is significant and his method artistic. *The End of the Affair* is not completely successful because it is Catholic in the narrowest meaning of the term. *Brighton Rock* and *The Power and the Glory* had been Catholic in a broad sense and, ultimately, had escaped the limitations of Roman Catholicism because of the warm humanism upon which they insisted. However, Evelyn Waugh, who had severely criticized Greene's "theology" in *The Heart of the Matter*, applauded Greene's ability in using the religious theme in *The End of the Affair*, perhaps because he found the theological implications more acceptable within the framework of a Roman Catholic belief closely akin to his own orthodox views. "Mr. Greene is to be congratulated," wrote Waugh in the *Commonweal*, "on a fresh achievement. He shows that in middle life his mind is suppler and his interests wider than in youth. . . . He has triumphantly passed his climacteric where so many talents fail."

The action of *The End of the Affair* is limited chiefly to the ultimately unsuccessful love affair between Sarah Miles and Maurice Bendrix, an author who had not yet made the mistake of becoming popular. In *The Power and the Glory*, Greene had made use of "Bystanders," characters the whiskey-priest had encountered on his progress to martyrdom. The purpose of introducing these Bystanders into the action had been simply to indicate the force of Catholic action; in other words, to indicate that all the priest represents would continue in one way or another. In *The End of the Affair* Bystanders are made use of again; but here they emerge as important aspects of the plot, for it is their function to authenticate the various "miracles" attributed to Sarah after her death. They also add their perspectives to the story of Sarah, exemplifying various aspects of her character; yet they do not, somehow, succeed.

Paradoxically, *The End of the Affair*, although Greene's least successful novel among those discussed here, is his most artistically conceived and most "modern" novel, if one will except *The Comedians*, published in 1966. The melodramatic and allegorical contrivances, although the theme of flight and pursuit is still the chief pattern of the action, are replaced by the devices of "modern" fiction: the skeptical narrator, stream-of-consciousness technique, flashback, diary, interior reverie, spiritual debate, the found or discovered letter—all are used with discrimination and insight. Indeed, *The End of the Affair* is the most Jamesian of Greene's novels and also the one that most confirms in his work the influences of François Mauriac and Ford Madox Ford.

The function of Bendrix, Sarah's lover and the chief narrator of the novel, is to maintain a secular perspective on the events of the affair and to comment on the religious—here it might be more applicable to say Catholic—aspects of the theme. Like Charles Ryder in Evelyn Waugh's *Brideshead Revisited*, Bendrix is skeptical about what he calls the religious "hanky-panky" of the action, yet is the one left to make a final assessment of the meaning of the love affair. His last physical action is to begin writing the story of his and Sarah's relationship, and the implication is that perhaps he too, will learn to accept the reality of a divine force.

Bendrix's account of the affair dwells on its carnal side, its passionate side. Having established this point of view, Greene allows Sarah's diary to fall into her jealous lover's hands; in this way Bendrix becomes aware of the spiritual struggle which is the basis of the novel. A third point of view is achieved by Parkis, an inept detective hired by Bendrix to spy on Sarah; a fourth by Sarah's husband Henry; and a fifth by Richard Smythe, a "rationalist" to whom Sarah goes in her need to deny the God who insists on her sanctity. But it is Bendrix who correlates and assesses these points of view. Here the reader finds himself in the same novelistic milieu that Ford Madox Ford so brilliantly describes in *The Good Soldier*, except that Bendrix's jealousy makes him infinitely more human than Dowell could ever be.

Sarah Miles's reluctant decision to prefer God over Bendrix is occasioned by her promise to give up Bendrix if God will allow him to live: she thinks he has been killed by a bomb that falls on the house where they have been making love. At first she tries to forget the promise, but she cannot. She suffers, as had Major Scobie before her, but her suffering teaches her to believe staunchly in the God who restored Bendrix. Her faith becomes her trust; and Greene insists that this trust is as firm as that which gave strength to the greatest saints. Sarah writes to Bendrix:

> I believe there's a God—I believe the whole bag of tricks; there's nothing I don't believe; they could subdivide the Trinity into a dozen parts and I'd believe. They could dig up records that Christ had been invented by Pilate to get himself promoted and I'd believe just the same. I've caught belief like a disease. I've fallen into belief like I fell in love.

The End of the Affair is technically Greene's masterpiece. The diary and the journal, the flashback, and the reverie all allow him not only to characterize his actors but also to present the various levels of Sarah and Bendrix's spiritual dilemmas. If *Brighton Rock* and *The Power and the Glory* owe something to Eliot's *The Waste Land*, then *The End of the Affair* owes as much to *Ash Wednesday*, for penance and acceptance condition the atmosphere of the novel. If Major Scobie fails in matters of trust, it is in these same matters of trust that Sarah Miles triumphs.

II

Allegory and all the excitement occasioned by the contrivances of melodrama had given Greene ample latitude to develop his themes in *Brighton Rock* and *The Power and the Glory*, and, to some extent, in *The Heart of the Matter*. The need to explain, clarify, and define had been a partial stimulus for his writing these books. But in *The End of the Affair* Greene discovered little need to allegorize, and melodrama was kept to a minimum. The four novels indeed describe a single pattern, a movement, from definition and qualification of a religious conviction to a thumping avowal of the reality of goodness in the real world. But one cannot forget that goodness had been present in the world of *Brighton Rock:* one need only compare Rose to Sarah Miles to understand what tremendous strides Greene made between 1938 and 1951 in both characterization and novelistic technique.

Between the publication of *The End of the Affair* in 1951 and the appearance of *The Comedians* in 1966, Greene wrote two major novels, *The Quiet American* in 1955, and *A Burnt-Out Case* in 1961. Set in Indo-China, *The Quiet American* exploits in terms of Conradian doubles the implications of political innocence and philosophical experience. The English journalist Fowler is paralleled by Alden Pyle, a naive American intent on establishing contact with a mysterious power cult headed by an equally mysterious General Thé. While paying lip service to the tenets of contemporary Existential thought, *The Quiet American* is in reality a further illustration of the themes that interested Greene in *The Ministry of Fear* and *The Heart of the Matter:* the fascination of power and its destructive potential.

Pyle's political innocence is paralleled by Fowler's knowledge of the politics centering on the war-ravaged zone surrounding Vietnam and its neighboring countries. At the novel's end Fowler is forced to betray Pyle in order to keep the "innocent" American from contributing to the deaths of innocent people. Criticized by many American reviewers for its anti-American feeling, *The Quiet American* nevertheless makes a cogent point in a startling manner: what Greene intends, first, is to demonstrate satirically his belief that money cannot buy peace and security in a world coerced by power addicts; and, second, to insist that in a world on the brink of destruction, a man must choose to remain human, even if his choice imperils a personal equanimity dearly bought and paid for.

At the end of the novel Fowler says of the man he had betrayed to the Communists, "Am I the only one who really cared for Pyle?" Although on the surface *The Quiet American* seems to exemplify the Existentialist formula of engagement and to give evidence of the *angoisse* necessary to a full appreciation of human involvement, the novel actually takes a sidewise glance at the theme of pity. Stripped of Major Scobie's sentimentality and high-sounding purpose, Fowler's reasons for betraying Pyle appear simply as egotism: the aspect of pity is perhaps replaced by that of compassion, much more difficult to appreciate. Fowler says, "I know myself and the depth of my selfishness. I cannot be at ease (and to be at ease is my chief wish) if someone is in pain. . . . Sometimes this is mistaken by the innocent for unselfishness, when all I am doing is sacrificing a small good . . . for the sake of a far greater good, a peace of mind, when I need think only of myself." Despite this assertion Fowler wishes after Pyle's death that there were someone to whom he could say he was sorry.

In the introduction to *A Burnt-Out Case*, Greene says that the task of writing the novel proved so difficult that he felt the effort involved in writing still another to be beyond him. Indeed, there is something enervated about *A Burnt-Out Case*, even though the craftsmanship of the novel is superb. The Conradian elements emerge clearly and forcibly, even humorously at times, but on the whole the novel remains unconvincing and the hero's plight unmoving. However, the ambience of *The Comedians*, published in 1966, must have renewed Greene's interest in the art of novel, and his effort was rewarded; it is one of the very best of his books and as exciting and compelling as any of those written between 1929 and 1951.

The Comedians is a black comedy, full of broad farcical touches paralleled by frightening melodramatic innuendoes. Perhaps the most significant aspect of the novel is that it gives evidence of a shifting attitude on Greene's part toward his Maker as well as toward his fellow man. *The Comedians* also elaborates more fully on the theme of innocence, best exploited previously in *The Quiet American.* There, Alden Pyle, thematically Fowler's alter ego, is the committed man; once investigated, however, the nature of his commitment is found wanting. Through Pyle Greene attempts to indicate that innocence uninformed by experience is dangerous in a world menaced by power cults. In *The Quiet American* Fowler is forced to sacrifice Pyle to the cause of what he hopes to be higher humanity, although he is by no means certain of his personal motivations. What Fowler does know, and know for certain, is that he cannot resist the appeal of the bodies mangled by the explosion of Pyle's plastic bombs. In *A Burnt-Out Case* the architect Querry makes his voyage into the heart of Africa to rediscover the springs of innocence. Led by Deo Gratias, a mutilated leper, to the very borders of innocence, Pendelé, Querry comes near to rediscovering the goodness he lost years before.

The hero, or rather antihero (for such he is), of *The Comedians* is a man simply named Brown. (There are also characters within the plot called Smith and Jones: the point, perhaps, is to lend an Everyman aspect to the narrative.) With Brown, Greene attempts to define further the nature of innocence and that experience which is its opposite. In Greene's world, power is one of the many disguises of evil, and in *The Comedians* the fear engendered by power becomes the device by which the question of innocence is forced into prominence. The fact of the matter is that Greene in his last three novels has moved away from the highly stylized and symbolical representations—representations first employed in *Brighton Rock* and set aside after *The End of the Affair*—and has entered a new dimension, the outlines of which can only now be perceived.

Greene entitles his latest book *The Comedians,* and in the course of the novel's activity attempts to define what he means by the word "comedians," which, in turn, requires his establishing a definition of comedy. "Neither of us would ever die for love," says Brown to his mistress, Martha. "We would grieve and separate and find another. We belong to the world of comedy and not of tragedy." If *The Comedians* is a comedy, it is certainly not one in the accepted meaning of the term, nor in the Dantean sense; rather, it is Greene's version of contemporary black humor: there is no movement from despair to happiness—there is movement only from horror to despair.

The comedians are the pretenders, those who play a part, those neither good enough nor grand enough for tragedy—perhaps because Greene's world no longer allows for tragic action. Martha's husband, the ambassador of a small, unnamed South American country, says, "Come on, cheer up . . . let us all be comedians together . . . it's an honorable profession. If we could be good ones the world might gain at least a sense of style." But it is difficult to recognize the comedians, for frequently those who appear to be best qualified to play a part reach a point at which the part overwhelms them—the reality and the drama coalesce, or, to borrow Yeats's phrase, the dancer becomes indistinguishable from the dance. Occasionally one who assumes a role becomes the character he portrays, yet ironically the face he presents to the world continues to reveal eccentricity and grotesqueness. The comedians are nevertheless the worthwhile. They form a small troupe of initiates in a power-coerced and fear-ridden world. Still, it would be wrong to call tragedians those who manage to transcend the limitations of the role they play, for Greene's world, having once accommodated tragic action, no longer does so: at the novel's end the Haitian patriots are found symbolically housed in an abandoned insane asylum in Santo Domingo.

This question of innocence is at once the crux of and the key to the novels and the entertainments (*Our Man in Havana* appeared in 1958) published since Greene left off working with the anatomy of sainthood in *The End of the Affair.* In Sarah Miles, the strongest of his women characters, Greene carries the theme he had first presented in *Brighton Rock* to a final and disquieting conclusion—the impossibility of recognizing sainthood in a world hostile to saints, a world seemingly dedicated to the destruction of goodness. The recently published story, "Beneath the Garden," included in the collection significantly entitled *A Sense of Reality* (1963), is a further illustration of Greene's renewed interest in the anatomy of innocence, for that story is an expressionistic, occasionally absurd, and frequently humorous attempt to rediscover the point at which innocence was lost, to be replaced by the cynicism of experience.

The setting of *The Comedians* is contemporary Haiti under the dictatorship of Dr. Duvalier, "Papa Doc." Greene writes:

> Poor Haiti itself and the character of Doctor Duvalier's rule are not invented, the latter not even blackened for dramatic effect. Impossible to deepen the night. The Tontons Macoute are full

> of men more evil than Concasseur; the interrupted funeral is drawn from fact; many a Joseph limps the streets of Port-au-Prince after his spell of torture, and, though I have never met the young Philipot, I have met guerrillas as courageous and as ill-trained in that former lunatic asylum near Santo Domingo. Only in Santo Domingo have things changed since I began this book—for the worse.

Like a Kafka enigma, Papa Doc remains mysteriously within his palace, his laws enforced by the Tontons Macoute, bogeymen, whose insignia are slouched hats and sunglasses, behind which they hide their uncertainties. The Voodoo element comes into play in the course of the novel's action, and an equation is drawn between Papa Doc and Baron Samedi, the prince of the dead of Voodoo belief. The Tontons approximate a mysterious fraternity of terror infinitely more menacing than that of the cultists. The chief representative of the power cult in the novel is Captain Concasseur, who is responsible for the mutilation and emasculation of Joseph, Brown's servant in the hotel Trianon.

Brown, Smith, and Jones arrive in Port-au-Prince on a Dutch vessel ominously called the *Medea*, Brown to return to his luxury hotel which he has been unsuccessfully trying to sell in the United States; Smith, a former presidential candidate who ran against Truman on a vegetarian ticket in 1948, together with his wife, to set up a vegetarian center; and Jones, an inept adventurer who calls himself "Major," to engage in a military maneuver of dubious nature.

Brown has been conducting a love affair with Martha Pineda, the wife of a South American diplomat. She is the mother of a five-year-old child, Angel, whose claims keep her from abandoning her family for Brown, whom she says she loves. The affair, bittersweet and reminiscent of many love triangles in Greene's fiction, is resumed the night Brown returns to Haiti. Brown admits several times that what he seeks in a love affair is not so much happiness as defeat; and ironically there is a sort of success at the novel's end—Brown and Martha both realize once they are safely over the border in Santo Domingo that their love affair belongs peculiarly to Port-au-Prince, that it was but the reflection of the horror and terror of the times.

Brown has been brought up a Catholic, but he is unlike the Catholics Greene has previously portrayed. The passionate pity of both Scobie and Fowler has given way to a tragicomic compassion, which is also the chief mood of the novel; Brown is much more tolerant of success than any of Greene's other heroes, but he is infinitely less loving. His Catholicism is not the leper's bell that it is to both the whiskey-priest and Sarah Miles; it is instead a cloak of indifference, a means whereby the stupidities and the atrocities of the world can be warded off, and perhaps explained. Brown's Catholicism becomes for him a standard of measurement, in Haiti a valid one, for Catholicism liberally sprinkled with Voodooism is the religion of the majority.

Through the Smiths, or perhaps because of the Smiths, Greene expresses a certain amount of anti-American sentiment reminiscent of *The Quiet American*. Dr. Magiot remarks at one point:

> We are an evil scum floating a few miles from Florida, and no American will help us with arms or money or counsel. We learned a few years back what their counsel meant. There was a resistance group here who were in touch with a sympathizer in the American embassy: they were promised all kinds of moral support, but the information went straight back to the C.I.A. by a very direct route to Papa Doc. You can imagine what happened to the group. The state department didn't want any disturbance in the Caribbean.

Although he bears much in common with Alden Pyle of *The Quiet American*, the good vegetarian Mr. Smith is by no means the same sort of deluded innocent. He is capable of appreciating the opportunism and graft-seeking of the corrupt Tontons Macoute; and he even has the courage to admit that his vision of setting up an American Vegetarian Center in either Port-au-Prince or the new city, Duvalierville, is impractical. Despite their being vehicles for caustic satire, Mr. and Mrs. Smith emerge as the two strongest characters in the novel; they are saved by their humanity, by their certainty that there is goodness in the world. Ultimately, it is their dedication to their cause, their sincere and straightforward desire to better the human predicament—by reducing acidity in the human body—that makes them acceptable.

It is also through the Smiths that the theme of commitment enters the novel, again satirically. As in *The Quiet American*, Existentialism is used as a philosophical determinant, but in this novel it is not so much obscured by religious considerations. Furthermore, the jargon of Existentialism is kept to a minimum and the theme emerges more cogently, demonstrated as it is in the action of the comedians who make up the drama.

"Major" Jones, who at first appears to be the biggest fraud of all, one of the "tarts," as he puts it, is a committed man by the novel's end; but his commitment is comically handled. He passes himself off as an organizer of military affairs, but he fools only those who wish to be fooled. He dreams, he invents, and he deludes, at times even himself. But there is something about the man that endears him to others. Tin Tin, the girl at Mère Catherine's bordello, likes him because he makes her laugh; and Brown's mistress Martha, in whose embassy Jones takes shelter when his bogus papers are discovered by Captain Concasseur, likes him too, and for the same reason—he makes her laugh. Brown, we are told, has never learned the trick of laughter.

Together with Dr. Magiot, a committed Communist, Brown arranges for Jones to escape the Tontons and to join the partisans, who under Philipot, a one-time Baudelairean poet, are attempting to unseat Papa Doc in bumbling and ineffectual ways. However, Brown's decision to help the partisans is motivated not by a feeling for the rightness of their cause, or by the danger and the excitement, or by his awareness of the childlike innocence of their exploit, but by the unreasoning jealousy that he feels toward Jones. Again, the reader is reminded of Fowler. Jones is a comedian within the broadest meaning of the term; but unlike Brown who cannot—perhaps because of early Roman Catholic training—he can follow the gleam, and there comes a point where the dream and reality coalesce. In his last glimpse of Jones, the reader sees him limping along, unable to keep up with the partisans because of his flat feet. He remains behind, a comical version of Hemingway's Robert Jordan, to fire upon the Tontons in order to make it possible for those he has grown to love to survive, it only temporarily.

Of all the major comedians, Brown alone remains uncommitted. He is a con man grown old, whose most successful venture had been peddling bad pictures of the nouveaux riches. His mother's postcard had brought him to the Trianon, and one of her first questions had been, "What part are you playing now?" After her death, Brown had discovered among her papers a note she had written to her young lover: "Marcel, I know I'm an old woman and as you say a bit of an actress. But please go on pretending. As long as we pretend we escape. Pretend that I love you like a mistress. Pretend that you love me like a lover. Pretend that I would die for you and that you would die for me." Brown's love affair with Martha, however, is something more than just pretending; it is a desperate attempt to capture stability in a fear-menaced world, and it is compounded as much of the desire to inflict pain as it is of a desire to dominate. For several years Brown has prospered, achieving a false sense of security; but the coming of Papa Doc and the Tontons has destroyed not only his business but his sense of belonging as well. He finds himself involved with innocence, with the Smiths and with Jones, who, thematically, serve to set off and to illustrate his failure.

The problem of Brown's Roman Catholicism is an important one in understanding both the characterization of Brown himself and the theme of the novel; it is indeed the chief challenge of the book. The Voodoo black mass in which Brown's servant Joseph participates makes a sensational counterpoint to the religious importunities of the novel; the figure of Baron Samedi is associated with Papa Doc, the personification of evil. But the black mass does not necessarily suggest a breakdown of religion. At the novel's end, it is contrasted with the mass the priest reads over the body of Joseph in the insane asylum in Santo Domingo where the partisans are cared for. Brown's failure, then, does not illustrate a religious breakdown; it is a failure of character.

Brown's failure is his inability to accept reality, and it can best be explained in Existential terms. He can detect innocence, appreciate goodness, admire courage, and—even if for the wrong motives—help the cause of right. But he is so good a comedian that he cannot transcend the limitations imposed by the role. All the religious implications seem like so much rationalization on Brown's part, and he fools neither himself nor the reader. Brown can appreciate commitment: to retain his self-esteem, to support his ego, he is forced into comedy. Although his sympathies are with Dr. Magiot, Philipot, and the partisan cause, Brown makes no real commitment to anything, not to love, not to religion, not to God, not to innocence. It is only right that at the novel's end Brown becomes a partner in the undertaking business. In his black suit and black hat he appears a comic Baron Samedi. He belongs to the world of the dead and not to that of the living, and symbolically and literally he serves the dead.

Since the appearance of *The Man Within* critics have accused Greene of being pessimistic. The truth of the matter is that he is not a cheerful writer, but *The Comedians*, tragicomic though it is, and full of comic touches and humor of a macabre and grotesque nature, is the gloomiest of his novels to date. At least Major Scobie loves God, in his own mistaken way; at least the whiskey-priest finds honor, albeit unwillingly; and Sarah Miles achieves a sort of gratuitous sainthood. Querry in *A Burnt-Out Case* finds the hint of an explanation; he glimpses Pendelé. But there is only a pathetic part left for Brown to play in *The Comedians*. There is not even the saving factor of remorse as in *The Quiet American;* for Fowler wishes at the end of that novel that there were someone to whom he could say he is sorry for his participation in Pyle's death. Fowler at least is spurred to action after witnessing the carnage caused by Pyle's plastic explosives. He does what he does because he loves. But there is no real love in Brown, only ego. Jones and Smith may indeed illustrate contrasting aspects of the theme of innocence, but within the pattern of the novel they serve merely as foils to set off the failure of the individual.

TERRY EAGLETON

Reluctant Heroes: The Novels of Graham Greene

At the end of *The Power and the Glory*, the whiskey-priest dismisses the half-caste who has betrayed him into the hands of the lieutenant of police with a gesture of forgiveness. "The priest waved his hand; he bore no grudge because he expected nothing else of anything human." It is a characteristic moment in Greene, and one which demands analysis. The priest's gesture embodies a paradox: it has the quality of Christian humanity, yet that humanity is ironically dependent on an overriding sense of man's cheapness. The forgiving wave dignifies and devalues man in a single gesture: in enacting a compassionate solidarity with human corruption, it endorses, at the same time, the unchanging reality of that corruption. Yet by the same token, the sceptical disillusion which makes forgiveness automatic qualifies any suggestion of outstanding sanctity on the priest's part: it is easy to forgive creatures from whom one expects little. Greene, then, allows his whiskey-priest a compassionate holiness while protecting him from the dangers of pride; because the priest devalues himself, knowing the half-caste's weakness within his own body, he can be safely dignified by his author. The priest is raised above corruption without being detached from it; it is by his sense of complicity with sin that he is able partially to transcend it. Through an image of despairing forgiveness, then, Greene is able to dramatise two qualities of feeling which are everywhere deeply interrelated in his work: a pitying compassion which confirms a kind of value without thereby challenging the fact of human worthlessness, and a potentially heroic virtue which is at the

---

From *Exiles and Emigres: Studies in Modern Literature.* Schocken Books, 1970.

same time fiercely or sceptically hostile to the notion of goodness. In both cases, it seems necessary to affirm and deny human value in the same moment.

After his fruitless interview with Father Rank in *The Heart of the Matter*, Scobie recognises that he is incapable of conforming to what he sees as orthodox Roman Catholicism. "I know the answers as well as he does. One should look after one's own soul at whatever cost to another, and that's what I can't do, what I shall never be able to do." Scobie's attitude here is essentially Greene's: given a tragic tension between the claims of human relationship and the demands of faith, the rigours of orthodoxy must be guiltily denied in the name of the human. The irony implicit in Greene's view, however, is more subtle than this simple counterpoising. For although an individualist "soul-saving" theology is rejected, the concomitant feelings crystallised around the same phase of Roman Catholic history—the sense of relationships as negative and treacherous, corrosive of personal integrity—are uncompromisingly retained. Indeed they are extended, at times, into a version of the human world as putrid corruption which moves beyond the Catholic tradition into forms of radical Protestantism. The result is a striking paradox: Greene's protagonists turn, at the risk of damnation, from a soul-saving theology to the insidious pressures of humanity, but only in the context of a continually undermining disbelief in the final validity of such claims. Orthodox Catholicism is denied in the name of "humanism"; yet that humanism is itself critically qualified by traditionally Catholic ways of feeling. The upshot of this is a kind of deadlock: the human value of men like Scobie or the whiskey-priest lies in their readiness to reject an orthodoxy in which they nevertheless continue to believe; yet to acknowledge the superior truth of that orthodoxy, in the act of refusing it, is to confront the inadequacy of the sheerly human commitments they embrace.

By affirming an absolute standard, then, Greene's characters are able to retain a sceptical detachment from human values: a detachment which lends them superiority, in the final analysis, to the rationalist or liberal humanist. Yet by failing that standard in action while endorsing it in consciousness, they can reveal qualities of compassion which are again superior to the humanist's ethic by virtue of the disillusion and damnation—and so lack of self-deception—in which they are rooted. To go through the motions of human love, in a nagging awareness of its inevitable partiality, emerges as a more courageously mature and disinterested attitude than that of the humanist, who trusts naïvely and destructively to an ultimate value in man. By a curious irony, scepticism, *dégagement* and disbelief furnish a more positive ethic than a committed faith in the possibilities of human good. The fundamental detachment from the mess of secular complexities which permits the Christian a deeper insight than the humanist also allows him to outstrip the humanist on his own territory.

The point may be usefully illustrated by *The Heart of the Matter.* Here, as in all Greene's novels, human relationship is inherently tragic: love, pity and innocence are lethal because they entice men out of their safely sterile *dégagements* into the corrupting complicities of passion and responsibility, into infectious and conflicting involvements which proliferate beyond control. This is the thesis which the novel is intended to illustrate, and it centres on Scobie because he alone is agonisedly conscious of the inescapable debt and damage implicit in the vulnerabilities of feeling. Because the thesis is given rather than argued, we are asked to admire Scobie's moral pragmatism: his sluggish, compassionate enactment of the motions of relationship, constantly penetrated by a desire for the peace of death, is offered as wiser than that ethic of decisive action which can belong only to the innocent, to those damagingly ignorant of the heart of the matter. Yet what is obvious in the novel is that this tragic version of life is the result, as well as the motivation, of Scobie's behaviour: his well-intentioned bungling, his rejection of truth for a patching-up of immediate pain which merely delays and complicates decision, his despairing half-commitment and wry passivity, his self-disgusted inability to value himself, his complicity in allowing others to live a lie, his sentimental attraction to suffering, his disbelief in the possibility of happiness—all these are offered as *responses* to a given hopelessness, but are, just as much, the sources of that paralysis. Scobie acts as he does because he sees the human condition as irreparable, but it is at least partially true that the human condition of the novel is irreparable because he acts as he does. (It is perhaps worth mentioning that the aspect of traditional Christian ethics which Scobie finds most unpalatable—their apparently intransigent insistence on the need to take a stand in certain situations at the cost of immediate damage—is related to a belief that the alternative is likely to be the kind of mess in which Scobie finds himself.) Because human relationships are viewed as inherently unviable, moral blame attaches, not chiefly to Scobie himself, but to the "conditions of life"; relationships fail "naturally," evil spreads by its own momentum, and what is then in question is not the quality of action, but the nature of intention, despite its inevitably negative effects. In this continuing concern with motive rather than effect, Greene is, ironically, very Roman Catholic in attitude. It is necessary that Scobie's efforts to redeem his situation should fail, since this validates the novel's thesis; but it is also essential that he should fail with good intentions, since this allows him a moral superiority to his situation without suggesting the possibility of a transforming morality which might effectively challenge that condition. Scobie's "anti-heroism," his failure to conform to his own absolute standard, is the source of his humanism, and thus of a moral worth greater than others—than his trivially malicious fellow-colonialists, for instance. Yet his conscious commitment to the standard he betrays both critically qualifies the humanism, lending him a perspective beyond its limits, and intensifies the price he pays for humane action in a way which renders it even more admirable. Once more, an affirmation of human goodness is accompanied with strict reservations about its validity.

Greene's "bad" Catholics, then, condemn themselves by the rigour of an absolute orthodoxy while consciously breaking its rules. Sanctity, like the damnation of Pinkie in *Brighton Rock*, consists in recognising and refusing the rules simultaneously; the two conditions are allied in this as in other respects. The characters' failure to conform to the standard is essential for humane action; their continued acceptance of it is necessary, not only if they are to be distinguished from non-Christian humanists, but if they are to experience that self-deprecating humility of failure which is, for Greene, the condition of holiness. The standard is refused in the name of the corrupting complexities of routine experience; yet precisely because that experience is still seen, from the standpoint of orthodoxy, as tangled, amorphous and self-defeating, it provides no basis for the formulation of any alternative ethic by which a man could press through to a questioning of orthodoxy itself. Orthodoxy is submitted to the test of experience, and its inadequacies exposed: but not to the point where it might be shown up as hollow—revealed, for instance, as bad theology—for that would be to slacken the tension between orthodoxy and humanity, and so to destroy that guilty self-disgust by which the believer is rendered superior to the rationalist. The orthodox standard reveals itself in a mainly negative way: in the characters' guilty scrupulousness in offending against it. Their anxiety at being bad Catholics is one of their most notably Catholic traits.

The novels, then, have to preserve a very fine tension between their characters' conscious commitment to orthodoxy and their active rejection of its limits. Yet there is more than one occasion where the effort to sustain the tension leads them into serious ambiguity and confusion. The behaviour of the priest in *The Power and the Glory* is a case in point. If the priest is to be saintly, he must infringe the orthodoxy; yet if he is to have the self-castigating humility of holiness, he must also remain convinced of its truth. The novel does not everywhere succeed in persuading us of the logicality of this paradox. In the prison scene, for instance, when the priest is confronted with the intolerably pious complacency of the middle-aged woman beside him in the darkness, he is almost able to articulate his "unorthodoxy" into an affirmative argument which could undermine the falsity of the woman's religious respectability. He refuses, for example, to accept her dogmatic assertion that the sexual intercourse of the couple in the dark corner of the cell is mortal sin, and allows only that "We don't know. It may be." Yet although he is here on the point of formulating his superior depth of experience into a "position," his criticism of established religion must not be allowed to develop into a radical assault, for this would be to deprive him of the very standard by which he measures his own humble unworthiness, and so the means by which he achieves a kind of heroism. Yet the problem persists: if the priest is able to extend forgiving leniency to the sexual sins of others, why is he unable to do this in his own case? The priest is extraordinarily stringent with himself, but ceaselessly liberal with others; he can perceive the bad faith of respectable Catholicism and its pressing dangers to the soul, but is at the same time gripped with scruples for such things as saying mass in mud-huts without an altar stone. The ambiguity is also evident at another point: in his self-accusation of sins which we are forced to take on credence because they are nowhere shown in the novel. "The words proud, lustful, envious, cowardly, ungrateful . . . he was all these things." There is a genuine obscurity here: either the priest is accurate in his self-evaluation, in which case his apparent virtue is cast damagingly into question; or he is self-deceived, in which case the novel can impress us with his humility only at the cost of implying in him a disturbing and ultimately unaccountable lack of insight. The novel effectively refuses to choose: either possibility would harm the image of the whiskey-priest which it is concerned to project. One is forced to conclude that the priest's self-estimation cannot really be true, since it obstinately refuses to accommodate itself to the novel's actual presentation of him; but neither can it really be false, since the authenticity of the priest's experience depends upon our giving at least some credence to the accuracy of his judgements and the reality of his sense of failure. To deny this is to conclude that the priest's perceptive insight into the condition of others consorts mysteriously with a peculiar obtuseness in his view of himself—an obtuseness which the term "humility" is too indiscriminate to cover.

Yet "humility" is, of course, the formal explanation which the novel offers for this incongruency: the priest's overbearing sense of inadequacy as a man of God. The inadequacy, however, lies largely in infringements of an orthodoxy which he recognises as actively harmful in the case of the woman prisoner, or, later in the novel, in the bourgeois religion of the hygienically Lutheran Lehrs. It is his humility which prevents him from pressing through his sense of these falsities into anything which might approach a radical criticism: he believes that the woman prisoner needs sympathy, not correction. Yet in emphasising this humility as his virtue, the novel also covertly indulges in the priest what is really a kind of defectiveness, akin to his nervous giggling and card-tricks; it exploits the priest's inability to take himself seriously in order to ward off criticisms of the Church, while at the same time giving the priest's experience a serious value. The novel, in other words, needs to endorse the significance of its protagonist's experience, but needs to prevent him from doing the same. The humility is part of a general experience which objectively aims a radical criticism at orthodoxy, but it is simultaneously used to forestall any subjective appropriation of such criticism on the part of the priest himself—a move which might lead the novel and its hero into the camp of the revolutionary lieutenant of police. When the priest confronts the lieutenant before his death, the novel's attitude is less than candid: the priest agrees, briefly and unspecifically, with the lieutenant's attack on the established Church, but then affirms the superiority of the Christian faith:

> "What an excuse it all was, what a fake. Sell all and give to the poor—that was the lesson, wasn't it? And Senora so-and-so, the druggist's wife, would say the family wasn't really deserving of charity, and Senor This, That and the Other would say that if they starved, what else did they deserve, they were Socialist anyway, and the priest—you—would notice who had done his Easter duty and paid his Easter offering. . . ."
>
> The priest said, "You are so right." He added quickly, "Wrong too, of course. . . ."
>
> "Well, we have ideas too," the lieutenant was saying. "No more money for saying prayers, no more money for building places to say prayers in. We'll give people food instead, teach them to read, give them books. We'll see they don't suffer."
>
> "But if they want to suffer. . . . We have facts, too, we don't try to alter—that the world's unhappy whether you are rich or poor—unless you are a saint and there aren't many of those. It's not worth bothering too much about a little pain here."

The area of real agreement between priest and policeman—their common dislike of established religion—is quickly blurred over, and the differences sharpened. The priest's callous attitude to suffering can be made more palatable by an appeal to his experience—he, after all, has known pain, and so his last statement can be made to seem courageous rather than cruel—but it is really a kind of trick. We are persuaded, by the depth and value of the priest's experience, to accept from his mouth an attitude we would be less willing to take from the pious clerics whose way of life he has renounced; and yet the statement is the kind of platitude which belongs essentially to their world. The novel appeals to the priest's wisdom only as a way of asking us to accept the persuasions of an orthodoxy which it has been part of that wisdom to criticise. So, once more, humane values are both affirmed and heavily qualified: the whiskey-priest is revealed as superior to bourgeois pieties by virtue of his humane compassion, but superior to humanism by virtue of his identification with orthodox piety. A precariously narrow line must be balanced between a rejection of love, and a belief that it can be in any sense effective.

There are similar unresolved ambiguities in almost all of Greene's "Catholic" novels. Why in any case does the unheroic whiskey-priest stay in the country at the risk of his life? Why does Scobie stay in his African colony? Why does Sarah Miles, in *The End of the Affair*, make a vow to a God she doesn't believe in? Why does she see herself as "a bitch and a fake?" Why does Querry, in *A Burnt-Out Case*, stay overnight in the forest to comfort his injured servant Deo Gratias? At the root of all these questions lies a common problem. Each of these facts counts to the credit of the character concerned: in different ways, they are evidence of moral distinction, of a capacity for some kind of love. Yet love, in the world of Greene's novels, is an even more treacherous passion than pity: "I don't believe in anyone who says love, love, love," says Louise Scobie, in response to the self-dramatising advances of Wilson: "It means self, self, self." And this is an attitude which Greene's novels on the whole endorse. Love is a self-regarding emotion or a destructive possessiveness; it is innocent of the reality of failure, and so dangerously naïve, finally indistinguishable from egoism. There is no alternative in Greene's world between the diseased compassion of a Scobie, dissolving the self's integrity into the shapelessness of a growing stain, and the callow self-assertiveness of a Wilson or the public-school bumptiousness of a Bagster. Each of the novels, then, confronts a crucial difficulty. If God's love is real, it must be in some sense incarnated in human living: Greene is sufficiently Roman Catholic to reject any non-incarnational view of divine love. Yet how is this to be shown, when human love is also seen, in an extreme Protestant mode, as merely one more deceptive form of the pride of self, one more sign of false consciousness and bad faith? In any final analysis, the issue is incapable of adequate resolution: all the novels can hope to do is to suggest the presence of charity in particular men and women while simultaneously protecting them from a pharisaic awareness of their own better feelings.

But this can be done only by convicting the protagonist of a curious lack of self-knowledge, or simply by obscuring vital evidence. The case of the priest in *The Power and the Glory* is again relevant: why does the giggling, frightened, self-doubting renegade risk death by refusing to join his fellow-clerics in their flight from the country? The question of motivation is not convincingly established:

> "That's another thing I don't understand," the lieutenant said, "why you—of all people—should have stayed when the others ran."
>
> "They didn't all run," the priest said.
>
> "But why did you stay?"
>
> "Once," the priest said, "I asked myself that. The fact is, a man isn't presented suddenly with two courses to follow: one good and one bad. He gets caught up. The first year—well, I didn't believe there was really any cause to run. Churches have been burnt before now. You know how often. It doesn't mean much. I thought I'd stay till next month, say, and see if things were better. Then—oh, you don't know how time can slip by. . . . Do you know I suddenly realised that I was the only priest left for miles around? There was one priest in particular—he had always disapproved of me. I have a tongue, you know, and it used to wag. He said—quite rightly—that I wasn't a firm character. He escaped. It felt—you'll laugh at this—just as it did at school when a bully I had been afraid of—for years—got too old for any more teaching and was turned out. . . ."
>
> "It was when he left I began to go to pieces. One thing went after another. I got careless about my duties. I began to drink. It would have been much better, I think, if I had gone too. Because pride was at work all the time. Not love of God. . . . I thought I was a fine fellow to have stayed when the others had gone. . . . I wasn't any use, but I stayed. At least, not much use. . . . It's a mistake one makes—to think just because a thing is difficult or dangerous. . . ." He made a flapping motion with his hands.

The priest has taken no definable moral decision: a man "gets caught up," and then "you don't know how time can slip by"; the vagueness of this is then concealed by a displacement of attention to the self-righteous fellow-priest who fled. That priest's flight throws the whiskey-priest himself into a morally favourable light, but also qualifies his courage: it was after that incident that he "began to go to pieces," and one thing led, automatically, to another. The priest then settles on pride as his motive, and in doing so once more appeals to a moral condition which, given the lack of essential evidence, the reader can neither confirm nor effectively question. Because of his pride, he "wasn't any use"; but that too explicitly demeaning comment is then instantly qualified: "At least, not much use." The priest's final comment trails off into inarticulate ambiguity: "It's a mistake one makes—to think just because a thing is difficult or dangerous. . . ." If this is to be interpreted as hinting that the priest consciously embraced those dangers, judging his action more valuable on their account, then, even if this too is merely to be dismissed as proud self-deception, it seems difficult to square its suggestion of conscious courage with the notion that he has simply been "caught up."

If the whiskey-priest was merely "caught up," the same can be said of Scobie. Scobie's inability actively to control his environment, to prevent the inexorable spreading of evil through the air breathed by innocents, is offered as part of the nature of things, a defeatism nurtured by the "conditions of life"; but it also allows him to be led passively into a possibly heroic posture, by the sheer logic of his unheroically fragmented situation-ethics. Scobie, too, gets "caught up," and like the whiskey-priest what he gets caught up in is a kind of sanctity which transcends pragmatism. It is important for the novel both to affirm the quality of virtue—to show it as more than mere circumstantial determinism—and yet to stress at the same time the seemingly inexorable, partial, piecemeal process by which it is attained, so as to avoid any damagingly pharisaic implication that it was a course of action he ever consciously chose. A kind of self-sacrifice possible only to the morally courageous must be endorsed, but not at the cost of questioning the wisdom of a pragmatic passivity. Once again, the novel has to tread an awkwardly narrow line between conscious and confused motivations, between the objective reality of goodness and a subjective unawareness of its presence. Scobie's impotent passivity, his chronic incapacity for decisive moral action, is a criticism of his behaviour; yet it is lessened in force, not only because the mood and comment of the novel co-operate in confirming the intelligence of this stance (even the climate is made to suggest its natural inevitability: "This isn't a climate for emotion . . . anything like hate or love drives a man off his head"), but because it is precisely his passivity, his desperately pragmatic scepticism, which leads him to a courageous act and at the same time shields him from any destructive belief in its value. Because Scobie is caught up by his very pragmatism into an action which both transcends that process and yet is also its last, logical step, the novel is able to validate and criticise this ethic at the same time. He is led, by decent, "rational" behaviour, to kind of courage which outstrips the behaviour of the decent rationalist.

A similar ambiguity is apparent in *The End of the Affair;* in this novel, however, it is built into the very structure of the work. The novel operates essentially at two distinct levels: on one level we are shown the conscious motives and actions of the characters; on a deeper level, the mysteriously obscure purposes which they are fulfilling, unknown to themselves, as the agents of God's devious love. In this way, Greene is able to provide himself with a structural framework for resolving the disparities of human self-estimation and the reality of the divine love at work within and between men. Because the action of God is now an unconscious process, insidiously and invisibly at work, the difficulties of accommodating the power of this love to corrupt human motive and behaviour are lessened; Sarah, Bendrix, Henry, Parkis and more minor characters can act consciously at one level while the true "meaning" of their behaviour is revealed only within a deeper dimension of which they are all for the most part unaware. In this way, Sarah's dramatic conversion may be squared with her previous agnosticism because it is an event for which she is really in no sense fully responsible; we are asked to believe that it is the organic culmination of that invisible process which began, unknown to herself, with her secret baptism as a child. Because Sarah is not fully responsible for her own holiness, she can be given moral value without this qualifying her own judgement on herself as "a bitch and a fake"; the two levels, divine and human, can co-exist without mutual interference, and one distinct advantage of this is that Greene is thereby able to preserve his thesis that common human life is sterile and corrupt. Yet at the same time the action of grace cannot be shown as wholly deterministic and invisibly disembodied, for this would be to equate Sarah the saint with Bendrix and Smythe the rationalists. Somehow, the two levels of meaning must interact—Sarah must be shown, as a person, to have the qualities of God's love—without one level being fully reconciled to the other, since this would suggest that men were of their own efforts capable of merit—a thesis the novel wants to reject. So once more there is a problem: we can neither believe, nor disbelieve, Sarah's judgement of herself. To believe it is to dislocate too radically the action of grace and the quality of persons; to render Sarah morally equal to Bendrix. But to disbelieve it is to suggest that the love of God can issue in outstanding human value—can actively redeem, at least in a local sense, that fallenness which for Greene is "given" from the outset. The ambiguity is "resolved," as it was in *The Power and the Glory*, by the tactic of concealing essential evidence. Sarah, much more than the whiskey-priest, is presented to us obliquely, by virtue of the novel's structure: she is seen either from the tendentious angle of Bendrix's own tortured account, or through her own self-demeaning record in her diary. In neither case is she seen "objectively." What we *see* would suggest that her low self-estimation springs from the deceptions of humility; yet, as with the whiskey-priest, it is vital, if we are not to miss the tension between human cheapness and divine power, that we do not entirely dismiss it as such.

There is a parallel obscurity in the question of Sarah's vow to a God in whom, at the time, she has no conscious belief. "Why did this promise stay," she asks herself, "like an ugly vase a friend has given and one waits for a maid to break it?" Sarah's own irritated bewilderment suggests an answer: it stayed because God wanted it to, against the grain of Sarah's own frustrated bitterness at the loss of Bendrix's love which was its result. Yet although responsibility for the persistence of the vow is to that extent removed from Sarah's own control, and any dangerous hint of consciously heroic love thereby avoided, it is not wholly that: for Sarah's commitment to her promise, against her own deepest instincts, *is* offered, elsewhere, as a distinguishing mark of personal sanctity. It is neither simply a question of a courageous decision which elevates her morally above others, nor simply a choice made for her by God himself: by sustaining this ambiguity, the novel refuses to choose clearly between seeing Sarah merely as the determined instrument of grace, or seeing her as a self-determining saint. Either alternative, in itself, would be detrimental to Greene's viewpoint. Thus, it is important that Sarah's death should be markedly unheroic—it results from her catching cold—yet it is also important that the cold should be caught in her efforts to avoid Bendrix, and so the temptation to betray God. Her death can neither be consciously chosen nor merely accidental: she must be protected alike from the falsities of both Christian martyrdom and sheerly human contingency. Once more, the possibility of outstanding virtue must be affirmed in the context of a radical suspicion of conscious goodness.

In a later novel, *A Burnt-Out Case*, the clash between "heroism" and "anti-heroism" becomes a dominant theme. Querry, the burnt-out architect, is cynically aware of his own worthlessness; yet his actions trigger off a conspiracy to enshrine him as a saint. The chief actions which lead us to be suspicious of his own radical self-disgust are his care of the injured African Deo Gratias, and his concern for the vulnerably innocent, maltreated Marie Rycker. Here is the incident where he follows Deo Gratias into the forest, vaguely aware that he may have met with an accident:

> His own presence here was hardly more explicable than that of Deo Gratias. The thought of his servant lying injured in the forest waiting for the call or footstep of any human being would perhaps at an earlier time have vexed him all night until he was

> forced into making a token gesture. But now that he cared for nothing, perhaps he was being driven only by a vestige of intellectual curiosity. What had brought Deo Gratias here out of the safety and familiarity of the leproserie? . . . What was the meaning of the sweat he had seen pouring down the man's face? . . . Interest began to move painfully in him like a nerve that had been frozen. He had lived with inertia so long that he examined his "interest" with clinical detachment.

At the end of the path into the forest, Querry finds the African injured and paralysed with fright:

> After ten minutes of struggle Querry managed to drag his limbs out of the water—it was all he could do. . . . The fingerless hand fell on Querry's arm like a hammer and held him there.
>
> There was nothing to be done but wait for the morning. . . . He took Deo Gratias' hand to reassure him. . . . Deo Gratias grunted twice, and then uttered a word. It wounded like "Pendélé."

Querry's motives for pursuing his servant are "inexplicable"; or, if a motive is demanded, it is "perhaps" merely curiosity. Yet that curiosity, while possibly "clinical," is itself obscurely related to what the novel sees as best in Querry: his persistent search, despite the conscious detachment, for the path which leads to "Pendélé," to a mysterious haven of peace. So while his concern for Deo Gratias is at one level an intellectual interest which is not allowed to count in his favour, the African's curious disappearance stirs in him, at a deeper level, that yearning for an absolute reality which renders him in some senses morally superior to those more committed rationalists or pragmatists who discount such strivings—Dr Colin, or the Father Superior. The decision to seek out Deo Gratias is "inexplicable" rather than clearly defined; and once this is taken, Querry is passively caught up in an act of charity, led on by his own half-conscious motive to the point where "There was nothing to be done but wait for the morning." That "nothing to be done" qualifies any hint of compassion by suggesting a circumstantial inevitability; yet the same comment cannot adequately explain his taking hold of the leper's hand to comfort him. One is forced to conclude that the novel is using here, rather less emphatically, something of the technique of *The End of the Affair*. Like Sarah, Querry's deepest motive is a search for God, but its very unconsciousness prevents him from being in possession of his own experience and so running the contaminating risks of valuing himself highly. Yet again, as in *The End of the Affair*, the meritorious motive cannot be allowed to remain wholly submerged: if it is to be more than mere determinism, it must find tangible expression at some point in the character's actual behaviour. And so the novel shows Querry perform a charitable act without, however, revealing his attitude: the account is kept scrupulously external. In a similar way, Querry's involvement with Marie Rycker appears to indicate in him a kind of negative humanity—it is chiefly through Querry's eyes that her brutally egoistic husband is exposed for what he is—yet once more the involvement which leads to the night in the hotel and so to Querry's death simply "happens" as an accumulation of trivial actions, a process within which no isolatable moment of commitment occurs. The balance, as usual, is precariously preserved: Querry's comments on the sterility of the Ryckers' marriage count to underscore his cynical view of man; yet they also count, at least in a negative sense, to reveal in him a moral sensitivity and insight. Again, Querry's journey to the leper-hospital is a conscious renunciation of humanity; yet he is anxious from the beginning to help with menial tasks, and the discrepancy of motive is not successfully accounted for. Once more, we cannot explain the incongruency by saying that Querry is merely self-deceived, for this would be finally to invalidate a misanthropy which the novel wishes at least in part to endorse, and to slip into the camp of those who wish to make Querry a cult-hero and destroy him in the process; but on the other hand, we are meant to see, as with Scobie and the whiskey-priest, that the very stringency of his self-condemnation discloses a negative moral value:

> He thought: there was only one thing I could do and that is reason enough for being here. I can promise you. Marie, *toute à toi*, all of you, never again from boredom or vanity to involve another human being in my lack of love. I shall do no more harm.

This both emphasises the deceptions of human feeling, and by the same token reveals a sort of humanity in Querry. The novel is able to reconcile its affirmation and rejection of human love by suggesting that affirmative qualities must be implicit in such a rejection. In a parallel way, the book also implies that there is value present in the very unflinching honesty with which Querry confronts his own worthlessness: it is his honesty, after all, which distinguishes his own "dark night of the soul" from Rycker's. To assert this is to lend Querry dignity without questioning his low self-estimation: in this novel, Greene can reconcile his paradox of a man being at once worthless and better than he thinks by finding his best qualities in the way he faces his worthlessness. The bad Catholic is redeemed by the very intensity of his scruples: "You must have had a lot of belief once to miss it the way you do," Colin tells Querry. It is no longer a case, as it was with Scobie and the whiskey-priest, that Querry is especially self-deceived: it is true, as the novel shows us, that he has little or no capacity for genuine love. Nevertheless, the man who continues to seek faith has already found it: once again value lies in good intentions, however obscure to consciousness. Querry shares the pragmatic rationalism of Dr Colin, against the pious egoism of Rycker or Father Thomas; yet his quest for an absolute value beyond the mess of human reality also lends him a certain superiority to the rationalists. He shares the Superior's lack of concern with moral theology, but also, in a way hardly evident to himself, Father Thomas's preoccupation with absolute questions; they are both, as Colin comments, "men of extremes," whereas Colin himself—the most positively admirable character in the novel—is not. Querry is thus protected from being completely identified either with materialistic rationalism or metaphysical dogmatism, with a conscious commitment to the human world or with an egoistic asceticism which rejects it. In the case of Querry, as of Scobie, Greene is able to have his pragmatic scepticism and reach beyond it at the same time.

It is worth turning at this point to *The Quiet American*. The book centres on a conflict, common to Greene's writing, between the destructive ruthlessness of innocence and principled action on the one hand, and the corrupting guilt of pragmatic humanism on the other. Pyle, the quiet American, is strong, innocent, decisive and so dangerous; Fowler is weak, cynical, compromised and corrupted, and so both inferior and superior to Pyle's kind of virtue. Like the priest of *The Power and the Glory*, Fowler opposes decisively radical social action; he does so in the name of a desire to preserve life which, like the priest's, is based on a belief in the unchanging meanness of human nature—a belief which Pyle is unable to challenge because it is founded on Fowler's "experience," as against the rigidities of his own "ideology." (The radically ideological nature of the stance to which Fowler's experience has led him is not, of course, allowed.) It is important that Fowler's jaundiced view of the human situation should not go uncriticised—indeed, as often with Greene, it is part of the quality of that view that its exponent should be self-critical. Fowler can see that Pyle is in many ways the "better" man, and so can we; indeed, given a wholly different context, there is in the relationship of Fowler and Pyle a faint but detectable resonance of the relationship of Pinkie and Rose in *Brighton Rock*. In both cases, the role of the innocent partner is unwittingly to reveal to the other his own corruption. But Fowler's self-disgust lends credence to his condemnation of Pyle at the same time as it permits him to acknowledge his inferiority: the self-disgust springs from the same depth of "experience" from which the criticism of Pyle's murderously naïve ideologising is launched. And because Fowler is empty of self-esteem, his dislike of Pyle can be seen as disinterested. In a better world, Pyle's energy and commitment would overshadow Fowler's flaccid cynicism, and to this extent Fowler is critically placed; but because Fowler's view that a better world is impossible is, despite the criticism, endorsed, Pyle can be rejected. (He is, in any case, something of a straw target, with his crew-cut and volumes of ideology; the effective humour reaped at his expense comes suspiciously easily.) The man who rates human potential highly is thus destructive; the man with a confused regard for life has a low estimation of its worth.

Yet once more Greene faces an intractable problem. If the rejection of Pyle's murderous innocence is to have validity, it must be made from a humane standpoint; yet what is being denied is in fact the view that significant human value exists. Fowler, then, must be allowed a certain humanity—enough, in fact, to let him conquer Pyle in ideological argument without convicting him of ideological views, and so of an articulate commitment to purposive action. Thus, when the two men are arguing in the watch-tower, Fowler can clinch the political discussion by commenting: "I've been here a long time. You know, it's lucky I'm not *engagé*, because there are things I might be tempted to do—because here in the East—well, I don't like Ike. I like—well, these two." "These two" are the silent Vietnamese soldiers who crouch with them in the tower; and Fowler's appeal to them is meant to undercut the "unreal" ideologising to the level of the simply human. "I'd like those two poor buggers there to be happy—that's all." He appeals to a life in which the Vietnamese peasants can simply get enough rice and avoid being shot at: "They want one day to be much the same as another."

Fowler's political position is, in fact, deeply confused. The question of how peace and enough rice are to be attained—the fact that it is, inescapably, a *political* question, and that it slides over certain additional issues, such as whether the peasants are to govern themselves or be governed by imperialist regimes—is seriously blurred. Fowler is, of course, rabidly anti-American, but to avoid the disruptions of "ideology" he must launch his satirical assault on U.S. imperialism from a non-political standpoint: from a commitment to "the human" which detaches it from its inevitably political embodiments, and which moreover must avoid imbuing "the human" itself with too much value. This is the point of his suggestion that the peasants merely want enough rice and a settled routine: to imply a sympathy with the peasant which at the same time contains the judgement that he lacks the capacity to see further than his stomach. Yet there is a further, more serious ambiguity in Fowler's attitude: the conflict between his passionate anti-Americanism and his carefully nurtured cult of dispassionately objective *dégagement*. The first would indicate a humane indignation; the second implies its opposite. The problem of resolving these attitudes is lessened to some degree by the fact that Fowler's anti-Americanism is for the most part less an objection to what the Americans *do*—and so, at least by implication, a commitment to their victims—than a criticism of what they *are*, an almost physical disgust for the trivia of hairstyle and manner. Fowler's anti-Americanism is closer to a vulgar snobbery than to a shrewd analysis of the brutalities of U.S. imperialism, a fact which the novel itself seems significantly not to question. Nevertheless, Fowler's anti-American feeling draws him emotionally towards an engagement he would intellectually repudiate: if he were not *dégagé*, there are things he "might be tempted to do," morally committed courses of action he might follow. These would be "temptation," since committed action is bound to fail and destroy: one of the novel's epigraphs is Arthur Clough's comment that "I do not like being moved: for the will is excited; and action is a most dangerous thing." Yet such tempting actions might also reveal a kind of moral fibre: they would have behind them the ratifying force of Fowler's "best self," his disgust at imperialist manipulation.

The climax of the novel is Fowler's submission to temptation. Swayed by a "moment of emotion," a swift response of shocked horror at the bomb-murders with which Pyle is involved, he betrays the American to his death. Again, there is no clearly defined moment of moral decision: having decided to have Pyle silenced, he gives him various chances to escape. Yet in taking this action, Fowler is obedient to the impulse of common humanity he felt for the soldiers in the tower: his detachment is exposed as self-deception and yields to principled decision. To the extent that his action emerges from the humanism which gives him a title to reject Pyle, it is related to what is most morally valuable in him: by performing it, he transcends his sterile cynicism and betrays a feeling for life. Yet to the extent to which the act of consigning Pyle to his death reaches beyond the confusions and half-commitments of pragmatism into serious involvement, it must fall under the strictures which Fowler himself has made on Pyle. Thus Fowler's action both substantiates a humanity which is, in the last analysis, more worthy than Pyle's fanaticism, and at the same time, through Fowler's guilt at having killed a kind and honourable man, serves to ratify the wisdom of his previous detachment. Both involvement and detachment are therefore criticised; but the "moral" is not quite that detachment is desirable, but impossible. Detachment is desirable, but only to the degree that it does not sterilise the humane feelings by which criticism of others' more committed (and so more destructive) involvements can be made. The uncommitted man must be shown as both inhumanly cynical and humanly sensitive: either perspective can be selected to attack the revolutionary, but both are necessary if the attack is to rest on a version of man both inferior and superior to the revolutionary's own. And this, essentially, is what Greene's novels want to do.

II

It is possible to express the tensions we have traced within Greene's work in slightly different terms. There is a sense in which the ethics of Greene's "bad" Catholic characters differ from the ethics of pragmatic humanism only in the guilt by which the actions they lead to are accompanied. Yet the guilt is an essential element: as we have seen, it allows humanism to be both qualified and endorsed. Greene's kind of Christianity, in fact, makes remarkably little difference to the quality of human life itself: it makes its difference felt chiefly at the end of life, in the reality of death. God is peace and love, the Pendélé at the end of the path through the decayed human jungle, glimpsed in frustrating moments through its undergrowth; in *The End of the Affair*, God is the presence which emerges when human relationships have broken down. Neither Bendrix nor Fowler are Christians, and the fact has some significance: because of it, Greene can distance himself to some extent from their crude acquisitiveness. Yet what is striking is how little difference belief would really make to either man's attitudes. Fowler himself defines what faith might mean to him in a way which suggests this fact: "The job of a reporter is to expose and record. I had never in my career discovered the inexplicable. . . . I had no visions or miracles in my repertoire of memories." Christianity is seen as the "inexplicable," which makes a difference to ordinary human life chiefly by not fitting in with it—by being superadded vision and miracle. And in this sense, it need not alter the sceptical version of man which Bendrix and Fowler hold. Through these men, Greene does not simply express a view of what the world seems like without God; he expresses what the world seems like with God too. It is just that, for Sarah and Deo Gratias, there is something beyond the world which the atheist does not recognise. Greene's attitude in this respect seems, indeed, to have become increasingly pessimistic as he has developed: it is true that divine grace makes a qualitative difference to the whiskey-priest's behaviour in *The Power and the Glory*, and still, although less true, in the case of Scobie; but in Sarah's case, the symbols of divine love are miracles which occur after her death. She is, so to speak, most effectively present in the world after she has left it.

There is a theological basis to this way of seeing. Although Greene's novels centre again and again on the truths of passion and crucifixion, the definitive event of Christian faith—resurrection—finds no place in their economy. God is not seen as the living power which sustains and renews human relationship; He is what is found among the debris of their collapse. We can return at this point to a problem touched on earlier: the tension between Greene's extreme Protestant view of men as radically corrupt, and his more orthodox belief in a divine love which is somehow tangibly incarnated. The novels escape this dilemma by seeing God as incarnate, not in human creativity, but in human failure. Failure, for Greene, is at once what is most essentially human about man (Scobie speaks of "the loyalty we all feel to unhappiness—the sense that that is where we really belong") and yet is also what reveals him in the least heroic or impressive light. It is therefore safe to love failure, as Sarah "loves" the disfigured Smythe, because it involves one in loving, not humanity, but its negation—in loving that in man which finally points beyond him. "I am kissing pain," says Sarah when she presses her lips to Smythe's strawberry-mark, "and pain belongs to You as happiness never does." The more men are exposed as broken and corrupted failures, the more one can love them and so have one's "humanism," but the more, by the same token, they endorse an anti-humanist view of their fallenness. The more you love men, the less you value them: "Here," says Scobie, "you could love human beings nearly as God loved them, knowing the worst." When the whiskey-priest ponders that "it needed a god to die for the half-hearted and the corrupt," he dignifies and demeans humanity at the same time. In the light of this, the humility of Greene's characters gains an added significance: what the novels do not see is that their characters' inability to value themselves is intimately related to their inability to value others. Their attitude is the direct reverse of the traditional Christian insight that, in order to be able genuinely to love another, one must also be able to love oneself.

The whiskey-priest's sense of solidarity with suffering, guilt and weakness is one instance of a pervasive belief, in almost all of Greene's novels, that it is here that God is most concretely present. It is only by the experience of suffering, guilt, weakness, and so of compassion, that the pharisaic egoisms of respectable religion, hygienic innocence and the ethic of success can be avoided. Yet this, while radical in its attitude towards orthodoxy ("God might forgive cowardice and passion, but was it possible to forgive the habit of piety?"), is at another point deeply conservative: it leads the whiskey-priest to a rejection of those beliefs which would hope to remove the unhappiness where men "really belong." Once men cannot be pitied they cannot be loved, since the love was, all along, only a form of pity. Scobie wants his wife Louise to be happy, but can't love success: "He thought: it was the hysterical woman who felt the world laughing behind her back that I loved. I love failure: I can't love success. And how successful she looks, sitting there: one of the saved." The extent to which pity degrades its object (the term is apt) is realised: it occurs to Scobie that Louise is "someone of human stature with her own sense of responsibility, not simply the object of his care and kindness." He half-recognises that, precisely because his "automatic terrible pity" goes out to *any* human need, regardless of the particular person involved, it is to that degree a kind of abstraction. Yet although the dangers of pity are seen, it is preferable, in the end, to the callow arrogance of love.

Greene's novels, then, have to accommodate their strong impulse towards a rejection of human experience itself as inherently flawed—the instinct of the police lieutenant, who wishes to "destroy everything" and begin afresh—to a tired respect for a pragmatic negotiation of ordinary life. It is worth looking finally at one of Greene's earliest novels, *Brighton Rock*, since there some of the tensions we have discussed seem least satisfactorily resolved. The evil of Pinkie, in *Brighton Rock*, lies in his uncompromisingly total rejection of ordinary human reality: of the texture of human experience itself. His evil is closely linked with his social and sexual ignorance: he embodies a kind of pure negation, an "annihilating eternity." Yet Pinkie's view of experience is time and again confirmed by the novel itself: his revolted rejection of life is underpinned by the book's mood and imagery, which remorselessly elaborate the selective sordidities of Brighton to the status of an entire human condition: "The sun slid off the sea and like a cuttlefish shot into the sky with the stain of agonies and endurances." Brighton, a seedy, flashy, candy-floss world, is seen by the novel with a coldly dehumanising perception which parallels Pinkie's own responses. "Down the steps of the Cosmopolitan came a couple of expensive women with bright brass hair and ermine coats and heads close together like parrots exchanging metallic confidences . . . they flashed their pointed painted nails at each other and cackled." "Bright," "brass," "metallic," "flashed," "painted," "cackled": these are the terms in which the whole of Brighton is seen, and the verbal artifice, the over-insistent, over-written dragooning of casual detail into tendentious effect, is characteristic of the whole book. The Brighton world finds its unreal epitome in Ida Arnold, the brassily sentimental whore who intervenes to save the innocent Rose from the evil Pinkie:

> "You leave her alone," the woman said. "I know all about you."
> It was as if she were in a strange country: the typical Englishwoman abroad. She hadn't even got a phrasebook. She was as

> far from either of them as she was from Hell—or Heaven. Good and evil lived in the same country, spoke the same language, came together like old friends, feeling the same completion, touching hands beside the iron bedstead.

Ida enters the metaphysical world of Pinkie and Rose as a self-righteous day-tripper from the land of pragmatic humanism; for all her knowledge of "human nature" she is a vulgar and irrelevant voice in the absolutist country into which she blunders. Pinkie and Rose belong to a metaphysical élite who have transcended the seedy ethics of quotidian experience for the superior world of those "real" enough to embrace or reject divine salvation. "She!" says Pinkie of Ida. "She's just nothing"; and the novel confirms his judgement.

Pinkie, then, is damned because of his incapacity to surrender himself to life; yet we are nowhere shown that life is particularly worth surrendering to. We condemn his murders, of course, but not from any standpoint of sympathy with his brutal or broken victims. If Ida Arnold and Pinkie's underworld friends are truly representative of the human condition, then it is difficult to avoid feeling that Pinkie is damned by his author for holding a view of life which the novel validates.

At least, this would be so if it were not for Rose, Pinkie's innocent girl. Rose is the mute, living embodiment of the terrible judgement in store for Pinkie, accompanying him everywhere, inseparable from his nature; it is Rose who incarnates that capacity for loving self-abandonment which manifests Pinkie as lost. Rose is the criterion by which Pinkie is damned, yet at least two facts in the novel work against the effectiveness of this. First, Rose's goodness is entirely passive: it cannot assume the form of positive action, for positive action belongs to the self-righteously ethical world of Ida Arnold, the realm of obtusely interfering do-gooding. Action, in any case, presumes a knowledge of the world which the incorruptible Rose cannot be allowed. Rose is the only person in the world who symbolises the love which Pinkie has denied, but she is hardly "in" the world at all: she belongs to Brighton no more than Pinkie. (It is significant, incidentally, that Brighton is where Pinkie grew up: by making his home a no-home, a seaside resort for London, a town usually thought of as a place people visit rather than inhabit, the novel detaches him from any natural locality and so renders his evil less environmentally explicable.) Secondly, Rose's association with Pinkie works as much in his favour as to his disadvantage: they are linked together as the complementary polarities of good and evil, and the differences between them are less significant, for both of them, than their mutual opposition to the shabbily unheroic world of Ida Arnold. Rose recognises what Pinkie is, in a world too flashily one-dimensional to evaluate the terrifying meaning of his life; Pinkie, unlike other Greene characters, is fully aware of his own metaphysical significance, and it is a criticism of the world that it cannot see this significance. Pinkie may be "evil," but he is not "corrupt": his evil is a pure, pristine integrity, a priestly asceticism which refuses the contaminations of ordinary living. Moreover, in this early novel, the disgusted desire to shake oneself free from experience is not emphasised as naïvety of false consciousness; the incidents which reveal Pinkie's unworldly integrity of evil—his sexual clumsiness with the girl in the car-park, for instance—count at least as much against social "decadence" as against Pinkie himself. Pinkie *is* innocent, but while he is damned for it, it is also a mark of his superiority to the Ida Arnolds of the world. His innocence is not a fault which could be corrected with time, as one could argue, perhaps, about Pyle in *The Quiet American:* it is integral to what he is, part of the essence of his evil. And to that degree it is part of his general, metaphysical superiority to the Brighton world. Pinkie cannot understand human reality, but the human reality we are shown has nothing substantial about it to be understood; Pinkie and Brighton are two negations linked in a fixed opposition. Pinkie regards human involvement as despicable weakness, and is damned for it; yet the novel's major image of such involvement is the despicable Ida.

Brighton Rock, then, has its share of the ambiguities we have seen elsewhere in Greene, but it also has its divergencies. By choosing a wholly evil figure as its focus, the book can indulge that vision of the world as putrid corruption which is a significant element of other novels without this leading to difficult tensions with a simultaneous suggestion of virtue. Virtue is affirmed elsewhere, in Rose; yet in a way which, as we have seen, connives at rather than qualifies the detailed imagery of fallenness. Again, by choosing an evil "hero" (and the term has, perhaps, some force), the novel is saved from later problems of accommodating conscious to unconscious motives. If it is of the essence of good for Greene that it should be to some degree humbly ignorant of itself, it is of the essence of evil that it should know itself for what it is: a man cannot be damned against his will.

As a consequence of this difference in the protagonist, there is a corresponding difference in the attitude towards corruption. The "good" men of Greene's later novels cannot take Pinkie's uncompromising stance towards the ordinary universe, although they are constantly attracted to some version of it; to do this would be to betray their goodness, which lies, precisely, in a solidarity with human weakness. What is interesting in *Brighton Rock,* in this respect, is the ambiguous characterisation of Ida Arnold; for Ida is both a warm, relaxed, lenient earth-mother, embracing all human weakness to her ample bosom, and yet, in her pursuit of Pinkie and Rose, a relentless avenger of wrong. The novel, in fact, has some difficulty in squaring these disparate aspects of Ida: in endowing her at once with a breezy hedonism and an adequate motivation in her remorseless quest for justice. The aesthetic weakness embodies a moral dilemma: it springs from the novel's desire to reveal ordinary life not only as corrupt, but also as crassly assertive and interfering, and so to engage it in a confrontation with metaphysics which will expose its inferiority. The attempt is unconvincing: it entails our belief in Ida as both amoral vitalist and indignant moralist. The novel, once more, is over-insistent: it is torn between an impulse to dismiss routine life as glitteringly empty, and a need to worst it in argument.

In Greene's next important novel, *The Power and the Glory,* the situation has significantly changed: corruption and self-righteousness are no longer clumsily combined within the same person, but confront each other as polarities. This is the condition we have examined throughout, with its attendant problems and ambivalences. The exploration of evil in *Brighton Rock* is in one sense a dead-end; Greene turns from it to a more subtle and shaded analysis, in which despair and virtue, value and cheapness, are intricately interwoven. One condition for doing this is the transplanting of the action outside England, to the tropics: for here a corruption which in the domestic setting of *Brighton Rock* is seen merely as flashily or brutally superficial becomes full-blooded and intense. Deaths, betrayals and despair are now no longer confined to a criminal underworld within the "sordid" respectabilities of a seaside resort, but become the fabric of a whole way of life. And so a different attitude may be taken to the "fallen" world: whereas the official world of Brighton is merely seedy, the worlds of Africa, Latin America and the East are seen as both seedy and extreme, decrepit and exotic. And because corruption is more exotic and intense, it can be connected with the imagery of redemption and damnation which in *Brighton Rock* was jealously confined to an élite. The half-caste of *The Power and the Glory* can be related to metaphysical conditions in a way impossible for Ida Arnold. In these situations, as we have seen, Greene is able to find in the realities of suffering and weakness a value absent in the earlier novel: by the dialectics of death and salvation, cynicism and heroism, meanness and moral worth, a compassionate engagement with those merely despised in *Brighton Rock* can be made to consort with a rejection of the human world, and of the possibilities of sanctity within it, which still owes much to Pinkie's way of seeing.

J. A. WARD

Henry James and Graham Greene

In Graham Greene's collected essays [*The Lost Childhood and Other Essays*] the dominant figure is Henry James. Not only is James the subject of five essays; he is also the novelist who receives Greene's highest tribute: "He is as solitary in the history of the novel as Shakespeare in the history of poetry." And the terms of the tribute are nearly unique when viewed in the context of all the critical praise that James has received:

> The technical qualities of Henry James's novels have been so often and so satisfactorily explored [the first essay begins] . . . that perhaps I may be forgiven for ignoring James as the fully conscious craftsman in order to try to track the instinctive, the poetic writer back to the source of his fantasies. In all writers there occurs a moment of crystallization when the dominant theme is plainly expressed, when the private universe becomes visible even to the least sensitive reader. . . . I think we may take the sentence in the scenario of *The Ivory Tower*, in which James speaks of "the black and merciless things that are behind great possessions" as an expression of the ruling fantasy which drove him to write: a sense of evil religious in intensity.

The observation, which lies behind all of Greene's appraisals of James, clearly raises problems. "Religious" and "evil" are among the loosest and most relative of concepts, especially since James, unlike Greene, had no interest

From *The Henry James Review* 1, no. 1 (November 1979).

in formal doctrine and only the vaguest sense of the supernatural (for instance in his ghost stories, wherein supernatural occurrences derive their validity from literary convention, not from observed experience). But recurrent comments in the essays on James make it impossible to define "religious" loosely, suggesting simply a conflict between good and evil or a concern for morals and ethics. Emphatically the Henry James honored by Graham Greene is a novelist of the supernatural order: quite simply, "James believed in the supernatural"; "the struggle between the beautiful and the treacherous is lent . . . the importance of the supernatural." Thus Greene associates James with Mauriac, and—consistent with his view that "with the death of James the religious sense was lost to the English novel"—regrets the exclusively secular dimension of the works of Forster and Virginia Woolf.

In several of his essays Greene notes the curious affinity of James and Joseph Conrad—of James whose characters are ladies and gentlemen at home only in the capitals of Europe and of Conrad whose characters are sailors and adventurers roving about in the most remote and primitive parts of the world. "It was a strange fate which brought these two to settle within a few miles of each other and produce from material gained at such odd extremes of life two of the great English novels of the last fifty years: *The Spoils of Poynton* and *Victory*." The relation of Conrad to James parallels the relation of Greene to James, even to the extent that Conrad and Greene are, in their own ambiguous ways, Catholic. Conrad's own essay on James, "The Historian of Fine Consciences," has much in common with Greene's essay "Henry James: The Private Universe," for it focuses on James's unique (for the Anglo-American novel) talent for making human intelligence a moral and spiritual faculty. Greene finds the Conrad-James relation an "amusing" one, for the apparent differences are strikingly insignificant. Lord Jim's Patusan is only geographically remote from Merton Densher's London and Venice (in James's *The Wings of the Dove*), as indeed is Scobie's west Africa (in Greene's *The Heart of the Matter*).

One inevitably fears that Greene is perhaps contriving a James in his own image—as a religious novelist, as "a Puritan with a nose for the Pit," as a believer in "supernatural evil, but not in supernatural good." At the very least, in the emphasis Greene gives to James's "world of treachery and deceit," he compels a refocusing. The center of *The Portrait of a Lady* is thus not Isabel Archer but Osmond and Madame Merle. James develops not from *The Europeans* (social comedy) but from *The American* (melodrama). His theme is not innocence but corruption. Yet if Greene seems to be acclimating certain of James's characters and plots to the world of his own novels—implying some essential resemblance between Osmond and Pinkie Brown—it is curious that James's villains, at least as Greene represents them, seem even more malignant than Greene's. Who in Greene's fiction possesses "an egotism so complete that you could believe that something inhuman, supernatural, was working through the poor devils it had chosen?" Even the malevolence of Pinkie Brown—certainly Greene's most sadistic character—has an obvious pathological foundation.

Whether the evil of betrayal is James's dominant theme is certainly open to question, but that the subject is pervasive is incontestable. Had James been as comfortable with a Christian vocabulary as with an aesthetic one, he might, like Greene, have used the figure of Judas as an archetype for many of his own characters. In novel after novel, James varies the theme of the innocent betrayed. But only in the earlier and simpler novels is the betrayer what might be called, in any conventional sense, a villain. In *The Awkward Age*, the agency of betrayal is a social situation or a complexity of good intentions. And in the later works the relation of betrayer to betrayed seems hardly ethical at all. Thus in *The Ambassadors* the adulterous woman who deceives the innocent American is a figure for whom we are intended to feel intense compassion. Ultimately in James it is the world that is menacing, and the world accepts as its victims (who are often indistinguishable from victimizers) all but the insensitive.

Greene dwells exclusively on the private deeds of betrayal in James; to him the major difference between Madame de Bellegarde and Charlotte Stant is in their creator's growth in artistic sophistication. Greene ignores James's steady movement towards an ambiguous representation of villainy and his association of villainy with specific societies and with civilization itself. He ignores, that is to say, James's increasing tendency to see evil in much the way Greene sees it—not as the exclusive condition of certain individuals but as a more-or-less universal condition, ambiguously but unmistakably present everywhere.

More significantly, James develops towards an association of evil with sexual passion, and in this regard he is very much like Greene. James plays recurrently on the problem of the relation between love and ethics. If the dilemma of Fleda Vetch is resolved in favor of denial—of passion thwarted so that decency may be preserved—Madame de Vionnet, Merton Densher, and Charlotte Stant submit to passion and thus deceive and exploit others in the cruelest of ways. That passion corrupts is the simple allegorical lesson of *The Sacred Fount*, wherein the victims of love are literally drained of life. Our final glimpses of Madame Merle, Madame de Vionnet, and Charlotte Stant are of persons ravaged by erotic compulsions. To Greene they are "damned": hopelessly desperate, tormented by guilt and humiliation. Also, such figures as these, rather than aloof egotists like Osmond, are strikingly similar to Greene's own haunted protagonists, who similarly discover that passion not only warps the moral sense but corrodes the soul. Greene's epigraph for *The Human Factor* is a quotation from Conrad: "I only know that he who forms a tie is lost. The germ of corruption has entered into his soul." By an obscure logic Greene requires that his characters who submit to passion—Scobie, Querry, Bendrix—are quickly involved in some insidious betrayal. In Greene and James the principle is harshly simple: as Greene puts it, "you must betray or, more fortunately perhaps, you must be betrayed."

Still one questions why Greene regards Jamesian evil, pervasive and destructive as it clearly is, as "religious in intensity." Greene respects James's "passionate distrust in human nature," his implicit rejection of mere psychological or sociological explanations of human pain and treachery. Greene writes that James shared with his father and older brother a "sense of daemonic possession": *The Turn of the Screw*, James's paradigmatic parable of damnation, thus centrally parallels *The Wings of the Dove* and *The Golden Bowl*, whose "incomparable figures of evil," Kate Croy and Charlotte Stant, are every bit as damned as Peter Quint and Miss Jessel. One must conclude, then, that an "evil religious in intensity" or a "supernatural evil" is such because the evil-doer is "driven," "possessed," and almost literally damned by some malign transcendent power.

Greene and Greene's James nowhere converge so directly as in their attitudes towards the evil-doer. To Greene it is a mark of James's greatness as a novelist that he shows "that a damned soul has its chains," that his suffering is to be pitied. The alter ego of Spencer Brydon of "The Jolly Corner" (to which Greene several times makes significant reference) is "a burnt-out case," devastated by a lifetime of ego-driven savagery, and pitiable in his very horror. Greene's James therefore has the most important attribute of Greene's God—mercy. So, too, these "damned" characters of James manifest a kind of inverse spirituality in the very intensity of their suffering. Charlotte Stant in her final agony reveals what is probably Greene's dominant theme—the extension of consciousness through suffering, especially the suffering of the damned. Each of the novels of James's major phase represents an end of an affair, and Greene's epigraph (from Leon Bloy) to his *The End of the Affair* could probably stand in Greene's mind as a suitable epigraph to these: "Man has places in his heart which do not yet exist, and into them enters suffering, in order that they may have existence."

The passage from James that Greene finds so revealing—"the black and merciless things that are behind great possessions"—refers not simply to the crimes that create fortunes, but, much more universally, to the depths of depravity that underlie and co-exist with all that we consider civilized. Clearly it is one of James's great themes; it may indeed be his "ruling fantasy." In James's fiction, such civilized properties as art, social style, and manners prevail not in spite of or in conflict with the baser capacities of man, but actually in alliance with them. In a raw society James's innocent Americans remain not only uncorrupted but incapable of corruption; to participate in a high culture they have no choice but to sacrifice their innocence to the "black and merciless things that are behind" it. And, as Greene acutely observes, these "things" are usually "treachery and deceit." Almost by definition, as James everywhere implies, civilization is institutionalized deviousness; its nobility and grandeur—though real, desirable, and finally indispensable—are at bottom pretenses, and one caught up in a traditional and artificial culture is not only required to sacrifice a great deal of his naturalness but also finds available a style whereby to enact his selfish pursuits—that is, to achieve some private gain at the expense of another person, all the while fulfilling his social role as perfect gentleman. Isabel Archer of *The Portrait of a Lady*, if she wishes to "experience" Europe fully, has no choice but to accept the morally corrupt principles of Madame Merle, the woman who deceives her. Isabel's recognition of an evil intrinsic in the civilized is similar to that of Maggie Verver of *The Golden Bowl*, who feels "the horror of finding evil seated, all at its ease, where she had only dreamed of good; the horror of the thing hideously *behind*, behind so much trusted, so much pretended, nobleness, cleverness, tenderness. . . . it had met her like some bad-faced stranger surprised in one of the thick-carpeted corridors of a house of quiet on a Sunday afternoon."

Given James's preoccupation with "civilization," Greene's sense of kinship with James (which the essays make patently clear) is rather paradoxical. For Greene's violent, squalid, and primitive situations seem totally different from James's hyper-genteel characters and settings. In addition, civilization in James's fiction does indeed mean something, positively as well as negatively. Negatively, it may mean hypocrisy or a mere facade of elegance purchased by great wealth; positively, however, it may mean something like a moral code, albeit no one can quite adhere to its sublime standards, though many recognize their existence. Figures such as Ralph Touchett of *The Portrait of a Lady*, Mr. Longdon of *The Awkward Age*, and Fleda Vetch of *The Spoils of Poynton*—all ultimately devastated by the less sensitive—require in their lives that manners achieve the dimension of morals, that the beauty of surface reflect honesty and goodness. In effect the idea of civilization is like the idea of moral theology. James's "civilization" is something like Greene's

Catholicism—a timeless and intensely ritualized moral order; a traditional and finally inviolable system of rules, values, and styles that gives meaning to individual actions by relating them to the universal and the beautiful. Of course James's civilization is nearly as decadent as Greene's Catholicism. Its hollow forms may be graceful, but its spirit can be found only in the souls of those alienated from actual society, spectators of and not participants in what Greene calls "the moral anarchy of the age." James's civilization, like Greene's Catholicism, has become all a matter of form; in all but a few of the representatives of each, its vital energies have been sacrificed to superficial observance of the rules. Ralph Touchett, like Greene's whiskey-priest, is the true believer; Gilbert Osmond, like the selfishly pious of *The Power and the Glory*, is the manipulator of external forms. As Greene wrote of James, "No writer was more conscious that he was at the end of a period, at the end of the society he knew. It was a revolution he quite explicitly foresaw." Many of Greene's novels suggest an imminent, and Orwell-like, apocalypse; *The Power and the Glory*, *The End of the Affair*, *Brighton Rock*, and even some of the "entertainments" suggest the collapse of a post-Jamesian liberal-bourgeois culture, to be replaced by rationalistic totalitarianism, as embodied, for example, in the emergent police state in *The Power and the Glory*. But if the revolution has not quite taken place, certainly traditional human and religious standards have long since died. No wonder, then, that Greene's Catholic protagonists seem so irrelevantly quixotic.

But if James's traditional civilization is doomed and Greene's Catholic culture is an antique abstraction, isolated and occasionally ridiculous reactionaries stand at the center of the books of each author. To them and their creators, their plights are comprehensible only within the contexts of vanished or vanishing moral or theological milieux. The moral norm is the outsider—the American in Europe, the Catholic in the modern secular world; both provide or conserve a set of values to which the existing society is blind, though these values at one time formed the bases of civilizations. The values are essentially those of innocence and moral seriousness. The challenge that James's Americans present to Europe is the question of whether their innate decency and passion for freedom are compatible with a traditional social order. Greene's Catholics challenge modern totalitarian politics and secular emptiness with their implicit demands for moral law and a recognition of the spiritual order.

I would like to explore in more detail certain resemblances between James's fiction and Greene's, using *The Wings of the Dove* (1902) and *The Heart of the Matter* (1948) as concrete illustrations. Admittedly, it is an arbitrary approach. But these novels are at the same time extraordinary achievements and generally representative works of their authors. Further, they have a common theme: a protagonist caught in the irresolvable dilemma of being committed simultaneously to two women. Though in itself a cliché, easily adaptable to the tritest of melodramatic treatments, the subject as handled by James and Greene is a profoundly and fundamentally moral one.

In *The Wings of the Dove* (which Greene calls James's "main study of corruption," a young, beautiful, but poor British girl, Kate Croy, is in love with the journalist Merton Densher, but because Densher is also poor and Kate, with her passion for "magnificence," is unwilling to forego her chances for wealth, she insists that her engagement to Densher be concealed and that the marriage be indefinitely delayed. The appearance on the scene of Milly Theale, a fabulously wealthy and sickly American girl, gives Kate the opportunity to resolve her problem. Kate gradually and even delicately schemes for Milly to fall in love with Densher, pressures Densher into courting her ("Since she's to die I'm to marry her?" Densher exclaims), and patiently awaits the expected results—the death of Milly and the acquisition of her fortune. The second half of the long novel comes almost entirely from Densher's point of view, so that it is his dilemma more than the wounded innocence of Milly or the amoral plotting of Kate that receives our attention.

The resemblance to Scobie's quandary in *The Heart of the Matter* is obvious. An English policeman in a West African colony in wartime, Scobie is involved in a dull and loveless marriage. Almost accidentally he has an affair with a young shipwreck victim. Torn by guilt, less for adultery than betrayal, Scobie finds his dilemma unresolvable except through suicide.

Densher and Scobie are remarkably sensitive, especially in contrast to the other characters, mainly callous egotists. But their situations differ considerably. For example, the two women who "surround" Densher compel a good deal more admiration than Scobie's nagging wife and rather ordinary mistress (so much so that Scobie's driving passion—"pity"—seems the only appropriate feeling that one could hold for either). Kate is a woman of brilliance, strength, and great social ability. Milly, in her vulnerability to life and desperate passion for human experience, possesses a kind of spiritual beauty. And Densher responds fully to the "capacity for life" of each.

The difference in stature between the women in the life of Densher and those in the life of Scobie is significant in a comparison of James and Greene. Greene's subordinate characters, those who frame the crises of his protagonists, have a pettiness and vulgarity rarely to be found in any but the most incidental characters in James. Vacuous types like the adults in *What Maisie Knew* hold no attraction for James's figures of intelligence. For all of her deviousness and unscrupulousness, Kate Croy is a commanding figure, not only beautiful but seductive in the very egotism and willfulness that make her monstrous. One understands Densher's love for her. It is considerably more difficult to understand Scobie's love (ambiguous though it is) for his wife and mistress, women whose fundamental second-rateness raises questions about the man who aligns himself with them. Ultimately James is more worldly than Greene. Love may be destructive, but it can also be enormously fulfilling. Madame de Vionnet, while "driven and damned," is yet "magnificent," in large measure because of her corruption. There is no one remotely like her in Graham Greene.

James and Greene grant their male protagonists a certain stature by stressing their moral refinement. Even so these are remarkably weak men. Offering no resistance, Scobie simply drifts into his crisis, a victim of the light pressures of domestic habit, reawakened libido, and mild compassion. Densher's passivity perhaps compels more respect, for the forces that direct his life are Kate's magisterial will and Milly's sublimity. Densher is a regular James type, the vacillating, hyper-scrupulous man, ever suspicious of human entanglements. But unlike his forbears in this line—unlike, for example, Vanderbank of *The Awkward Age* and Marcher of *The Beast in the Jungle*—Densher allows himself to fall in love. His squeamish inner deliberations occur after he makes his commitment.

Though no adulterer, Densher resembles Scobie in his anxiety and sense of guilt for betrayal. Yet the inner pain of each exceeds the stereotype. For both Densher and Scobie, emotional involvement creates the necessity for the subtlest moral discriminations. Love leads to commitment, hence to duty. Both Densher and Scobie regard promises of fidelity as absolutely binding commitments; to them pledges are as important as persons. But each realizes the hopelessness of moral resolution, the ineffectuality of moral scrupulousness. Passively, indeed inevitably (in their own minds), they succumb to an emotion, hence to commitment, all the while observing their own desperation with full sensitivity. Scobie compares his failing with that of his fellow officers: "They had been corrupted by money, and he had been corrupted by sentiment. Sentiment was the more dangerous, because you couldn't name its price." Densher is less brutally honest with himself than is Scobie. His feelings are more of immediate pain, guilt, and frustration than of ultimate judgment. It is the impossibility of his situation that most distresses him. Trying to evade the discomfort of his mock courtship of Milly, he strolls aimlessly and endlessly about Venice, all the time meditating his predicament. Stopping in a cafe, he thinks:

> Anything he should do, or he shouldn't, would have reference, directly, to her life, which was thus absolutely in his hands—

> and ought never to have reference to anything else. It was on the cards for him that he might kill her. . . . The fear in this thought made him let everything go, kept him there, actually, motionless, for three hours on end. . . . What had come out for him had come out, with this first intensity, as a terror; so that action itself, of any sort, the right as well as the wrong—if the difference even survived—had heard in it a vivid "Hush!" . . . He was mixed up in her fate, or her fate, if that were better, was mixed up in *him*, so that a single false motion might, either way, snap the coil.

Like Scobie, Densher experiences paralysis of will, not an inability to act but a recognition of the inadequacy of any act to even slightly modify the urgency of the human situation. This sense heightens the awareness of hypocrisy as Scobie continues to make love to Helen and Densher to visit Milly. Scobie's solution is literal suicide—less to escape than to avoid giving pain to others—but Densher experiences a kind of psychic suicide, an ultimate extension of the emotional impotence that Kate has produced in him, relegating him "to mere spectatorship." At the last stage of his brutal—especially brutal because passive—betrayal of Milly, he is the helpless spectator of his own wretchedness.

The evil of goodness (or, what is the same, the goodness of evil) is the fascinating and oppressive subject of James's and Greene's novels. To both writers, human situations, especially those involving love relationships, are so complex that decent motives seem inevitably to result in betrayal and deceit. Scobie "realized the pain inevitable in any human relationship—pain suffered and pain inflicted." James and Greene show not only that those most capable of love are those most sensitive to pain—their own and others'—but that love, or its variants—like pity and compassion—is a destructive energy. The nature of the world frustrates love and turns it to the appearance, if not the reality, of its opposite. Hence Densher and Scobie are the victims of their good will, their fundamental decency and sensitivity. (Were they simply callous opportunists, their problems would vanish, but to both "decency" is the supreme virtue.) However, they torture others as well—though it should be said that Scobie's wife and mistress are far less vulnerable to his duplicitous position than is Milly Theale to Densher's: when Milly ultimately learns of Densher's deceit she loses the will to live and soon dies, hopelessly in love with the man who has falsely courted her.

Densher becomes disgusted with his own promiscuous kindness. "It was that he liked too much everyone concerned willingly to show himself merely impracticable. He liked Kate, goodness knew, and he also, clearly enough, liked Mrs. Lowder [Kate's aunt]. He liked in particular Milly herself;

and hadn't it come up for him . . . that he quite liked even Susan Shepherd [Milly's guardian]?" And after Milly's death, Densher scornfully tells Kate: "What a brute then I must be! . . . To have pleased so many people." Similarly, Scobie finds his compulsion to please others hopelessly at odds with the given conditions of life. Rationally he well recognizes that "no human being can really understand another and no one can arrange another's happiness." But it is ultimately neither neurosis nor misdirected compassion that leads Densher and Scobie to their destructive actions and inactions. It is the sheer complexity and obscurity of human motive; it is the pressure of fate. This fate ("an evil religious in intensity" because finally beyond human control) is forcefully conveyed in the two novels through the protagonists' sense of will-lessness, of being pursued and pressured, of being manipulated by forces they barely comprehend. But here again, one should not overlook the passivity and weakness of Densher and Scobie. People such as these tend to exaggerate the power of fate or circumstance out of control.

A desperate anxiety leads Densher and Scobie to seek, against all odds, some release, some abatement of pain. Scobie finds fitful relief in the tedious details of his job. "He could see in that driver's mirror Ali nodding and beaming. It seemed to him that this was all he needed of love or friendship. He could be happy with no more in the world than this—the grinding van, the hot tea against his lips, the heavy damp weight of the forest, even the aching head, the loneliness." Densher irrationally yearns for some power to "let him off." Milly, the victim of the conspiracy in which Densher plays an unwilling part, for a while simply refuses to leave her palace rooms, preferring isolation to what James calls "some abysmal trap" into which she is doomed to fall. Thus Milly sighs, "Ah, not to go down—never, never to go down." James's image for the world from which Densher and Milly crave release remains "the abyss"—with all its implications of death, obscurity, and inevitability.

The abyss is the world of human sin, a world that the sensitive yet vulnerable characters of James and Greene both contribute to and suffer from. The abyss is a human creation and yet, in its unvarying corruption, inevitably and preternaturally evil. I have spoken of the suggestion of fatalism in *The Wings of the Dove* and *The Heart of the Matter*. Not only do Densher and Scobie agonize over their helplessness, but James and Greene create a sense of almost demonic fatality that transcends the awareness of individual characters. As strong as the sense of evil of Densher and Scobie may be, that of the reader is stronger.

Such an effect is gained essentially in three ways: through the twists of plot that create the sense of the trap, luring good-natured victims into hopeless moral quandaries; through a concentration on the inner anguish of the victims of passions that lead them to betrayal; and through a symbolic use of setting—an equation of physical decay with a pervasive moral decay. The unnamed West African country of *The Heart of the Matter*, with its political corruption, its disease, its racial and national hostilities, its excesses of weather, and its squalid buildings, is both an obvious and an ironic environment for the drama of deceit and betrayal enacted by seemingly civilized, even religious, people. The physical decay of Greene's coastal village reflects a moral rottenness: "The houses were as white as bones in the moonlight; the quiet streets stretched out on either side like the arms of a skeleton, and the faint sweet smell of flowers lay on the air."

Of course the principal environments of *The Wings of the Dove*—Lancaster Gate in fashionable London and the Palazzo Leporelli in Venice—have little in common with west Africa. Yet the novel begins (significantly it is a betrayal scene) when Kate visits her father in his sordid rooms,

> changing her place, moving from the shabby sofa to the armchair upholstered in a glazed cloth that gave at once—she had tried it—the sense of the slippery and of the sticky. She had looked at the sallow prints on the walls and at the lonely magazine, a year old, that combined, with a small lamp in coloured glass and a knitted white centrepiece wanting in freshness, to enhance the effect of the purplish cloth on the principal table; she had above all, from time to time, taken a brief stand on the small balcony to which the pair of long windows gave access. The vulgar little street, in this view, offered scant relief from the vulgar little room.

It is from such places as this that Kate wishes escape; indeed, her dread of vulgarity impels her scheme—which is the plot of the novel. Yet Jamesian squalor is not solely a matter of dingy rooms and dilapidated furniture, for as Kate does "advance" the reader notes, if Kate does not, that the London mansion into which she at first moves is simply ostentatious (as are the Londoners who gather there) and hence vulgar as well. Milly's rented Venetian palace is a rotting museum, its style every bit as archaic as Lancaster Gate's is artificial. But like Greene, James heightens our sense of evil in place through using certain environments as moral symbols. In a way suggestive of Mann's *Death in Venice* and Eliot's "Burbank with Baedeker," he evokes from Venice an atmosphere of historical evil. Venetians seem "a race in whom vacancy was but a nest of darknesses—not a vain surface, but a place of withdrawal in which something obscure, something always ominous, indistinguishably lived."

Greene's characters are often inexplicably drawn to the most disgusting of environments. In *A Burnt-Out Case*, the distinguished architect Querry feels at home only in a leprosarium in an African jungle, "where the boat goes no further." But a similar if less apparent compulsion to seek out the loathsome is sometimes found in James's characters as well. The tawdry Bloomsbury shop where the Prince and Charlotte discover the golden bowl introduces us to the sordidness that underlies the apparently brilliant marriages of the Ververs. The elegant and wealthy characters of *The Princess Casamassima* find themselves drawn to the slums of London; their repudiation of country houses and elegant mansions for the dingy neighborhoods may be obscurely romantic in their own minds, but there is a raw reality in the ugliness that they find perversely alluring.

Curiously, both James and Greene use weather to reflect the darker human passions. At the height of Scobie's agony, "The sky wept endlessly around him; he had the sense of wounds that never healed." Similarly, it storms as Densher stalks through Venice, aware that Milly knows of his duplicity: "It was a Venice all of evil that had broken out for them alike, so that they were together in their anxiety, if they really could have met on it; a Venice of cold, lashing rain from a low black sky, of wicked wind raging through narrow passes, of general arrest and interruption."

It is a mark of their sensibilities that Densher and Scobie respond to the symbolic dimension of their decayed environments. Their fascination with an external corruption corresponds to their absorption in their own corruption. Densher, ineffectual as he is, cannot leave Venice. Scobie, to his wife's astonishment, actually likes his place of assignment: "Why, he wondered, swerving the car to avoid a dead pye-dog, do I love this place so much? Is it because here human nature hasn't had time to disguise itself? Nobody here could ever talk about a heaven on earth. Heaven remained rigidly in its proper place on the other side of death, and on this side flourished the injustices, the cruelties, the meannesses, that elsewhere people so cleverly hushed up."

The "moral chaos" of *The Wings of the Dove* and *The Heart of the Matter* is defined more exactly through a dramatization of a social environment than through a depiction of physical atmosphere. Both James and Greene work directly in the tradition of the English novel of manners, that of Thackeray and Trollope and of Forster and Waugh. Central in the tradition is an identification of snobbery with viciousness. The mainly English characters who surround Milly, Kate, and Densher are shallow, unconsciously cruel, selfish, and insensitive (hence Densher, also an Englishman, is a remarkable exception: his cruelty is quite conscious; the basis of his treachery is love, not greed or pride). In spite of their apparent civility, the English have an inordinate regard for wealth; thus Kate and Aunt Maud, as well as the lesser figures who fill spaces at dinner parties, equate Milly totally with her money. Milly's early suspicions of her English friends are well-founded: "she had, on the spot, with her first plunge into the obscure depths of a society constituted from far back, encountered the interesting phenomenon of complicated, of possibly sinister motive."

One of James's recurrent observations on immorality is what he calls "the high brutality of good intentions"—the destructive capacity of the well-meaning. Lord Mark, the unsuccessful suitor of Kate Croy, reveals to Milly that Densher is secretly engaged to Kate. Mark is solemn and vacuous, certain in his own mind that it is his "duty" to speak the truth to Milly, though the knowledge shortly has the effect of killing her. As Milly's guardian remarks to Densher, Mark "is an idiot of idiots":

> "An idiot of idiots." For a moment, on it all, on the stupid doom in it, they looked at each other. "Yet he's thought so awfully clever."
>
> "So awfully. . . . One could almost pity him—he has had such a good conscience."

In *The Heart of the Matter*, the subordinate figures are about as petty and morally indifferent as those in *The Wings of the Dove*. Scobie's moral earnestness is absurdly inappropriate in a community where displaced British officers mainly amuse themselves with frivolous gossip, occasionally muted by sentimental old-school-tie nostalgia. They lack even the "cleverness" of Lord Mark and the social authority of Aunt Maud. As Scobie observes a gathering of his junior officers, "He told himself: Be careful. This isn't a climate for emotion. It's a climate for meanness, malice, snobbery, but anything like hate or love drives a man off his head." He notes his wife: "Beside the bookshelves Louise was talking happily to Wilson, but he could feel the malice and snobbery of the world padding up like wolves about her." Wilson, actually a government spy though supposedly an accountant, betrays Scobie—to his wife and superiors—in a manner somewhat like that of Lord Mark. But if Mark is simply stupid and self-righteous, Wilson is calculatingly self-serving: by ruining Scobie he can more easily take his wife as a lover. Deceit for Wilson is simply an acquired habit: "His profession was to lie, to have the quick story ready, never to give himself away, and his private life was taking the same pattern."

James called such characters as Lord Mark "fools"—fundamentally stupid people whose insensitivity and compulsion to interfere clumsily in the lives of others bring catastrophe to those of delicate conscience. Fleda Vetch cannot survive the oafishness of Mona Brigstock. In *A Burnt-Out Case,* the desperate Querry is finally hounded from his refuge—the leprosarium—and murdered by the idiotic Rycker.

The moral turmoil of Scobie, like that of Densher, seems a near irrelevance, since to most of the other characters (or "fools") moral issues are simply non-existent. Indeed *The Heart of the Matter* is a considerably more cynical book than *The Wings of the Dove,* for after Scobie's suicide we find that his wife and mistress are at best indifferent and at worst relieved that this troublesome man is no longer around and that they are free to take other lovers. By contrast, Densher, though a failure on his own terms, has at least deeply affected the two women in his life.

Indeed the ultimate irony is that Scobie's pity is wasted. He projects a sensitivity in Helen and Louise; the pain that he feels he causes is a fantasy. Densher however responds acutely to the actual rather than the imagined suffering of Milly Theale, just as he responds to her beauty and her love. One sometimes suspects that Scobie exaggerates his own importance; no one really loves him or even much cares for him. He is a protector and a consoler, by no means irreplaceable.

There is another way in which Greene, the "Catholic" novelist, presents a considerably bleaker interpretation of human suffering than does James. Sir Luke Strett, the eminent physician in *The Wings of the Dove,* is a detached counselor, wise and compassionate. Almost clairvoyantly, he perceives the needs and sufferings of Milly and Densher. Though finally very limited in what he can do, he yet provides a large sense of dispassionate concern. His role is priestlike. Indeed he seems more priestlike than the literal priest in *The Heart of the Matter*, Father Rank, who, like Sir Luke, stands outside the story as occasional observer and advisor. But Greene sharply distinguishes Father Rank's human and ecclesiastic identities. As a man he is friendly and decent, but also a gossip and a gourmand. Whatever benefits he may confer are through the sacraments he administers. On the human level—which is the level of the novel—Sir Luke Strett is more religious than is Father Rank.

Greene's cynicism, I think, reflects a radical distrust of goodness, and in this respect he crucially differs from James. In his essay on "The Religious Aspect" of James, Greene writes that James's "religion was always a mirror of his experience. Experience taught him to believe in supernatural evil, but not in supernatural good." Now if Greene means by this that evil is stronger than good in James, of course he is right. But I think it is also true that there is a good in James purer than any in Greene (who seems compelled to present his good people as weak and quirky); it is also true that James sometimes presents his good people in something like a supernatural aura (the principal instance being Milly Theale). In Greene's fictional world there is an inferno and a purgatory, but no paradise. That is, there are the mindlessly corrupt and the tormented who struggle against temptation, but there is no grace. Goodness exists beyond the grave; it is known only through the teachings of the Church. Tortured and defeated idealists like Scobie and the whiskey-priest represent all that can be expected of man in the novels of Greene. To James, however, human beings may at their best be agents of grace, may love purely and absolutely, may even suggest the transcendent. (In his commentary on James, Greene completely rejects this idea.) Such a person is Milly Theale, of whom there is no remote equivalent in *The Heart of the Matter*. The final turn of *The Wings of the Dove* is the spiritual conversion of Merton Densher. Milly has loved him to her death in spite of his betrayal of her. Densher's ultimate awareness is of something sublime: "The essence was that something had happened to him too beautiful and too sacred to describe. He had been, to his recovered sense, forgiven, dedicated, blessed; but this he couldn't coherently express." Densher's vision of grace indicates that James, at times at least, had not only a sense of evil but a sense of good "religious in intensity."

ROGER SHARROCK

Love and Pity: The Honorary Consul *and* The Human Factor

In construction and execution *The Comedians* [1966] is a very good novel and its successor *The Honorary Consul* (1973) is even better (*Travels with my Aunt* [1969], which appeared between them, is a purely comic novel).

The theme of political commitment and the political duty of a Christian in an unjust society is even more to the fore in *The Honorary Consul* than in *The Comedians.* Father Rivas is a Catholic priest who has become a Marxist revolutionary, and his school friend Dr Plarr, the representative of indifference, takes sides for the sake of Rivas far more decisively than Brown does for Jones, since he loses his life in doing so. So if the discussion of the novel seems restricted, though I admire it as much as any by Greene, and he himself considers it his best, it is partly because it is a subtle and accomplished variation on a continuing theme. It has the tolerance and the mellowed wryness of attitude to be found in all the later novels; the tiredness of life is no longer an extreme disease but another mask among many to be assumed, and there is admission of the existence of a disconcerting reserve of human freedom enabling the wearer to put down the masks and be himself to his own terror and amazement. Perhaps also there is a sense in which, like Tolstoy's happy families, all controlled, calmly good novels are alike, and therefore to some extent immune to critical discussion; they are not, like the great flawed novels, sustained by dreams and personal obsessions, for example, most of Hardy, or indeed *The Power and the Glory* and *The Heart of*

From *Saints, Sinners and Comedians: The Novels Of Graham Greene.* University of Notre Dame Press, 1984.

the Matter. Therefore my restricted discussion will dwell principally on features which cannot be classed as repetition or variation.

The setting of *The Honorary Consul* is a small port on the shores of the great river Paraná in northern Argentina which forms the border with Paraguay. The mood is even more elegiac than that of *The Comedians*, breathing the sadness and the missed opportunities of middle age. In the first scene a plume of smoke on the further shore lies across the red bars of the sunset "like a stripe on a national flag"; "It was an evening which, by some mysterious combination of failing light and the smell of an unrecognized plant, brings back to some men the sense of childhood and of future hope and to others the sense of something which has been lost and nearly forgotten."

Eduardo Plarr, a man in his thirties and a doctor, is, like so many Argentines, of mixed descent, the son of an English father and a Paraguyan mother. The elder Plarr is an opponent of General Stroessner's régime in Paraguay and supposed to be in prison. When Plarr was a boy his father had sent him for safety with his mother down the river to Argentina. The mother "had mislaid her beauty and become querulous," and lives in Buenos Aires eating too many cream-cakes in fashionable tea-rooms. Plarr feels the guilt of middle-class comfort and is his father's son in his sympathy with the poor: "In the *barrio* of the poor I am aware of doing something he would have liked to see me do." Apart from this he is emotionally cold, sleeping without love with a succession of married women, an exile from any community and any form of belief.

Then comes the shocking intervention of chance and danger into the deadening round of his life: his old school friend Leon Rivas, leading a small group of Paraguyan terrorists, plans to kidnap the American ambassador as a publicity stunt and in order to bargain for the freedom of those imprisoned across the border. By their amateurish blunder they capture instead Charlie Fortnum, a very minor British official, not a real consul but an honorary one in the port. He is wounded during the kidnapping and they need a doctor; so Plarr becomes involved and is brought to their hiding-place in the *barrio* of the poor.

The ironies multiply. Plarr is the lover of Charlie Fortnum's wife Clara, a former prostitute in the local brothel. The possible release of his father might have been a good motive for Plarr's assisting the terrorists but he now learns from them that his father has been shot trying to escape. Though the main motive for his helping the terrorists is now removed, he, the egoist and cynic, finds that he cannot abandon his old friend Leon or the friend he has cuckolded, Charlie Fortnum. He goes to Buenos Aires and tries to prevail on the British ambassador to intervene but Fortnum is not important enough for a diplomatic representation. "The trouble is, Plarr," says the ambassador, "Fortnum is such pitiably small beer." His smallness not only controls the course of the plot: it is the source of the spiritual humility which makes him loving and tender to his wife, the ex-whore, and more interesting than other characters who are sustained by power or self-sufficiency. In fact the others, including Plarr, are comedians in the sense used in the previous novel, and Charlie Fortnum is not (although he is a figure of fun to all). Plarr, like Jones, leaves off comedy to die for his friends and possibly also for an ideal he did not know he had entertained associated with the respect he feels for his father.

Still hoping for an intervention at a high level to raise a ransom, Plarr proposes the foundation of a local Anglo-Argentinian society; there will only be two members, himself and a British expatriate Humphreys, but the president will be an Argentinian novelist of some reputation, Jorge Julio Saavedra, who is to write a stirring letter on Fortnum's behalf to national and international papers. Meanwhile Plarr has several interviews with Colonel Perez the chief of police who suspects him of connivance at the kidnapping both because of his father's politics and his known liaison with Clara. The ironies are emotional, too: Charlie loves Clara even when he learns she has been unfaithful to him; Clara, pregnant by Eduardo Plarr, begins to understand that she loves him; Plarr, too resolute in resisting the claims of others really to know himself, does not know where he stands:

> If for once he had been aware of a sickness he could describe in no other terms, he would have unhesitatingly used the phrase "I love," but he had always been able to attribute the emotion he felt to a quite different malady—to loneliness, pride, physical desire, or even a simple sense of curiosity.

Colonel Perez and a paratroop detachment find the hut where the terrorists and their prisoner are hidden and close in. A time limit for their surrender is announced over a loudspeaker. Plarr goes outside the hut to plead for them and is immediately shot. Leon goes to his assistance and is shot down too. Leon says as he is dying, "I am sorry . . . I beg pardon." He is presumably apologizing for letting his friend become involved; but Plarr, intending to make the sort of joke they had made as boys against the formulae of the Church, says, "*Ego te absolvo.*" The words of absolution thus uttered take on a serious resonance since a para approaches to finish him off and in a few seconds they are both dead.

Once again Greene has practised the journalistic skill of being the right man in the right place to present an incident which bears within itself the seed of future events. The book shares this prophetic quality with *The Quiet American:* the tactical failure of the French to control the jungle war in Indo-China, emphasized in the latter work, forecasts the futility of the American military effort fifteen years later, just as Pyle's ideas foreshadow the inadequate policies leading to the military débâcle. A year after the publication of *The Honorary Consul* the British ambassador to Argentina, Geoffrey Jackson, was kidnapped by the Tupamaro guerillas and held for several months before obtaining his release, a period in which his unflagging resolution and capacity for engaging in intelligent dialogue gained for him the respect of his captors. Once again Greene is reporter as well as creator, and the imaginative impact of the novel is qualified by its function as interpretation of that frightening public world reflected more coarsely in the mass media.

The Argentine has terrorists, and indeed secret police, but, unlike Haiti, is not at the time of which Greene is writing a terrorist society. It is however a very peculiar society, a country, in its urban centres, of exiles and expatriates, often hankering after their European roots and priding themselves on their superiority to other Latin American nations. Nostalgia for French culture and Europe in general alternates uneasily with a different national myth: the home-grown cult of the *gauchos,* the horsemen of the pampas, as celebrated in the popular epic *Martin Fierro.* This is the cult of male honour and courage, the *machismo* that often finds its expression in a knife fight to the death against impossible odds. It is not too fanciful to suggest that if the Foreign Office had circulated *The Honorary Consul* in the right quarters as an ancillary state paper in the early months of 1982 our commanders in the Falklands might have been better prepared to comprehend the temper of the Argentine pilots who flew their planes to almost certain death over San Carlos Water.

Eduardo Plarr is personally and racially an Argentine, with some roots in another country, fluctuating in the strength of his sense of identity but desperate to establish it. But the chief exponent of *machismo* in the book is the novelist Saavedra: he writes melancholy books, one about Castillo the fisherman who wages an unending struggle with the sea for a small reward, another about passionate love and jealousy which ends in the ritual knife fight. Saavedra is an aging man whose reputation has not grown; he has been deeply wounded by a young critic Montez whom he had helped to get his books published and who has now written a mordant article on his work denouncing the whole cult of *machismo.* He is comparatively poor, living in a tiny room with two suits on hangers and a few books, his own works. Under a surface of sheer comedy Greene exposes his essential dignity, as he had done with the old German doctor Hasselbacher in *Our Man in Havana* or Parkis the private inquiry agent in *The End of the Affair.* He goes to Señora

Sanchez' brothel merely in order to prevent inordinate desires coming between him and his work.

The climax of the comedy, involving his total attention to style in life and art, is when he agrees to write the letter to the newspapers for the Anglo-Argentinian society, but, regardless of urgency, insists on correcting the draft and turning it into an artistic work of psychological delicacy:

> Do you believe writing is as easy as that? Would you do a delicate operation, on the spur of the moment, on this table? I will sit up all night if necessary. The quality of the letter I write you will more than make up for the delay, even in translation. By the way who is going to translate it—you or Dr Humphreys? I would like to check the translation before you send it abroad. I trust your accuracy, of course, but it is a question of style. In a letter like this we have to move the reader, to bring home to him the character of this poor man . . . It is a situation in which such a man either succumbs to fear or he grows in stature . . . I saw, behind the superficial gaiety, a profound melancholy.

The irony is revealing, because although Saavedra is forcing Charlie Fortnum's character into his own romantic-heroic idiom, he does hit upon the real depth of the latter's nature which underlies his unselfish love for Clara: *machismo*, like Communism or Catholicism, is an interpretative tool that can be applied to all lives. Nobly and extravagantly Saavedra offers himself as a hostage in Fortnum's place, and Plarr thinks that in such a country the scheme might work; Saavedra has of course a personal reason: "At least I will show young Montez that *machismo* is not an invention of the author of *Martin Fierro*." C. S. Lewis wrote that courage was the necessary underpinning of all the virtues, and *machismo* is a cultural melodramatization of the quality of courage; in the context of terrorism the other characters tend to fall into the style of *machismo*, Leon and his companions holding out against the whole state apparatus, and Plarr walking out of the hut to face the bullets of the paras. It is inevitable that at the end it should be Saavedra who pronounces Plarr's funeral oration in which the facts are twisted and the sentiment translated into the melancholy national idiom:

> You were a friend to each of your patients—even to the poorest among them. All of us know how unsparingly you worked in the *barrio* of the poor without recompense—from a sense of love and justice. What tragic fate then it was that you, who had toiled so hard for the destitute, died at the hands of their so-called defenders.

Only Charlie Fortnum, the survivor, is immune to *machismo* for he displays virtues that are without a cultural solvent: charity and humility.

A far more famous writer than Saavedra is depicted to be must have given Greene material to enrich the ethos of the fictional character. Amongst the great variety and subtlety of his work Jorge Luis Borges has several stories celebrating the moral tradition of *Martin Fierro,* including one which actually celebrates the hero himself. In another a man convalescent from an illness returns to his old home in the rural south of Argentina; some louts pick a fight with him, an old *gaucho* throws him a knife, and he goes out with them on to the plain, "firmly clutching the knife, which he perhaps would not know how to wield." It is all there, as in the novels of Saavedra and in the parody deaths outside the hut of men whose private search for identity must be interpreted in terms of the myth of masculine identity embraced in a chosen moment of death. The norm of the myth is typified in the terrorist Aquino, one of Leon's companions, who writes poetry and whose favourite poem is "Death is a common weed, Requires no rain."

In a masculine culture like this the authority of the father is a dominant force; fear of the father's anger and disapproval is the spur towards daring action, whether making love to women or risking death with other men. Charlie Fortnum had been humiliated by a father who was a bully, but now he feels lost without him and drinks too much in compensation (his repeated comic tags are that he "knows his measure" and a reference to his beloved Land Rover as "Fortnum's Pride"):

> I used to be angry with my father. He didn't understand me, I thought, or care a nickel about me. I hated him. All the same I was bloody lonely when he died . . . I even imitate him. Though he drank more than I do.

His father was always accusing him of cowardice, of crying too easily. But in his ordeal Charlie shows no self-pity and behaves better than the obvious exponents of *machismo;* in a childhood incident his father had abused him for babyishness in crying over a lizard he had squashed; his reply had been, "I'm crying for the lizard, not for me." He alone among the personages of the novel demonstrates a capacity for a truly outgoing love; in the incongruous realm that is human nature he alone, the clown and drunkard, is a fully grown up person:

> He was not crying now for himself. The tears were for Clara and a few of them for Fortnum's Pride, both left alone and defenceless. Loneliness, as he knew from experience, was a worse thing to suffer.

Charlie, then, has finally freed himself from obsession by a father whom he had loved and hated. In comparison Plarr knows himself but slenderly and has never quite come to terms with the loss of a far nobler father whom he had infinitely revered. The relationship is perhaps only fully satisfied when he goes out of the hut to his death; previously he can only try to come near his father's code of justice by working in the *barrio* of the poor, or escape from his unsatisfactory mother in the arms of other women. It is significant that when one of his former mistresses, Señora Escobar, straddles him in a chair while her husband sleeps in another corner of the room, and asks him to go on saying something, he can only remember the nursery rhyme, "This is the way the postboy rides, gallopy, gallopy, gallopy," which his father had recited, dandling him on his knee.

His love for Clara begins as mere physical curiosity. She has the thin child's immature body which in Rose, Helen, Phuong and Marie Rycker has provided a magnet to other alienated men. He wonders if a man too rational to fall in love is destined for a worse fate, to become subject to an obsession. But gradually tenderness replaces lust, though he will still not recognize the change in his feelings or in those of Clara. When he comes to her at the beginning of her pregnancy and after the kidnapping of Charlie Fortnum, she touches his cheek and says, "Do you remember that time at the camp when I told you I was pretending? But, *caro*, I was not pretending. Now when you make love to me I pretend. I pretend I feel nothing. I bite my lip so as to pretend. Is it because I love you, Eduardo?" Her tender and naive question cannot penetrate the protective shell of his cautious egoism; as he goes away he has almost forgotten it: "It could not have been very important. The only questions of importance were those a man asked himself." It is only under the stress of the ordeal in the hut that he begins to recognize his own emotion; he is jealous of Charlie's selfless love for Clara, and his jealousy, together with the wish to repay the debt to his father, impel him towards his last gesture: "I don't know how to love. Poor drunken Charlie Fortnum wins the game." At the end, after Plarr's funeral, Charlie takes comfort from the fact that Clara genuinely loved Plarr and that he in a fashion came to love her. They will call the child Eduardo. His magnanimity is impressive, a sort of *machismo* in reverse; though Clara delicately denies that she had loved Plarr he knows that this is not true and rejoices:

> Her lie meant nothing to him now at all. It was contradicted too plainly by her tears. In an affair of this kind it was the right thing to lie. He felt a sense of immense relief. It was as though, after what seemed an interminable time of anxious waiting in the ante-

> room of death, someone came to him with the good news that he had never expected to hear. Someone he loved would survive. He realized that never before had she been so close to him as she was now.

A major success of the book lies in its ability to present convincing images like this of the extraordinary range and frequent bewildering incongruity of the relations of men and women. As Leon says, "When I was a young priest, I used to try to unravel what motives a man or woman had, what temptations and self-delusions. But I soon learned to give all that up, because there was never a straight answer. No one was simple enough for me to understand." Greene, however, does probe these complicated motives in a prose that is spare and functional now and freer from imagery. Short blunt sentences convey immediate emotional facts; the longer ones, varying the rhythm, explore more tentatively the realizations of intimacy that lie on the edge of consciousness; no wonder Saavedra is treated with sympathy since he helps to define the style of the book: "The opening sentence is the key to the rest. One has to strike the right tone, even the right rhythm. The right rhythm in prose is every bit as important as the right metre in a poem."

There is an apparent fissure in the novel between the personal motives which guide Fortnum and Plarr, and indeed Saavedra, and the political ideology of liberation as expounded by Leon to Plarr in the hut on their last night alive. This fissure is not an artistic fault, since the division of values is never reconciled and is perpetuated in a constant debate. Even the almost accidental formula of contrition and absolution between Leon and Plarr at their death remains a problematic and ironic gesture in the direction of the Catholicism they have both left behind. The debate between Plarr and Leon is a more mature and telling version of an argument that has existed since the formalized and over-simple morality dialogue of the priest and the lieutenant in *The Power and the Glory*. The perfected version of the debate is to be found in the long conversations of the priest and his friend the Communist mayor in Greene's *Monsignor Quixote* (1982), where there is the leisure of the road in place of prison or siege with a mortal crisis hanging over the participants. Leon's case certainly does not simplify the issues: he has taken a wife, embraced violence, and been excommunicated by the Church, but he considers that, since he follows his conscience against outright hypocrisy and oppression, he is separated from the Church by mutual consent, not divorce. He looks forward to a renewed Church beyond "the temporary Church of these terrible years." Many details contribute to the picture of him as "a priest for ever" attempting to live out his priesthood on a new and strange plane. He breaks eggs over a pan and as he holds the shells the position of his fingers reminds Charlie Fortnum of the priest breaking the Host over the chalice. The faint trace of the tonsure through the hair that has grown is "like a prehistoric camp in a field seen from a plane." The debate is also complex because Plarr is not the exponent of traditional Christianity but of the wickedness of God, if there is a God, in such an evil world; and Leon shares something with him and the uprooted comedians of the novel since he too is trying to resolve an unsatisfied relationship with his father: in his case he is reacting against a rich and powerful father who had been a successful lawyer for the rich and for the ruling party in Paraguay.

The crux of the debate in the hut is reached when Leon attempts to counter Plarr's belief that the God who has created this world must be a monster, "that horror up there sitting in the clouds of heaven." "He does so by disarmingly accepting the responsibility of God for man's evil. He made us in his image—and so our evil is His evil too. How could I love God if he were not like me?" Responsibility is tempered by a belief in an evolving universe which recalls the echoes of Teilhard de Chardin in *A Burnt-Out Case:*

> When you speak of the horror, Eduardo, you are speaking of the night-side of God. I believe that the time will come when the night-side will wither away, like your communist state, Aquino, and we shall see only the simple daylight of the good God. It is a long struggle and a long suffering, evolution, and I believe God is suffering the same evolution that we are, but perhaps with more pain. . . .
>
> . . . I believe in Christ, I believe in the Cross and the Redemption. The Redemption of God as well as of Man. I believe that the day-side of God, in one moment of happy creation, produced perfect goodness, as a man might paint one perfect picture. God's good intention was for once completely fulfilled so that the night-side can never win more than a little victory here and there.

It is noteworthy here that the daring or unorthodoxy lies entirely in the luxury of speculation, and the speculation is used to buttress an unshakeable acceptance of the divinity of God in Christ and his love for men, and to reconcile that acceptance with "belief" in the intellectual or emotional sense in the fallen world evacuated by God. Leon, under pressure of his Indian wife Marta, says a Mass for his besieged band, without vestments or an altar. Before the *Domine, non sum dignus* the loudspeaker blares out its last message, "You have exactly one hour left to send out the Consul to us and save your lives." This again recalls the hurried Mass in the village in *The Power and the Glory* before the arrival of the police. In the circumstances of contemporary violence the rites of a religion of hope are celebrated, without ecclesiastical trappings, without intellectual assurance, but persisting along the road of choice and the assent of will. The apogee of this Christianity made naked is to be found in *Monsignor Quixote* when the absent God is sacrificed and worshipped through the mere motions of the Eucharist.

II

The love that is described in *The Honorary Consul* and the next novel, *The Human Factor* (1978), is, unusually for Greene, happy, or, at any rate, living, married love. No doubt this needs some qualification in regard to Clara and Charlie Fortnum: Clara is too passively simple to claim an active happiness, and her passivity is perhaps only stirred by Plarr; but the moment of communion Charlie feels with her at the end suggests a more harmonious future. It is a highly traditional realist novel ending in that it obliges the reader to think forward into continuing existences outside the text; yet the openness of Greene in handling the decisions of his characters in the course of the text precludes any dictatorial control by the author over what the future holds. The reader can only know that the text is not closed in upon itself but has referents in an imagined world of which it is merely a partial report, that Lady Macbeth indeed had children. Will Charlie go on drinking? Will Clara again be unfaithful? Even so, will the new bond between them somehow persist? (There will be the child of course, the conventional cementing of a marriage in so many stories, another instance of how Greene adapts and transforms the formulae of novelistic convention and of poor human nature.) The questions are as easy or difficult to answer as it is to decide the balance between selfishness and altruism in Brown's engineering Jones's escape in *The Comedians.* The printed pages of the text and the white pages of futurity are equally open, equally random in the strain they put upon human volition.

We do not encounter this degree of openness in *The Human Factor.* In the forefront of the book is a happy and equal marriage between a white man and a black woman of comparable intelligence and education with a child to whom they are attached. They are Greene's happiest couple, but their treatment by the plot is of the cruellest, leading to their apparently permanent separation in circumstances inimical to the peace of mind of each. One is bound to reflect that Greene is more inclined to favour the twisted and the fallen, a drunk and an ex-prostitute, than the normally happy; it is the same in the novella *Doctor Fischer of Geneva or the Bomb Party* (1980), where an idyllic marriage is shattered by the girl's early, fortuitous death in a skiing accident: but on the author's behalf it should be remembered that poor nature and traditional wisdom afford sufficient instances of such early deaths. What does emerge from what I call the "normality" of Maurice Castle and Sarah in *The Human Factor* is a certain externality of treatment: it is the divided, those at odds with the man within—Plarr, Brown, Querry, Fowler, Scobie—who enjoy the dubious luxury of a rich inner life.

Sarah is normal, or more ordinary, in another way. She is not a thin-boned waif-like child like so many of Greene's earlier women characters, Rose, Helen, Phuong and Clara. The temper of these women moves along an arc between two poles: at one pole they represent a challenging purity, as does Elizabeth in *The Man Within*, at the other extreme they offer the passive promiscuity of the whore to the men who are obsessed by their physique. The men are the isolated ones who have lost countries and beliefs, exiles from their own identity, and their obsession leads to the dangerous form of love that is pity. At this other pole the passivity of the child-women extinguishes their individuality and they move in flocks, chattering together like birds, as do Phuong and her sister, or the well-behaved girls in Mère Cathérine's brothel or in that of Señora Sanchez. For the permanently exiled the brothel becomes a home, a place for a pure and basic sexuality without the corruptions of any social superstructure, a nostalgic attempt to recover infantile joys. The primal scene of this regained domesticity is the table at which the girls quietly sit with their madam talking and sowing. We meet the scene again in *Monsignor Quixote* but there with a still more extraordinary viewpoint: the scene, which the exiles had found almost innocent as a point of rest amid the disturbance of their lives, is now seen through truly innocent eyes and from a life that is not disturbed. Maurice and Sarah live in a different emotional world: they do not need to recover childhood innocence: their son Sam (her child by another man before her marriage) can do that for them.

Maurice Castle works with his friend Davis in Section 6A of the Intelligence Services which deals with the affairs of Southern Africa. There is a suspected leak of information to Soviet Russia and a new head of security, Colonel Daintry, begins to investigate. The spy is in fact Maurice; he has been supplying secrets to the Russians for years, not for ideological reasons but to discharge a personal debt of his own estimation. He had worked under cover in South Africa and been assisted by Sarah and a Communist, Carson. When Maurice and Sarah become lovers the affair becomes known to the South African security police and the law moves against them. Maurice has to flee to Mozambique, leaving Sarah behind, but Carson is faithful to his promise to smuggle her out of the country to join him. The is the moral obligation, to a man and not to a party, which drives Maurice to disloyalty. His every clandestine act is a sacrifice to the freedom and safety of Sarah and Sam: the assumption is that states and organizations do not really exist as moral entities deserving obedience. The old man under the island's advice to cultivate disloyalty (in "Under the Garden") is now put into practice in a strangely manufactured situation. Humaneness and sentiment condone Maurice's action; so do the madness and unpleasantness of most of those in the organization he is supposed to serve: but his conscientious betrayal leads only to misery for the wife and child he loves. Since Maurice is a quiet man and happily married, suspicion over the leaks falls on his colleague Davis: Davis drinks too much, gambles, and is hopelessly in love with one of the girls in the office, Cynthia. The unpleasant Dr Percival, who is ostensibly a medical man but in actuality has an executive post in the service, undertakes to remove Davis by means of a new poison Aflotoxin, the symptoms of which may be confused with those of cirrhosis of the liver. It is noticeable at this point that Maurice must have become aware that Davis is suspected and under surveillance; the poison is being administered in gradual doses by Dr Percival and he is experiencing weakness in his legs and arms.

Is there here another instance of the betrayal of a friend by a man of sensitivity caught in a trap of conflicting loyalties, Scobie betraying Ali, Fowler sacrificing Pyle? It is not possible to give a positive answer to the question since Maurice does not apparently begin to suspect poisoning until after Davis's death. Maurice realizes that danger is coming near to him and wishes to resign but it is impossible at this stage.

A new operation is being planned, Operation Uncle Remus: it involves the close co-operation of the U.S. and Britain in the defence of the South African Republic by early warning systems and tactical nuclear weapons. Though Maurice has sent what purports to be his last report by a secret "drop" in a hollow tree on the common near his home, he considers that his Soviet masters must hear about Uncle Remus. He resorts to his usual channel of communication, a book code; the book he uses is Tolstoy's *War and Peace;* he has bought it, as he has bought other books, from Mr Halliday's respectable second-hand shop in Soho, opposite Mr Halliday's son's shop which is a pornographic establishment. He had always understood that it was the son who was his letter-box and he now gives Mr Halliday an urgent message for him; the son is picked up by the police on account of his business and Maurice waits for what he thinks must be certain arrest. Muller, the South African security officer who had been his opponent in the past and who is now connected with Uncle Remus, has an intuition of his treachery and informs Colonel Daintry. The latter visits Maurice and questions him but takes no immediate action. When "they" act to get him out of the country, their representative is the totally unexpected Mr Halliday, an underground Communist since his time as a Soviet prisoner after the post–World War I Archangel campaign. He is disguised and put on a plane to Paris as a blind man. His final destination is Moscow.

The epilogue is unrelievedly chilling. There is an account of Maurice's early days in Moscow, "under wraps" in almost complete isolation, of his reunion with his old contact Boris and of his beginning to learn Russian. Meanwhile Sarah is miserable in Surrey with her snobbish and narrow-minded mother-in-law. She learns from Dr Percival that since Sam is not on her passport she would never be able to rejoin Maurice unless she went alone: mother and son would not be allowed to go together. In Moscow Maurice has learned the same and the book ends with a desperately frustrated telephone conversation between husband and wife in which they exchange unconvincing hopes for reunion in the future until the line goes dead.

The Human Factor is not a novel of the high, confident distinction to be met in *The Comedians* and *The Honorary Consul.* It does however possess valuable qualities which are liable to be overlooked on a first reading. This is because of the book's relation to the genus of the spy thriller. Though light years away from James Bond, Greene clearly invites comparison with practitioners of the secret service romance like Len Deighton and John Le Carré. The comparison is very much to his advantage. It is as if an old cat had come away from the fireside to show that he can catch mice too as well or better than the frisking kittens. All the appurtenances are there, the drab realism of office routine, exposing the fact that most secret service work is deadly boring; the chief always called "C" (like the wartime chief of SIS); the oblique, fencing conversations of the principals over lunches at the Travellers or the Reform; the arcane vocabulary of "traces," "drops" and "covers"; the ultimate bestiality underneath the routine in the shape of the slow murder of the feckless and attractive Davis. Moreover, the plot of intrigue and eventual exposure is complex but not too complex; Greene does not indulge in the wanton obfuscation which some of his would-be rivals have substituted for subtlety, any more than he practises the exaggerated use of the "metaphysical" simile, modelled on his own earlier imagery. The whole sequence of the escape, from the appearance of Mr Halliday as *deus ex machina* to the safe arrival of Maurice on the Paris flight, is a brilliant achievement of adventure writing comparable to the episode of Brown and Jones on the road to Les Cayes or the account of the night spent by Fowler and Pyle in the watchtower and then in the paddy-field.

The effectiveness of all this has its dangers: it tends to mask the ways in which Greene is transforming the genre he has adopted (he had of course written a secret service thriller before largely for burlesque purposes in *Our Man in Havana*). Greene's major effort is towards humanizing the thriller form. In Le Carré and others this effort remains a pretension rather than an accomplished fact. The prime example of this humanity is the live marriage of Sarah and Maurice. Their life in the home counties moves quite apart from the corridors of power; its lowness of key is conveyed by the fact that Maurice has no car and goes to and from the station on a bicycle; the boy Sam is skilfully drawn, and there is a dog Buller, a rounded character, the epitome of a lovable but stupid animal, and surely a rare intrusion from children's fiction into a serious novel (Buller, like his master and mistress meets a terrible end: Maurice has to shoot him in order to escape quietly). Colonel Daintry does not like his work and he is last seen after the exposure of Maurice preparing his resignation; Sir John Hargreaves—"C"—is an old African hand who does not like the South African policeman Muller and regretfully remembers times in the bush when his boy was preparing his chop: between them they inevitably recall the Assistant Commissioner in *It's a Battlefield*, and are contrasted with the wholly horrible and contented Dr Percival who enjoys the game for its own sake but wants to be on the side that wins in his lifetime: since he has no real loyalties he is incapable of treachery. Early in the novel, looking at a Ben Nicholson on his host's wall with its boxes of colour, he reflects on the fragmented lives of people who live in their separate boxes:

> Take a look at that Nicholson. Such a clever balance. Squares of different colour. And yet living so happily together. No clash. The man has a wonderful eye. Change just one of the colours—even the size of the square, and it would be no good at all . . . There's your section 6. That's your square from now on. You don't need to worry about the blue and the red. All you have to do is to pinpoint our man and then tell me. You've no responsibility for what happens in the blue and red squares. In fact not even in the yellow. You just report. No bad conscience. No guilt.

But the integrated human beings in the book are those capable of feeling guilt and worrying about what goes on in the blue and red squares, in South Africa, for instance. Reference is again made to the coloured boxes of the abstract picture when Muller tells Maurice that, since they are now on the same side, they had better concentrate on seeing the same picture and Maurice replies "In fact we're in the same box?" There is a difficulty here for any more common view of moral obligation. Is not Maurice's conduct very far from being an integrated view of behaviour? Does not his betrayal of country and colleagues make him a partial man like others, concentrating on one box, in his case the red one? Greene would, one imagines, meet these objections by reminding us that Maurice is not a Communist and has not embraced an ideology: he is acting purely on a personal motive. Yet presumably once his choice has been made he can not abstain from weighing the camps against Dresden and Hiroshima, Hungary and Czechoslovakia against the Bay of Pigs, and so on. There is no sign that he does this. As for the ordinary human revulsion from treason, Greene's peculiar consciousness of human failure in relationships allows him to minimize any such shock. As he writes of the double agent Philby whom he compares to an English Catholic working for Spain in the reign of Elizabeth: " 'He betrayed his country'—yes, perhaps he did, but who among us has not committed treason to someone or something more important than a country?" He admires Philby for adhering to the faith he has found with "logical fanaticism" and not allowing liberal qualms to turn him into "a querulous outcast of the Koestler-Crankshaw-Muggeridge variety." But Maurice is not such a fanatic, and since his treason is only justifiable on personal and emotional grounds, we are bound to think of his indirect responsibility for the death of Davis.

Greene's peculiar belief in the entirely private valuation of action, as if decisions were taken quite apart from group codes or inherited standards, means that his study of Maurice has no room to examine the tensions and conflicts we would normally associate with the life of a sensitive man acting as a double agent. Maurice is just a good ordinary man who happens to be found out. Is it that his weakness is loving too much, for it is certainly his love for Sarah that launches him on his career as a double agent? The idea of an excessively scrupulous love, a love that becomes a devouring pity, is deliberately excluded. In fact it looks as if the earlier condemnation of pity is in process of revision:

> Why are some of us, he wondered, unable to love success or power or great beauty? Because we feel unworthy of them, because we feel more at home with failure? He didn't believe that was the reason. Perhaps one wanted the right balance, just as Christ had, that legendary figure whom he would have liked to believe in. "Come unto me all ye that travail and are heavy laden." . . . It wasn't pity, any more than it had been pity when he fell in love with Sarah pregnant by another man. He was there to right the balance. That was all.

This righting the balance, which excludes the inordinate pride of pitying others and is an imitation of the "legendary" Christ, is the moral spring of Maurice's action in a world where prescriptive morality is already suspended or tainted by the *Realpolitik* of the Dr Percivals. Righting the balance is a principle that reflects back on the conduct of Charlie Fortnum in *The Honorary Consul;* we might have expected, on the premisses of *The Heart of the Matter*, that in taking Clara out of the brothel his feelings for her would be contaminated by the superiority of pity, but this is not so: a balance has been adjusted, a burden lifted, and the conclusion leaves promise of more equal interchange.

The question remains of the narrow limits placed on human decision in Maurice's case. He is like Scobie in being caught in a trap, and he does not have Scobie's final clutching at faith as a way of release. He picks his last random sentence from *War and Peace:* "You say: I am not free. But I have lifted my hand and let it fall." But this freedom, whether in London or Moscow, is so curtailed as to be derisory. Like Scobie again finding peace in the bush, like Daintry and Hargreaves missing a simpler and more expansive past, or Davis wanting to exchange his office for Mozambique, he hankers after a state of things from which the perpetual nagging of detail and choice would be absent: " . . . a city where he could be accepted as a citizen, as a citizen without any pledge of faith, not the City of God or Marx, but the city called Peace of Mind."

The Human Factor is full of allusions to Greene's past and to his earlier work. Maurice's home is in Berkhamstead where Greene grew up; the story is strongly localized in the station, the canal, particularly the common. Sam plays at hide and seek there with his father and Davis, as Greene had done, and the game corresponds to the adult games of secret service. The poems Sam likes Maurice to read reproduce the intense early emotions stimulated by poetry as they are described in *A Sort of Life*. There is also a confessional episode: Maurice goes into a Catholic church in Watford but encounters an unsympathetic priest who tells him he is wasting his time and that what he needs is a doctor. The theme of the clash between the need of the penitent and the advice received stretches back through the severity of Father Rank towards Scobie in the confessional to Greene's own experience when, planning marriage and afraid that he might be epileptic, he was advised simply to trust in God.

These allusions to recurring themes in the fiction and to crucial experiences in his past endow the book with a special character which marks it off from the common genre of the spy thriller, however excellently written. Greene has indeed humanized the thriller form but he has done something else too. He has written a sort of running commentary on his own kind of novel. Every novelist with each new novel creates a fresh disguise for the single novel he is writing all the time; and the novelist late in his career and at the summit of his skills finds that his remaining subject-matter lies more and more in the fruits of his past inventions and in his experience as a writer. Greene had in *Travels with my Aunt* (1969) already begun the game of literary allusions based on his earlier work; there is a visit to Brighton, and the introduction in person of the elderly crook Visconti who is a humorous reincarnation of the evil Renaissance tyrant who had thrilled the boy Greene in the pages of Marjorie Bowen.

In *The Human Factor* the function of the allusiveness is to bring the writer home to Berkhamstead. The theme of the frontier between custom and moral choice is approached by a return to the psychic origins: the spy-game on the familiar common merges into reality. As Greene quotes elsewhere from AE: "In the lost boyhood of Judas Christ was betrayed." A childhood hiding-place becomes a letter-box and a "drop" for a real coded message. The relating of the past to the present at both the fictional and the personal levels, Castle's and Greene's, makes the drama of espionage the vehicle for a statement about aging. Maurice Castle's treachery is mitigated in its impact on the reader, not simply because he is a decent person and not a political fanatic, but because the real betrayer is time. His loyalty is to his wife, a son, and the memory of a friend, not to Communist ideology; but the past catches up with him and separates him from his wife. He had identified himself with her plight under the "colour bar" in South Africa: now an even more cruel exile divides them. The son is not his son, and his very growth, the excited happiness of the all too suggestive game of hide and seek he plays with Davis on the common, throws Castle's aging into relief, as all children must do. The friend whose generosity of spirit was his main incentive in his clandestine course, dies, and again the past recedes leaving him stranded by his choices. So the final frustrated telephone conversation with Sarah and the interrupted line have been long prepared.

There is thus an elegiac quality about the book and an isolation of its central character which form its distinctive features. Maurice bears his isolation, even in its final form, with dignity, yet there results from it an inevitable narrowing of the scope of the work, beset as he and his family are by the sinister mad hatter's tea-party of the secret world embodied in Dr Percival and his vision of life as an amoral pattern of abstract squares. Seen in these terms, of time, closed inherited choices, and the ensuing constriction, the novel is a considerable achievement. It lacks however the openness and expansive scope of *The Honorary Consul*, and the contrast enables us to recognize the outstanding merit of the latter book. It is not just that the freedom of the characters, of Plarr, Charlie, Clara and Leon, allows us to hope, and thus provides some humanistic palliative, a guarantee that history can encroach thus far upon us and no further. That is not at all a message to be deduced from a text where history presses hard enough on both sides of the great river, the Parana. We have already seen that the freedom and the hope do not produce certainties, since the future of Charlie and Clara, the survivors, remains problematic. But the freedom, like the vast air, the huge pampas, the thick jungle beyond the river, is a freedom for the characters to grow. Plarr changes as a man, not like Brown in *The Comedians* by making a few right decisions and then resuming the comedian's role, but by learning at least a jealous love in place of indifference; Clara falls in love indeed, while Charlie discovers within his foolish private self enormous reserves of strength and moral tact. It is this growth of the characters within the text which is a new departure for Greene, and which, demonstrated through an assured and transparent technical assurance, communicates to the reader a sense of exhilarating freedom.

GRAHAME SMITH

A Burnt-Out Case

Greene himself is at pains to stress the "new elements" [in *A Burnt-Out Case*] and believes that it "marked a turning-point in my work . . . in it I think I succeeded . . . in breaking the pattern in the carpet." However, this shift is not quite so straightforward as Greene suggests. I have argued [elsewhere] that *Our Man in Havana* represents a change of direction in both its comedy and in the tenderness with which it treats human relationships. But, such is the inconvenience of creative writers to critics, this new tone is hardly apparent in the next novel, not at any rate at its artistic centre, the character and situation of Querry. Comedy is present in the savage treatment of Rycker and Parkinson, although of a decidedly dark kind, and there is tenderness perhaps around the edges of the book, in the innocent gaiety of the priests and in what we infer of Dr Colin's relationship with his now dead wife.

So there is continuity as well as development here, and possibly the most interesting link with *Our Man in Havana* is the extension of Greene's creative response to the role of the media in the modern world and, within this, the special place of the serious writer. Personal experience is, once again, relevant to our understanding of the work of art. After what he calls the "great vulgar" success of *The Heart of the Matter*, Greene was transformed into a public figure, at the mercy of intrusions into his life of every possible kind. This characteristic process of modern civilisation is bound to be trivialising, invariably ignoring the complexities of creative work itself in favour of gossip and personality. Many years ago, the *Daily Express* newspaper found

From *The Achievement of Graham Greene*. © 1986 by Grahame Smith. Barnes & Noble Books, Totowa, New Jersey, 1986.

it necessary to tell its no doubt bemused readers that the once, in its view, monkishly reclusive T. S. Eliot was now taking dancing lessons; a photograph of an equally bemused Mr Eliot was intended to validate his newfound joy in the pleasures of the ordinary man. A favourite target for this colour-supplement treatment was Picasso whose "life-style" was clearly grist to the mill of bourgeois fantasies of *la vie de Bohème*. The process, dependent on such technological advances as photography and widespread newspaper distribution, began at least as early as the middle of the nineteenth century, one of its first victim-beneficiaries being Dickens. The extraordinary popular success of *The Pickwick Papers* was partly a media event in its own day and led to a whole range of commercial "spin-offs" in the shape of clothes modelled on those of Dickens's characters, pottery figures, engravings, and so on. Dickens's attitude to all this was clearly much more ambiguous than Greene's; whatever its irritations, he gloried in what he saw as an almost personal involvement with a huge audience. But he was nonetheless public property and so vulnerable to a whole range of demands. Perhaps the most insistent were begging-letters, a source of exasperation in life which Dickens transforms into a great comic fantasy of importunity in the novels. When Greene found himself translated instantly into a Catholic author by the success of *The Heart of the Matter*, he was deluged by letters demanding spiritual comfort (and, on occasion, something more) by hosts of people, above all priests and women, a dilemma transformed into hilariously bitter comedy in *Ways of Escape*. But whatever the laughter this induces in the reader, it was obviously no joke for the recipient. Greene felt himself "used and exhausted by the victims of religion," maddened by "cries for spiritual assistance" in the face of which he felt impotent.

Some of this sense of a world moulded by press and publicity gets into *Our Man in Havana*. In *A Burnt-Out Case*, however, truly savage reprisals are taken against its agents and abettors. The grotesquely fat journalist, Parkinson, draws a vampire-like sustenance from his three million readers of the *Post* which makes him believe that he can manipulate Querry's reputation at will: "I told you I was going to build you up. . . . Unless . . . I find it makes a better story to pull you down" (part 6, chap. 2). And Greene parodies his yellow-press style with consummate ease, from his muddled use of Conrad's *Heart of Darkness* to his picture of Querry as a St Francis with "birds shitting in your hair" (part 4, chap. 3). But the novel moves beyond this wickedly accurate caricature to reveal how media distortion has its roots in the media-distortions of "ordinary" life. It is worth quoting at some length Rycker's (the local factory manager) response to Querry's arrival, probably Greene's most repellently critical portrait of a Roman Catholic:

> In my opinion . . . he may well be the greatest thing to happen in Africa since Schweitzer, and Schweitzer after all is a Protestant. I found him a most interesting companion when he stayed with us. And have you heard the latest story? . . . He went out into the bush two weeks ago, they say, to find a leper who had run away. He spent the whole night with him in the forest, arguing and praying, and he persuaded the man to return and complete his treatment. It rained in the night and the man was sick with fever, so he covered him with his body.
>
> (part 3, chap. 1)

This is language emptied of all personal content, used not in the service of thought and feeling, but as a mould that will force Querry's actions into some preconceived pattern regardless of his own motives or intentions. Just as his wife's romantic, and ultimately disastrous, fantasies are embodied in the language of her women's magazine, *Chantal*, so Rycker's speech and vision of the world are taken from the works of popular theology in which he is so immersed. Spontaneous living is thus nullified by a betrayal of language which instantly hardens it into a series of meaningless gestures and moral clichés.

There is evidently an element of corrosive self-criticism at work here. Parkinson is like a grotesque parody of Greene's journalistic activities, dragging his huge bulk into dangerous places in search of a story while he fires off his absurdly wrongly attributed quotations. With brilliant wit, Greene presents him as the apostle and martyr of a new faith, that three million readers of the *Post* cannot be wrong. His Remington portable and Rolleiflex camera are placed like the first and second thief on either side of Father Thomas's crucifix and, when he complains of what he has suffered in the cause—"Three times in a restaurant somebody hit me"—for "a moment he sounded like St Paul" (part 6, chap. 2). The cruelly comic deflation of Parkinson is apt and just, but deeper issues are raised also. Parkinson is a user, or misuser, of language, the same medium as that of the novelist, and his apparently widely accepted corruption of the medium of communication between human beings casts doubt on the novelist's ability to rehabilitate the language of the tribe. Perhaps three million readers of the *Post* can't be wrong. However mistakenly, Greene seems to have felt himself to be a part of this debilitating process for he writes of *The Heart of the Matter*, with cruel self-condemnation, that there "must have been something corrupt there, for the book appealed too often to weak elements in its readers." The problem is clarified by a passage from *Our Man in Havana* when Beatrice and Wormald sit watching a pornographic film, a "blue print of love. Similar movements of the body had once meant more to them than anything else the world had to offer. The act of lust and the act of love are the same" (bk. 4, chap. 1). The language of the body and the language of words have this much in common, that their outer identity may clothe entirely different feelings and motives. But although the physical movements which express love and lust are the same, it might be argued that the differences between Parkinson's writing and Greene's are obvious enough. Greene, however, refuses to let himself off so lightly at this stage in his career. The crisis engendered by *The Heart of the Matter* was a matter of style in a radically serious sense and he was made agonisingly aware of the pitfalls into which a false style might lure the unwary. My own view is that it is wrong to blame aspirin for the use that fools make of it, but one must admire the sense of responsibility towards his readers, and his craft, revealed in Greene's fear that his novel had proved a spiritual morass for those of uncertain faith.

That these preoccupations were in the forefront of his mind in the period leading up to *A Burnt-Out Case* is demonstrated by his return to Conrad after abandoning him "about 1932 because his influence on me was too great and too disastrous." As he rereads *Heart of Darkness* on his own journey upriver Conrad's "heavy hypnotic style falls round me again, and I am aware of the poverty of my own." Again, the judgement is cruelly harsh, even allowing for Greene's lapses into banal local colour, the over-use of simile, the sometimes mechanical reliance on key words such as "peace." But out of this harshness Greene reaps a rich reward, both for *A Burnt-Out Case* and for his later work. His next novel, *The Comedians*, will command a rich expansiveness quite without padding or decoration, but for *A Burnt-Out Case* a kind of stylistic purity seemed perhaps the only way to meet the challenge of human suffering on a plane of complete seriousness. Greene's fertility of invention is remarkable here, for the novel's theme and subject-matter might have suggested a return to the visionary intensity of the period beginning with *Brighton Rock*. Instead of his harking back, however, Greene discovers a totally new manner which answers perfectly to the note he wants to strike in this work. Despite the circumstances surrounding its genesis, there is none of the exhaustion so evident in *The Quiet American*. The burnt-out quality present throughout the novel is, in fact, a telling embodiment of the state of mind and feeling, or absence of feeling, that Greene is seeking to convey.

Querry's, and Greene's, journey is an inner one, a voyage to the interior of the self in a Congo which is a "region of the mind" (Dedication) and so any hint of mere exoticism in the writing would be totally out of place. Instead of this, setting is touched in only lightly:

> White flowers had opened with twilight on the long avenue; fires were being lit for the evening meal, and the mercy of darkness was falling at last over the ugly and the deformed. The wrangles of the night had not yet begun, and peace was there, something you could touch like a petal or smell like wood smoke. Querry said to Colin, "You know I am happy here." He closed his mouth on the phrase too late; it had escaped him on the sweet evening air like an admission.
>
> (part 4, chap. 2)

This delicacy comes from a writer who complains of the poverty of his style! And its sparse beauty is characteristic of every aspect of the novel. The setting is rigorously limited, with just enough trips away from the *leproserie* to avoid monotony. Language is spare, supple, free of clogging adjectives, and similes seem to float naturally to the surface of Greene's prose rather than being snatched from some storehouse of strained comparisons: "Every rib in the child's body showed. It was like a cage over which a dark cloth has been flung at night to keep a bird asleep, and like a bird his breath moved under the cloth" (part 2, chap. 3). Characterisation is deft and sure-footed. Dr Colin is beautifully realised through dialogue and action, with only occasional shifts into his point of view, and the sparseness of our information about him in no way impedes his sense of life. Even Querry lacks the tortured complexity of, say, Scobie. His pain is the pain of being unable to feel and his "case" is fairly straightforward.

This achieved simplicity is, however, the very reverse of simple-minded. Greene made his journey with a novel already beginning to form in his consciousness and the processes lying behind its full realisation are recorded in "Congo Journal" with an interest, excitement even, that gives the reader an awareness of the joys, as well as the trials, of creation. The journeyings here are manifold: Querry's and Greene's literal and metaphorical journeys, the exploration represented by the completed novel, and then the voyage into the creative process itself experienced through "Congo Journal." One moment in this last journey has a peculiar intensity of interest, Greene's discovery of the "fit" between the novel's various elements, above all between Querry and the setting:

> Leprosy cases whose disease has been arrested and cured only after the loss of fingers or toes are known as burnt-out cases. This is the parallel I have been seeking between my character X and the lepers. Psychologically and morally he has been burnt-out.

Here perhaps one can find an explanation of how the book's pared-down quality is perfectly compatible with various kinds of complexity. The complete fusion of character, setting, theme and language allows a richness and intensity of meaning to arise with unforced naturalness. This intensity, too, has its own special quality in the novel. Intensity may stem from the fusion of levels we find in, say *The Heart of the Matter* and *The End of the Affair*. The intensity of *A Burnt-Out Case* comes from a stripping away of the surface elements of human life in order to reveal a bedrock of character and theme.

This burning away of inessentials, to put it another way, suggests that Greene's fictional mode here is, in yet another new development, essentially allegorical and many features of the novel substantiate this. Taking a perhaps unconscious hint from Conrad's Kurtz, Greene worries in "Congo Journey" over the necessity of naming his central character because he is "unwilling to give him a definite nationality." The problem is neatly solved in the novel itself: " 'My name is Querry,' he introduced himself, speaking in an accent which Colin could not quite place as French or Flemish any more than he could immediately identify the nationality of the name" (part 1, chap. 2). In thus loosing his protagonist at such an early stage from the moorings of realism, Greene opens the way to a voyage of inner exploration through a figure with more than a hint of Everyman. The arresting oddity of his name also pushes one towards an allegorical reading: "query" and "quest" come irresistibly to mind. There's an element of risk and daring here which surely justifies Greene's belief that the novel contains "new elements." Another example is the mysterious Pendélé which echoes so strangely throughout the book. We're deeply familiar by now with the importance of "peace" in Greene's imaginative vocabulary. It's often identified with a generalised state of being, sometimes it is located in early childhood, but never before has it borne a specific name with its implied avowal of the possibility of an actual place of peace. Querry hears it first when he journeys into the forest in search of Deo Gratias, an experience which he later feels "seemed a night when things began": "Deo Gratias grunted twice, and uttered a word. It sounded like 'Pendélé.' In the darkness the knuckles felt like a rock that has been eroded for years by the weather" (part 1, chap 4). The whole episode is a perfect little exemplar of the novel's general method. It is completely acceptable on the realistic level; Deo Gratias falls into a hole and Querry, in whom interest "began to move painfully . . . like a nerve that has been frozen" (part 1, chap. 4), goes to look for him. But an allegorical quest fits easily with the vividly realised little adventure just as Deo Gratias's fingerless hand has a rock-like quality completely in keeping with the novel's attempt to reach down to solid foundations. Querry evokes a Pendélé for Marie Rycker, of the simplicities of her family life as an unmarried girl, and dreams of sailing to it himself by going even deeper into the jungle than the *leproserie*, just before his peace of mind is destroyed by Parkinson's newspaper article on him. But Querry's tragedy is that he was clearly in the process of finding his Pendélé within the *leproserie* itself. "*Nouse étions heureux*," says Deo Gratias in reply to Querry's questioning about the past he was evidently seeking to rediscover when he was lost and injured in the jungle, and Querry's own admissions of growing contentment, peace, happiness even, suggest that his Pendélé was around him if he could have remained safe from the intrusions of Parkinson, the agent of the gossip column and media publicity.

Yet another allegorical feature is suggested by Greene's Dedication to the doctor of the Yonda Missions where he stayed while gathering material for the novel:

> This is not a *roman à clef*, but an attempt to give dramatic expression to various types of belief, half-belief, and non-belief, in the kind of setting, removed from world-politics and household-preoccupations, where such differences are felt acutely and find expression.

This pin-points the book's element of metaphysical discussion which emerges through its series of fascinating exchanges between Querry, Dr Colin, the Superior, Rycker, and so on. Greene skilfully avoids the dangers inherent in fictional debate: one thinks of those achingly long pages of discussion in *The Magic Mountain* or Stephen's disquisition on aesthetics to Cranly at the end of *A Portrait of the Artist as a Young Man*. Greene's exchanges are pithy without being superficial and they gain complexity from their unforced relationship to a perfectly chosen setting. The characters' arguments about God's existence and nature take place in a context which is both a test of belief and a justification for unbelief for, as we are unobtrusively reminded, they frequently occur within sight of monstrous human suffering. A passage quite early in the book demonstrates a compassion with neither sentimentality nor voyeurism:

> The air in the hospital lay heavily and sweetly upon them: it was never moved by a fan or a breeze. Querry was conscious of the squalor of the bedding—cleanliness was not important to the leper, only to the healthy. The patients brought their own mattresses which they had probably possessed for a lifetime—rough sacking from which the straw had escaped. The bandaged feet lay in the straw like ill-wrapped packages of meat. On the veranda the walking cases sat out of the sun—if you could call a walking

> case a man who, when he moved, had to support his huge swollen testicles with both hands. A woman with palsied eyelids who could not close her eyes or even blink sat in a patch of shade out of the merciless light. A man without fingers nursed a baby on his knee, and another man lay flat on the veranda with one breast long and drooping and teated like a woman's.
>
> (part 2, chap. 3)

In this context, theological discussion is the reverse of academic, honed to a cutting edge by the implacable presence of the outer limits of human misery.

But however strong the allegorical emphasis of *A Burnt-Out Case*, its meanings are finally worked through in the life of a central personality, Querry, although here too the allegorical mode shapes Greene's characterisation. Querry has gone so far down the road of human nullity that his regeneration is marked not by a melodramatic transformation, but by the simplest evidence of what it means to be human, conveyed in fictional motifs of naked simplicity. Querry detests "laughter like a bad smell" (part 1, chap. 1) and is, in fact, physically incapable of laughing or even smiling. His capacity for feeling is frozen; as it thaws he begins to develop a "twitch of the mouth that Colin was beginning to recognize as a rudimentary smile" (part 4, chap. 1). This most basic form of human communication—we see the baby's smile as one of the first signs of its developing humanity—becomes possible as the atrophied nerves of Querry's emotions and interest in others begin to flicker into life. Greene's art succeeds triumphantly in this area of potential banality by convincing us that the change, simple as it appears, is momentous for Querry. And the danger of over-simplification is avoided by the irony that his new-found capacity for laughter is the direct cause of his death when the murderously jealous Rycker interprets Querry's "odd awkward sound" (part 6, chap. 3) as directed at himself.

Given that *A Burnt-Out Case* is such a relatively short novel, Greene is remarkably successful in suggesting the passage of time and, with it, a series of worked-out and believable changes in Querry's character. This is partly achieved by a skilful manipulation of memory, centering on an opposition between discomfort and suffering. Towards the end of the book Querry remarks to Dr Colin " 'I suffer, therefore I am.' I wrote something like that once in my diary, but I can't remember what or when, and the word wasn't 'suffer' " (part 6, chap. 3). What he did write, in the novel's first sentence, was "a parody of Descartes: 'I feel discomfort, therefore I am alive.' " Discomfort is entirely personal, of course; an itch, an ache, a bad smell are powerful reminders of the self, capable of distracting us from the beauty of art, nature, another person. Suffering, on the other hand, can hardly be entirely egotistical. However self-pitying we may be, suffering brings us inescapably into relation with others, either in what is done to us or in what we do. Querry believes that his moral and spiritual mutilation has gone so far that suffering is impossible for him and asks Dr Colin to teach him how to suffer because "I only know the mosquito-bites" (part 5, chap. 1). Again, this is an echo from something much earlier when the Superior of a mission had remarked, in response to Querry's admission of emotional deadness, "Oh well, you know, suffering is something which will always be provided when it is required" (part 1, chap. 1). Querry learns to feel suffering again through the awakening of his personal interest in Deo Gratias, as well as in the general plight of the lepers, but the context in which this is achieved is, once more, crucial. Paradoxically, Querry finds suffering through the peace of the mission. The atheist Dr Colin and the Catholic priests are united in one thing, their overriding involvement in bettering the lepers' existence. Their lives are so dominated by practicalities that they have no time or inclination to badger Querry with either pleas for help or spiritual enquiries. In short, they leave him in peace and this, all unwittingly, becomes a therapy through which Querry is able to feel his way back into human concerns; a peace threatened and ultimately destroyed by the pestering intrusions of the media-dominated outer world in the person of Parkinson with his determination to turn Querry into the Hermit of the Congo.

Mention of Parkinson returns us to those themes of writing, publicity, gossip and the role of the novelist with which I began and which may help us to see an important link between the novel and Greene's own life. Greene clearly dreads the simple-minded reader's equation of a central character with himself; indeed, one of his most frequently repeated admonitions concerns the necessity of making an absolute separation between author and protagonist. This makes all the more interesting an admission which occurs in a fascinating exchange of letters with Evelyn Waugh recorded in *Ways of Escape:*

> With a writer of your genius and insight I certainly would not attempt to hide behind the time-old gag that an author can never be identified with his characters. Of course in some of Querry's reactions there are reactions of mine, just as in some of Fowler's reactions in *The Quiet American* there are reactions of mine. I suppose the points where an author is in agreement with his character lend what force or warmth there is to the expression. At the same time I think one can say that a parallel must not be

> drawn all down the line and not necessarily to the conclusion of the line. Fowler, I hope, was a more jealous man than I am, and Querry, I fear, was a better man than I am. I wanted to give expression to various states or modes of belief and unbelief.

The justness of these comments is undeniable and in no way negates the writer/character dichotomy. Eliot's separation of the man who suffers and the writer who creates was surely a stratagem to obscure the personal suffering that lay behind *The Waste Land* rather than a critical dictum of universal value. Can anyone seriously believe that Shakespeare was in a totally equable frame of mind when he wrote *King Lear?* This no more equates Shakespeare with Lear than it does Greene with Querry; rather, it reminds us of a balance of forces necessary for the creation of art. The Turkish-bath of total subjectivism and the icy chill of complete objectivity are equally undesirable. Personal feeling dramatised in character, image and action is the hallmark of good literature. At any rate, all the evidence suggests that it is this combination that makes *A Burnt-Out Case* such a powerful book.

As with Wormald in *Our Man in Havana*, we are reminded of similarities between Querry and the novelist, sometimes by Querry himself:

> A writer doesn't write for his readers, does he? Yet he has to take elementary precautions all the same to make them comfortable. My interest was in space, light, proportion. New materials interested me only in the effect they might have on those three. . . . Materials are the architect's plot. They are not his motive for work. . . . The subject of a novel is not the plot. Who remembers what happened to Lucien de Rubempré in the end?
>
> (part 2, chap. 3)

But these hints of similarity are, finally, only a preparation for the extraordinary "parable" he recounts to Marie Rycker to pass a sleepless night. The allegorical mode is successfully dominant at this point, in Greene's reliance on a device which seems to echo the interpolated tales of eighteenth and nineteenth-century fiction and which encapsulates his theme with a directness barred to the realist, despite Querry's built-in denial of an autobiographical interest: "No, you mustn't draw close parallels. They always say a novelist chooses from his general experience of life, not from special facts" (part 6, chap. 1). The underlying seriousness of this astonishing episode in no way inhibits its brilliance. At one point, Querry accuses Marie of being "like so many critics. You want me to write your own sort of story," a moment at which Greene's personal exasperation with his own critics surfaces with mordant relish. When Querry's protagonist ceases to believe in the King (God, of course) he fashions exquisite objects for frivolous and morally doubtful purposes, but this makes no difference to the judges of his work who see moral seriousness (" 'satires on the age' ") despite the protagonist's intentions. Intentionality is a key aspect of the parable, in fact, as it is of *A Burnt-Out Case* itself. In their different ways, Parkinson and Father Thomas totally disregard Querry's motives in coming to the Congo; indeed, there is something maddening in the perversity with which they ignore the reality of his existence in their determination to shape it for their own purposes. The novelist who happens to be a Catholic—rather than a Catholic novelist—has his revenge here as he flicks his scourge over those who perpetrate on Querry's protagonist such critical fatuities as *The Toad in the Hole: The Art of Fallen Man* and who persist in regarding him as "the Jeweller of Original Sin."

The despair generated by misunderstanding is, however, not far below this amusing surface. Plato's parable of the perfectly unjust man comes to mind as Querry's ambiguous hero—Marie quickly realises that he is an architect as well as a jeweller and it's not hard for the reader to see that he is also a novelist—moves triumphantly through life: "articles in the papers praised his jewellery, women cheated their husbands and went to bed with him, and servants of the King acclaimed him as a loyal and faithful subject." Even his sexual behaviour can be accounted for as a "great capacity for love," the formula used by the mission's intelligent and sympathetic Superior puzzling over Querry's relationship with Marie Rycker after his death: "Judging from Parkinson's second article he would seem to have been a man with a great capacity—well—for love" (part 6, chap. 3).

But if Querry's parable is straightforwardly allegorical in its equation of the King with God and the Jeweller with Querry and, ultimately, Greene himself (the "time-old gag" cannot be perpetrated here surely), there is nothing schematic about its meaning. Greene excoriates his *bête noire*, the suburban Catholicism which sees the Christian life as a simple matter of rewards and punishments. In Querry's story, the "good" often apparently suffer in temporal life while the "wicked" prosper ("the girl was more beautiful with her virginity gone"), but "that made no difference because the King was the King of the dead too and you couldn't tell what terrible things he might do to them in the grave." The protagonist's boredom and spiritual emptiness aren't, however, the end of the matter: "I wouldn't know, but I'm told that there were moments when he wondered if his unbelief were not after all a final conclusive proof of the King's existence. This total vacancy might be his punishment for the rules he had wilfully broken." Querry and Greene himself I think, shy away from this problem which is "complicated to the point of absurdity," just as Greene himself loathes the labyrinthine complications foisted on such problems as whether or not Scobie is saved as he falls to the floor from the effects of his overdose. What is unproblematic is that telling his "sad story" gives Querry a "sense of freedom and release," that his confession—for it is nothing else—leaves him sitting in an "hour of coolness" with the thought "the King is dead, long live the King. Perhaps he had found here a country and a life" (part 6, chap. 1).

In the same way his death leads to a final, unresolved, debate between the Superior and Dr Colin in which each seeks to claim Querry for his own. Uncertainty is followed by horror at the realisation that a child of three, a small and delightful presence in the novel, has become infected with leprosy. These emotions are balanced, however, although not cancelled, by the fact that Querry has left behind something of permanent value, the hospital which had come to play a central role in his existence: "The roof-tree had been battered and bent by the storm, but it was held in place still by its strong palm-fibre thongs" (part 6, chap. 3).

Chronology

1904	Born October 2, at Berkhamsted, Hertfordshire.
1922–25	Student at Balliol College, Oxford.
1925	Publishes a book of verse, *Babbling April.*
1925–26	Works as a reporter for the *Nottingham Journal.*
1926	Is received into the Catholic Church, and begins working as an assistant editor for *The Times,* in London.
1929	*The Man Within.*
1930	*The Name of Action.*
1931	*Rumour at Nightfall.*
1932	*Stamboul Train.*
1934	*It's a Battlefield.* Journeys through West Africa, Liberia, and Sierra Leone.
1935	Publishes a book of stories, *The Basement Room.* Begins working as a film critic for the *Spectator.*
1936	*A Gun for Sale* (U.S. title: *This Gun for Hire*).
1938	*Brighton Rock.* Takes a trip through Mexico, about which he publishes the travel book *The Lawless Roads* in 1939.
1940	*The Power and the Glory.* Works as literary editor for the *Spectator.*
1941–44	Receives station in the British Foreign Office. Film version of *A Gun for Sale* produced in Hollywood in 1942. Agent with the British Secret Service in Sierra Leone, 1942–43.
1943	*Ministry of Fear.*

1947 *Nineteen Stories.*

1948 *The Heart of the Matter.*

1951 *The Lost Childhood* (essays) and *The End of the Affair.* Employed as a foreign correspondent in Kenya and Malaya.

1953 *The Living Room* (play) published and produced in London.

1954 *Twenty-One Stories.* Foreign correspondent in Indo-China for *The New Republic.*

1955 *Loser Take All* and *The Quiet American.*

1957 *The Potting Shed* (play) published and produced in London.

1958 *Our Man in Havana.*

1959 *The Complaisant Lover* (play) published and produced in London. Takes a trip to the Congo.

1961 *A Burnt-Out Case.*

1963 *In Search of Reality.*

1964 The play *Carving a Statue* produced in London.

1966 *The Comedians.*

1967 *May We Borrow Your Husband?* (collection of stories).

1969 *Collected Essays, Travels with My Aunt.*

1971 *A Sort of Life* (autobiography).

1973 *The Honorary Consul.*

1974 *Lord Rochester's Monkey* (biography).

1977 Member of the Panamanian delegation to Washington for the signing of the Canal Treaty.

1978 *The Human Factor.*

1980 *Doctor Fischer of Geneva, or the Bomb Party* and the autobiographical work *Ways of Escape.*

1982 *Monsignor Quixote.*

1983 Grand Cross Order of Vasco Núñez de Balboa, awarded by Panama.

1984 *Getting to Know the Generals.*

1985 *The Tenth Man.*

Contributors

HAROLD BLOOM, Sterling Professor of the Humanities at Yale University, is the author of *The Anxiety of Influence*, *Poetry and Repression*, and many other volumes of literary criticism. His forthcoming study, *Freud: Transference and Authority*, attempts a full-scale reading of all of Freud's major writings. A MacArthur Prize Fellow, he is general editor of five series of literary criticism published by Chelsea House.

R. W. B. LEWIS, author of *The American Adam* and *The Picaresque Saint*, has also edited critical volumes of Whitman, Melville, and Edith Wharton. He was awarded the Pulitzer Prize for his biography of Wharton in 1976. He is the Gray Professor of Rhetoric at Yale University.

FRANK KERMODE was King Edward VII Professor of English Literature at Cambridge University, and is now Professor of English at Columbia University. He is the author of critical works on Lawrence, Shakespeare, Donne, and Wallace Stevens, and works of critical theory, such as *The Sense of an Ending*, *The Genesis of Secrecy*, *Forms of Attention*, and *The Classic*.

ELIZABETH HARDWICK is a novelist and essayist, whose works include *Sleepless Nights* and *A View of My Own*. She has been a frequent contributor to *The New York Review of Books* and *The New Yorker*.

FREDERICK R. KARL has written Reader's Guides to the *Eighteenth Century Novel*, the *Nineteenth Century British Novel*, and the *Contemporary English Novel*.

MIRIAM ALLOTT has edited volumes of Keats, Shelley, Emily Bronte, and Charlotte Bronte.

A. A. DEVITIS, in addition to his critical volume on Graham Greene, is the author of *Roman Holiday: The Catholic Novels of Evelyn Waugh*. He is Professor of English at Purdue University.

TERRY EAGLETON is best known for his works on critical theory, particularly Marxist literary criticism. His most recent work is *Against the Grain*, a collection of essays.

J. A. WARD teaches at Rice University and is the author of *The Imagination of Disaster: Evil in the Fiction of Henry James* and *The Search for Form: Studies in the Structure of James' Fiction*.

ROGER SHARROCK is the editor of volumes of Dryden and Wordsworth, and is the author of *John Bunyan* and *Saints, Sinners and Comedians*.

GRAHAME SMITH is the author of *The Achievement of Graham Greene* and *The Novel and Society: Defoe to George Eliot*.

Bibliography

Allen, W. Gore. "Evelyn Waugh and Graham Greene." *Irish Monthly* 77 (1949): 16–22.

Allen, Walter. "The Novels of Graham Greene." In *Writers of Today*, edited by Denys Val Baker, 15–27. London: Sedgewick & Jackson, 1946.

Barnes, Robert J. "Two Modes of Fiction: Hemingway and Greene." *Renascence* 14 (1962): 193–98.

Boardman, Gwenn R. *Graham Greene: The Aesthetics of Exploration*. Gainesville: University of Florida Press, 1971.

Bowen, Elizabeth. "Story, Theme, and Situation." *Listener* 56, no. 1439 (1956): 651–52.

Brock, D. Heyward, and James M. Welsh. "Graham Greene and the Structure of Salvation." *Renascence* 27 (1974): 31–39.

Connelly, Francis X. "Inside Modern Man: The Spiritual Adventures of Graham Greene." *Renascence* 1 (1949): 16–23.

Cosman, Max. "An Early Chapter in Graham Greene." *Arizona Quarterly* 11 (1955): 143–47.

Costello, D. P. "Graham Greene and the Catholic Press." *Renascence* 12 (1959): 3–28.

Coulthard, A. R. "Graham Greene's 'The Hint of an Explanation.' " *Studies in Short Fiction* 8 (1971): 601–5.

DeVitis, A. A. "The Entertaining Mr. Greene." *Renascence* 14 (1961): 8–24.

Dinkins, Paul. "Graham Greene: The Incomplete Version." *Catholic World* 176 (1952): 96–102.

Downing, Francis. "Graham Greene and the Case for Disloyalty." *Commonweal* 55 (1952): 564–66.

Duffy, Joseph M. "The Lost World of Graham Greene." *Thought* 33 no. 129 (1958): 229–47.

Ellis, William D., Jr. "The Grand Theme of Graham Greene," *Southwest Review* 41 (1956): 239–50.

Fetrow, Fred M. "The Function of Geography in *The Power and the Glory*." *Descant* 23, no. 3 (1979): 40–48.

Fytton, Francis. "Graham Greene: Catholicism and Controversy." *Catholic World* 180 (1954): 172–75.

Gaston, G. M. "The Structure of Salvation in *The Quiet American*." *Renascence* 31 (1979): 93–106.

Glicksberg, Charles I. "Graham Greene: Catholicism and Fiction." *Criticism* 1 (1959): 339–53.

Graff, Hilda. "Graham Greene." In *Modern Gloom and Christian Hope*, 84–97. Chicago: Regnery, 1959.

Grob, Alan. "*The Power and the Glory:* Graham Greene's Argument from Design." *Criticism* 11 (1969): 1–30.

Grubbs, Henry A. "Albert Camus and Graham Greene." *Modern Language Quarterly* 10 (1949): 33–42.

Hoskins, Robert. "Hale, Pinkie, and the Pentecost Theme in *Brighton Rock*." *Modern British Literature* 3 (1978): 56–66.

Isaacs, Rita. "Three Levels of Allegory in Graham Greene's *End of the Affair*." *Linguistics in Literature* 1, no. 1 (1975): 29–52.

Jones, Graham C. "Graham Greene and the Legend of Peguy." *Comparative Literature* 2 (1969): 139–45.

Jones, James Land. "Graham Greene and the Structure of the Moral Imagination." *Phoenix* 2 (1966): 34–56.

Kaplan, Carola. "Graham Greene's Pinkie Brown and Flannery O'Connor's Misfit: The Psychopathic Killer and the Mystery of God's Grace." *Renascence* 32 (1980): 116–28.

Karnath, David. "Bernamos, Greene, and the Novel of Convention." *Contemporary Literature* 19 (1978): 205–29.

King, James. "In the Lost Boyhood of Judas: Graham Greene's Early Novels of Hell." *Dalhousie Review* 49 (1969): 229–36.

Kunkel, Francis L. "The Priest as Scapegoat in the Modern Catholic Novel." *Ramparts* 1 (1963): 72–78.

Lodge, David. *Graham Greene*. New York: Columbia University Press, 1966.

Lohf, Kenneth A. "Graham Greene and the Problem of Evil." *Catholic World* 173 (1951): 196–99.

Marshall, Bruce. "Graham Greene and Evelyn Waugh." *Commonweal* 51 (1950): 551–53.

McCall, Dan. "*Brighton Rock:* The Price of Order." *English Language Notes* 3 (1966): 290–94.

McCarthy, Mary. "Graham Greene and the Intelligentsia." *Partisan Review* 11 (1944): 228–30.

McDougal, Stuart Y. "Visual Tropes: An Analysis of *The Fallen Idol*." *Style* 9 (1973): 502–13.

O'Faolain, Sean. "Graham Greene, or, 'I suffer, therefore I am.' " In *The Vanishing Hero: Studies in Novelists of the Twenties*, 71–97. London: Eyre & Spottiswoode, 1956.

Pryce-Jones, David. *Graham Greene*. New York: Barnes & Noble, 1968.

Rolo, Charles J. "The Man and the Message." *The Atlantic Monthly* 207, no. 5 (1961): 60–65.

Savage, D. S. "Graham Greene and Belief." *Dalhousie Review* 38 (1978): 205–29.

Seward, Barbara. "Graham Greene: A Hint of an Explanation." *Western Review* 22 (1958): 83–95.

Sewell, Elizabeth. "The Imagination of Graham Greene." *Thought* 29, no. 112 (1954): 51–60.

Shuttleworth, Martin and Simon Raven. "The Art of Fiction III: Graham Greene." *Paris Review* 1, no. 3 (1953): 24–41.
Sternlicht, Sanford. "The Sad Comedies: Graham Greene's Later Novels." *Florida Quarterly* 4 (1968): 65–67.
Voorhees, Richard J. "The World of Graham Greene." *The South Atlantic Quarterly* 50 (1951): 389–98.
Woodcock, George. "Graham Greene." In *The Writer and Politics*, 125–53. London: Porcupine Press, 1948.
Zabel, Morton D. "Graham Greene: The Best and the Worst." In *Craft and Character in Modern Fiction*, 276–96. New York: Viking, 1957.

Acknowledgments

"The 'Trilogy' " (originally entitled "Graham Greene") by R. W. B. Lewis from *The Picaresque Saint: Representative Figures in Contemporary Fiction* by R. W. B. Lewis, © 1956, 1958 by R. W. B. Lewis. Reprinted by permission of the author and J. B. Lippincott & Co.

"Mr. Greene's Eggs and Crosses" by Frank Kermode from *Encounter* 16, no. 4 (April 1961), © 1961 by Frank Kermode. Reprinted by permission.

"Loveless Love" (originally entitled "Loveless Love: Graham Greene") by Elizabeth Hardwick from *A View of My Own: Essays on Literature and Society* by Elizabeth Hardwick, © 1961 by Elizabeth Hardwick. Reprinted by permission of the author and Farrar, Straus & Giroux, Inc.

"Graham Greene's Demonical Heroes" by Frederick R. Karl from *The Contemporary English Novel* by Frederick R. Karl, © 1962 by Frederick R. Karl. Reprinted by permission of Farrar, Straus & Giroux, Inc.

"The Moral Situation in *The Quiet American*" by Miriam Allott from *Graham Greene: Some Critical Considerations*, edited by Robert O. Evans, © 1963 by the University of Kentucky Press. Reprinted by permission of the publishers.

"Religious Aspects in the Novels of Graham Greene" by A. A. DeVitis from *The Shapeless God: Essays on Modern Fiction*, edited by Harry J. Mooney, Jr., and Thomas F. Staley, © 1968 by the University of Pittsburgh Press. Reprinted by permission.

"Reluctant Heroes: The Novels of Graham Greene" by Terry Eagleton from *Exiles and Emigres: Studies in Modern Literature* by Terry Eagleton, © 1970 by Terry Eagleton. Reprinted by permission of the author and Schocken Books, Inc.

"Henry James and Graham Greene" by J. A. Ward from *The Henry James Review* 1, no. 1 (November 1979), © 1979 by the Henry James Society. Reprinted by permission.

"Love and Pity: *The Honorary Counsul* and *The Human Factor*" (originally entitled "Love and Pity") by Roger Sharrock from *Saints, Sinners and Comedians: The Novels of Graham Greene* by Roger Sharrock, © 1984 by Roger Sharrock. Reprinted by permission of the author and the University of Notre Dame Press.

"*A Burnt-Out Case*" by Grahame Smith from *The Achievement of Graham Greene* by Grahame Smith, © 1986 by Grahame Smith. Reprinted by permission of the author and Barnes & Noble Books, Totowa, New Jersey.

Index